PRAYERS THAT MOVE ALMIGHTY GOD TO ACTION:

Prayers of Jesus and Humans

Dr. Franklin D. R. Jackson

GoToPublish LLC
1-888-337-1724
www.gotopublish.com
info@gotopublish.com

CONTENTS

I dedicate this book to all individuals who strive to initiate, strengthen, enhance and maintain a personal relationship with God the Father, Jesus Christ the Son, and the Holy Spirit through an effectual, fervent prayer life. In addition, I dedicate this book to you who are searching for inner peace that is attainable only through the gift of the Holy Spirit, which is a function of praying, believing, and accepting Jesus Christ as your personal Lord and Savior.

This book was written with you in mind. If you desire to have your prayers reach and touch the heart of God and for God to act, this book is for you. If you long to pray with the power of the Holy Spirit and you seek Jesus's assistance to respond to your prayers, the book is for you. If you want Jesus to answer your prayer so Jesus will glorify His Father, God, this book is dedicated to you with abundant blessings and love!

Foreword

For over a decade, I have had the blessing of a special light in my life, and his name is Dr. Franklin Delano Roosevelt Jackson. I first met Dr. Franklin, as I like to call him, when he arrived at Virginia State University in 2008. As the associate dean of Cooperative Extension, Dr. Franklin was my direct supervisor and he was unlike any supervisor I had met. He spoke freely of God's power and grace in every conversation we had, and he demonstrated to me what it meant to not be ashamed of God as a believer in Jesus Christ. I saw firsthand how he trusted in God no matter what the circumstances he faced and that he truly had God's favor through the ups and downs of life.

Many times, during his tenure at Virginia State University, Dr. Franklin and I prayed together for protection and strength. We prayed in gratitude for God's many blessings and even at times when the outlook was bleak. We prayed together for friends and colleagues who had fallen ill or went to be with the Lord. A lot happened during the time that Dr. Franklin was my boss, and I thank God that I was blessed to have a praying supervisor. Now that Dr. Franklin has retired from Virginia State University, there is not a day I do not pray for him. It seems his praying spirit is still here. I am so thankful I can still call Dr. Franklin my friend to this day.

For these reasons, I give my heartfelt support for this book on how to pray effectively by understanding the examples of prayer depicted in the Bible written by my boss, mentor, and friend, Dr. Franklin. In this book, Dr. Franklin discusses both Old Testament and New Testament prayers and how they were answered by God and, most importantly, points out key characteristics of effective prayers and how to apply them in our own prayer life.

What truly amazes me is that this book has made the prayers of the Bible become more accessible to me and made me look at how I prayed in the past and why my prayers may not have been effective at the time of my requests to God. After reading and applying many lessons learned in this book, I am more confident in my personal prayers being pleasing to God and being aligned with God's Will. It is my prayer for anyone reading this book that you will be encouraged to look to the Bible, the timeless Word of God to truly understand God and what He wants for your purpose-filled life. Prayer is the key to opening up a fulfilling, exciting, expectant life of joy and wisdom that only comes from a meaningful relationship and continuous dialog with your Creator, Savior and Comforter in the triune God, Jesus Christ and Holy Spirit. May God use this book to open the door of effective prayer in your life!

Dr. Theresa J. Nartea

Associate Professor-Extension Specialist

Virginia State University-Cooperative Extension, Petersburg, VA

October 16, 2020

Preface

Thank you for reading this book. It is my deep hope that through the Holy Spirit, this book will have a profound, positive, spiritual, and physical impact on you. I believe the Holy Spirit inspired me to write this little book to benefit you and others who are similar to you, as well as others who may be quite different from you. As a result of reading this book, you will begin thinking about prayers and the manner in which you pray differently.

You may be quite surprised, as I am, that minimal teaching and preaching are done on the actual powerful prayers of Jesus; even though much preaching and teaching are done regarding the Disciples' Model Prayer—the prayer which Jesus taught His disciples.

This prayer is generally referred to as the Lord's Prayer, which is really a misnomer. This book includes some of the most passionate and often painful prayers of Jesus—from the prayer when He was rejected by His own people at Nazareth to Jesus's prayer for the forgiveness of those who were crucifying Him.

Very seldom have I heard anyone mention powerful prayers recorded in the Bible, including those in the Old and New Testaments and those which Jesus prayed during

His earthly ministry. Many of these timeless prayers are still relevant for us today. One example is the prayer which God instructed Solomon and other people who are called by His name to pray when there is calamity on the land. A second example is the prayer of Jesus for the sanctification, protection, and empowerment of His disciples and subsequent followers of Jesus—Christians, believers. I hope you will accept Jesus's prayer and its benefits for your life.

I have included in this book some of the most powerful prayers in the Bible—prayers which received God's immediate attention and response. These prayers will inspire you to say, "Yes, I can. Yes, I will," or in some cases, "No I cannot, no I will not." I have presented and discussed some of the most heart-wrenching, spirit-heightened, and emotionally intensive prayers of both humans and Jesus—prayers which will sadden your hearts, and prayers which make you shout for joy. I wanted to pull the prayers together in an easy to get to way that they may be a blessing and source of affirmation for those seeking God's assistance in our troubled world.

I will share with you one of my prayers in which I asked God to help me when I was in extremely difficult situations—with no way out. I hope these treasured prayers will inspire, transform, and take you to a different level in your spirituality.

Through the prayers and comments within this book, you may experience enhanced physical, emotional, and spiritual well-being. If you find this book helpful in your life, please share this inspired book with your family, loved ones, friends, and neighbors. Please remember the teaching of the Apostle James that states, "The effectual fervent prayer of the righteous man availeth much" (James 5:16).

I am truly excited for you and am praying with you. When you are through reading this book or while you are reading it or meditating on what you have read, you will affirm your belief that sincere prayers get God's immediate attention and action.

God changes circumstances and situations. God changes the way you react to your circumstances and situations as a result of prayers, (your own, those of Jesus, the Holy Spirit) and those of others praying on your behalf. You will enhance your trust in God, and you will really trust Him and expect an answer to every prayer.

By the time that you finish reading this book, you will decide that with prayer you can do what needs to be done and a whole lot more. May the God, the Father of our Lord and Savior Jesus Christ, shower you with special blessings, and may the Holy Spirit guide your reading, understanding, and the application of the prayers in this little book.

Prayerfully,

Franklin D. R. Jackson

Acknowledgments

I want to thank my mother who taught me the Lord's Prayer (Disciples' Prayer) when I was a child and the Sunday school which made sure that all of us in the class were able to recite the prayer without errors. I thank the deacons and pastors who prayed so loudly that I thought that God was either far away or did not hear very well; however, I was convinced that once God heard, God answered. They were thanking God in advance, for answering their prayers because they were sure that He would answer; even though I sometimes did not see the answer. It was those individuals, including my mother, who engrafted in me the belief that God hears and answers prayers. It is that early childlike belief in prayer which caused me to pray every time I had a difficult task or needed protection from the evil one as I walked in dark places at night.

The influence of those blessed persons resulted in my regular praying long before I openly confessed a belief in Jesus Christ as my Lord and my Savior and was baptized. I owe so much to those wonderful persons and just want to say thank you to them!

In addition, I want to acknowledge the inspiration I received and am receiving from prayer warriors in our churches, Bible-study classes, and Sunday-school classes who poured out and continue to pour out their souls to God for me and for others. May God answer their prayers according to His will and timeframe, and may they be ready to accept God's answer to their prayers. May they keep on praying without ceasing, and not faint!

I am deeply indebted to my long-time Tuskegeean friend, Dr. Sarah Yvonne Johnson for conducting the final editing of this book in a greatly abbreviated period of time. She accepted my request with much enthusiasm and competed the editing with expediency. Thank you Yvonne!

Scripture quotations or paraphrases are from the King James Version (KJV) of the Holy Bible, unless otherwise stated.

INTRODUCTION

SELECTED PRAYERS IN THE BIBLE
AND THEIR IMPACT

To use the superlative *most* to give a statistical description of any situation for which you do not have empirical data to support your claim may be risky, at best, and foolish, at worst. Nevertheless, I am stating the belief that most Christians, who are minimally conversant with the Bible, are familiar with the prayer, which is often referred to as the Lord's Prayer. This beautiful short prayer is recorded in two of the New Testament Gospels: Matthew 6:9–13 and Luke 11:1–4. A less popular version of the prayer is recorded in the Gospel according to Mark 11:24–26.

I used to call this wonderful prayer the Lord's Prayer for many years before I came to the realization that this prayer is the Model Prayer that Jesus taught His disciples. Nowhere in the Gospels of Matthew, Mark, or Luke is the prayer called the Lord's Prayer. On further research, I concluded that this comprehensive, yet succinct Model Prayer is the disciples'— our—prayer.

There are several prayers which Jesus prayed which may appropriately be termed the Lord's Prayers. I have pulled together prayers of Jesus, which I believe you may appropriate, and accept the answers. I call them the Lord's Prayers. I discuss them at length in the subsequent chapters of this book. Jesus prayed some prayers specifically for you. You do not want to dishonor or reject Jesus's prayers as many rejected Jesus when He walked the earth as a sinless, righteous man.

Many Christians are familiar with the disciples' Model Prayer, "Our Father which art in heaven . . ." However, many are not aware or as aware of the gut-wrenching, emotionally heightened, and spiritually impactful prayers Jesus prayed for many, especially for those who were closest to Him—His disciples, you and me.

The Bible is replete with individuals—patriarchs, prophets, kings, barren women, a blind man—and others who prayed to God and received immediate responses to their prayers. Who are some of these people, and why are the prayers of Jesus superior to those of such God-fearing people? I explore these questions and more in this book.

You will take another look at the prayers of Eliezer of Damascus, Isaac, Jacob, Moses, Joshua, Hannah, Esther, Elijah, David, Solomon, Jabez, Zacharias, Mary, Bartimaeus, and Simeon. You will see how God answered the specific prayers of these human beings—from the great patriarchs Isaac and Jacob and the great kings David and Solomon—to a blind beggar and an old man who was longing to die.

You will appreciate how God answered specific requests—prayers of humans in specific way—and you will recognize and proclaim how much more He has answered the prayers of His only begotten Son, Jesus Christ. You will accept the prayers which Jesus prayed for you while He was on earth as God and a righteous Man. You will appreciate that through the sacrificial atonement of Jesus, you may accept Jesus Christ as your Lord and Savior. When you are a child of God, you will live with the power, protection, sanctification, and knowledge which Jesus's prayers provide for you.

All Things Work Together for Good: The Reassuring Consolation!

"And we know that all things work together for the good to them that love God, to them who are the called according to his purpose" (Rom. 8:28).

I am taking a pause from the flow of my discussion to share with you my recent experience, just a few days ago of which, at first, I did not see a good outcome. While I was typing this manuscript quickly, using two fingers—one on the left hand and one on the right hand—ideas were flowing to my mind like wildfire on a dry, parched hillside. I was typing away, impressed with the flow of ideas, really profound ideas, about Biblical, historical, and contemporary individuals and events which touched mankind and the world profoundly. Many of the events and individuals were memorialized, praised, condemned, or simply forgotten.

I was typing at a personally impressive rate of maybe thirty words per minute, using primarily the middle finger on the right hand. Then I decided to cut and paste three pages of this work of this "typing genius" (me), and you guessed it, my "uneducated" left middle finger hit the control button prematurely. I accidently deleted the three newly typed pages. All my intellectual, intense, hard labor work was gone. Of course, I did not know then that I should have tried right away to retrieve the unsaved, deleted file.

My best work ever, I thought at the moment, went down the proverbial drain in the twinkling of an eye. My rhetorical question was this: "How does this 'tragedy' work for my good? Does Romans 8:28 apply here?" I wondered. I was devastated for a little while. I researched Google and YouTube learning everything I could about retrieving unsaved deleted documents. I worked at this for about two hours with no success because I waited too long before I tried to retrieve the unsaved pages. I was frustrated and almost gave up. I did not know if I could reconstruct the "brilliant" ideas which flowed to my mind when I was typing (pecking) the manuscript. I prayed and asked God for immediate help. God responded to my SOS; urgent action was needed. So what did I gain from the typing error experience?

In the process of trying to retrieve the unsaved document, I learned a lot about storing and retrieving documents, and the working of the computer and software. Although I did not retrieve the unsaved, deleted file, I learned a lot.

Firstly, I learned that the computer has an auto save feature and that I may adjust the interval at which auto saving is done. Secondly, I believe that I was led to go in a different direction with the introduction of this book, and you are the beneficiary of this improved introduction.

So Romans 8:28 is true. However, you must respond to the call of God's purpose for you in a timely and intentional manner. This is something that I did not do in trying to retrieve the unsaved, deleted document. I waited too long to start the retrieving process. I encourage you to *look for the good* when things, circumstances, and even people go awry because they will. But look for the good in every situation. A bad experience is profitable if you do not allow it to frustrate you, and you learn something of value from it.

One outcome of my new insight, as I contemplated on my "hyperbolic, massive" setback, is to devote a section of the book on Jesus as the perfect oxymoron and on prayers which moved God to immediate action. The more I researched the Scripture—and I must confess that the King James Version of the Bible is my primary reading source for this book—and the more I listened to the still, small voice of the Holy Spirit within me, the more I became convinced to develop that God responds immediately to urgent prayers and the selected prayers in the Old and New Testaments of the Bible.

I believe that you will be touched by the book or rather be inspired by the prayers, regardless of who you are. You will be particularly blessed when you read the subsequent chapters and apply faith and actions similarly to the prayer warriors mentioned in the book. You probably are already familiar with many of the prayer warriors and prayers; however, you will think of them in new ways as you meditate on their prayers and God's response to them. You will want to emulate one or more of those praying with confident expectation, outcome-achieving persons whose prayers are included in each chapter.

Unless you are a Bible scholar, an informed religious leader and or a practicing Christian-believer, you may be surprised with my discussion on how many individuals misinterpret or misunderstand what God told Solomon in 2 Chronicles 7:13–14. It is probably one of the most misapplied passages in the Old Testament, yet it complies with God's instruction in the previously mentioned passage, and could have a profound positive impact on our nation. You will understand and appreciate the disciples' (believers') prayer, which the Lord taught His disciples, and us, as the Model Prayer. And you will appreciate Jesus's passionate prayers and the occasions of these prayers. I have heard many sermons, and you have probably heard some as well, but I have never heard a sermon on how Jesus prays or on His posture when He prays.

You are undoubtedly aware that in the Model Prayer, Jesus taught His disciples to address God as "Our Father." But how did Jesus address God, His Father, in His own prayers to God? I have explored a few examples in the book. You will certainly appreciate, if you have not in the past, the importance of praying with confident expectation. You will see how ordinary persons were blessed with extraordinary results as God answered their prayers. You will realize that God is ready and willing to answer your prayer when you pray according to His will and His guidance and in the name of Jesus.

In the book, I provide brief descriptions of some powerful prayers, which I mentioned earlier. I selected these prayers arbitrarily; however, they are somewhat representative of impactful prayers in the Old and New Testaments. The prayers are presented in a fairly chronological manner, based on how they appear in the Bible. You will benefit more from each prayer when you read verses before and after the prayer and perhaps more so if you read the entire incident relative to the prayer. This will assist you in better understanding the context or situation which precipitated the prayer.

Prayer: A Christian's Greatest Weapon of Defense and Offence

What is prayer?

For the purpose of this book, I define prayer as a conversation of one or more persons with God at some particular time. In other words, a prayer is a two-way dialog between one or more persons speaking with God. God chooses to respond or not respond as well as chooses how and when to respond to the individual(s) speaking with Him.

I am aware that Jesus Christ prayed to God and God responded; however, I will treat prayers between Jesus and God differently than the prayers of humans to God. In addition, I will focus on the prayers of individual persons, rather than on groups of persons with just a few exceptions. Since a prayer is communication between God and one or more human beings, prayer may be initiated by God or by the person praying. God may initiate the prayer by giving a person a dream or a vision or by some incident in a person's life. It may be sickness, a near accident, a near-death experience, or the presence of uneasiness or discomfort in a person's mind.

The following purposes of prayers are discussed in the book. This is not an exhausted list:

- Use of prayer for thanksgiving and praise
- Use of prayer for defense
- Use of prayer for offence

- Use of prayer for supplication, petition, and intervention
- Use of prayer for peace of mind

God Responds Immediately to Urgent Prayers!

The following chapters are descriptions and some discussions on prayers in the Bible for which manifestation of God's response was immediate. In some cases, God's response was not immediately manifested. The Prophet Isaiah tells us that God answers our prayers before we pray. However, sometimes the answer is not immediately revealed or discerned. I want you to know, to believe, to expect that God will answer your prayers as He did for the individuals mentioned in this book, with the condition that you believe and the Spirit of Jesus is in you. I want you to always remember the teaching of the Apostle James, "The effectual [expecting desired outcome], fervent [earnest, sincere, unceasing] prayer of the righteous [believer] availeth much [gets results] (James 5:16).

The Bible is replete with beautiful prayers of all types—confessions, repentance, remorse, petitions, thanksgiving, praises—and the list goes on. The Book of Psalms, Chronicles, Nehemiah, Daniel, and other books of the Old Testament include beautiful, powerful prayers. The Gospels and Epistles include an abundance of passionate prayers. In this book I am focusing primarily on prayers for which the manifestation of God's response is immediate with a few exceptions. In addition, I have included one prayer of David to which God did not give David a response, accepting that David recognized the manifestation of God's response when God did not answer his prayer in accordance with his request.

I have divided the prayers into two categories—those in the Old and New Testaments. I have identified prayers where God granted the requests and those that He answered but did not grant what was requested. These prayers should inspire you and strengthen your trust in God. It is with the guidance of the Holy Spirit, that these prayers are included in this book. I make no claim that this book includes an exhaustive listing of the prayers in the Bible. Some prayers are short and to the point while others are long. Some prayers are uttered aloud while some prayers are not audible. There are prayers of praise, prayers of thanksgiving, prayers of confession, prayers seeking forgiveness, prayers of blessings, prayers of petitions, prayers of intercession, prayers that are of multiple purposes. God hears and answers all sorts of effectual, fervent prayers. He hears them all and answers or does not answer according to His will and His timeframe!

CHAPTER ONE

SELECTED PRAYERS IN THE OLD TESTAMENT

Abraham Prays on Behalf of Ishmael!

Abraham was ninety-nine years old. God appeared to him and said unto him, "I am the Almighty God; walk before me, and be thou perfect" (Gen. 17:1). Then God went on to tell Abraham, "As for me, behold, my covenant is with thee, and thou shall be a father of many nations. Neither shall thy name anymore be called Abram, but thy name shall be Abraham; for a father of many nations have I made thee" (Gen. 17:4–5). God told Abraham that He was establishing a covenant with him and he would be father of many nations. God sealed the covenant with a symbolism of changing his name—from Abram (exalted father) to Abraham (father of many nations).

God Says No to Abraham

Shortly after God made a covenant with Abraham to make him the father of many nations, Abraham prayed to God, asking that God would allow Ishmael, his son with Sarah's maid, to carry out his legacy. Abraham was ninety-nine years old and Sarah, his wife, was eighty-nine years old. Abraham was probably thinking that he and his wife were too old to have and or be able to handle a baby. Ishmael was about twelve years old at the time. Abraham prayed on behalf of Ishmael and perhaps on his own behalf, "And Abraham said unto God, O that Ishmael might live before thee!" (Gen. 17:18). That was not God's plan, and God would not answer Abraham's prayer in the affirmative. God had made a promise to Abraham, but the promise would not be fulfilled through Ishmael.

It is interesting to note that God did not simply dismiss the prayer of the righteous man He had selected to be the father of many nations. Instead He explained that Ishmael would receive his blessings. God had a better plan for Abraham's legacy. God answered Abraham's prayer in this manner: "And as for Ishmael, I have heard thee: Behold, I have blessed him, and will make him fruitful, and will multiply him exceedingly: twenty princes shall he beget, and I will make him a great nation" (Gen. 17:20). God had a plan for Ishmael. He would be the ancestor of great nations, but he would not be the person, son, through whom Abraham's legacy would be carried out.

God answered Abraham's prayer; however, God did not grant Abraham's request. Rather, God gave Abraham the answer which was consistent with God's plan and right for Abraham. God had promised Abraham that his descendants would be as numerous as the stars, "So shall thy seed be. And he believed in the LORD; and he [God] counted to him [Abraham] for righteousness" (Gen. 15:5–6). Although Abraham believed, he was seemingly in a hurry to receive God's promise for the descendant who would carry out his legacy. He wanted God to substitute Ishmael for the son in God's plan. It was similar impatience which he and Sarah exhibited twelve years before that resulted in Abraham fathering Ishmael through Sarah's Egyptian maid, Hagar, in the first place (Gen. 16:1–4, 11, and 16).

This was at the suggestion of Sarah who was barren and wanted to please Abraham, and satisfy her own desire and longing for a child.

Once God said no to Abraham's prayer regarding Ishmael, Abraham accepted God's answer. Ishmael would not be the one to carry on his legacy. Abraham would have to wait another year for his son, Isaac, who would carry on his legacy. In fact, from the time God promised Abraham that his descendants would be as numerous as the stars to the time his promised son, Isaac was born in about fifteen years (Gen. 15:5–6; 21:1–3).

It is alright for you to ask God for interventions and blessings,; however, at the end of your request be certain to ask God that His will be done. You should be more concerned that God answers your prayer than you are with the answer He gives and the timing of His answer. God's answers are always right and on time.

There are many Christians who believe that only when God says yes to their requests that He answers their prayers. However, when God says no to a request, that no is the answer to that request-prayer! I regularly ask God to block doors through which He would prefer me not to enter and to nullify requests-and prayers which are not consistent with His plan for me. God sees yesterday, today, and tomorrow—the big picture; therefore, like Abraham, you should be willing and ready to accept God's answer to your prayers.

Abraham Prays for Sodom and Gomorrah: God Answers!

James reminds us that "The effectual fervent prayer of the righteous man availeth much" (James 5:16); yet we learn that when the man, who God considered righteously prayed, did not receive the response which the righteous man wanted. The Bible records, "And he [Abraham] believed in the LORD; and he [God] counted it to him for righteousness" (Gen. 15:6). God loved Abraham dearly, considered him righteous, and selected him to be the father of many nations, the father of God's special people.

God Says No to Abraham a Second Time

Abraham was not an ordinary man. The writer of Hebrews describes Abraham's faith in this manner: "By faith Abraham, when he was called to go out into a place which he should after receive for an inheritance, obeyed; and he went out, not knowing whither he went" (Heb. 11:8). Yet when Abraham prayed to God, pleaded with God to save Sodom, God would not say yes to that fervent, earnest prayer. Abraham negotiated with God on the conditions on which that evil city could be spared. God was willing to spare the city if the conditions agreed to with Abraham were met. God would have spared the city if as few as ten righteous persons were found in the city. However, even with the leniency of God to continue to accept Abraham's decrease of the number of righteous persons for whom God would spare the city—from fifty to forty-five, to forty, to thirty, to twenty, to ten—ten could not be found. God would have spared Sodom and Gomorrah if there were just ten righteous persons in those cities as a favor to Abraham, the righteous man. Unfortunately, ten righteous persons could not be found in those cities, so Abraham ended the negotiation.

It was Abraham who discontinued lowering his criteria for God's mercy, perhaps out of embarrassment or out of the realization that a single righteous person, not even his nephew Lot, would be found in Sodom. What sorrow must have pierced the proverbial merciful heart of God when He could not have granted the first big request which His righteous servant made of Him.

God is a merciful God, slow to anger, and eager to forgive; however, He is a just God as well. God could not grant an affirmative answer to Abraham's intercessory prayer and pleading because those for whom Abram prayed were not seeking forgiveness and asking for mercy. Even though this did not happen, God extended mercy to Lot and his family, undoubtedly on behalf of his righteous servant, Abraham. God then executed judgment on Sodom by giving Sodom what that unrepentant city rightly deserved (Gen. 18:23–32).

God does not always answer the prayer of the righteous/ believer in the affirmative; sometimes He answers prayers exactly opposite to the request. That happened when David, a man after God's own heart, prayed for the healing of the son he fathered with Uriah's wife. Instead of healing the little boy, God caused him to die. I discuss this incident later in this book. I have taught and will teach that we should not be concerned about how and when God answers our prayers; rather we should be concerned that He hears and answers our every prayer (2 Sam. 12:12–20).

Abraham Prays for Abimelech

After God destroyed Sodom and Gomorrah, Abraham journeyed from Mamre to Gerar. While in Gerar, Abraham was afraid that the people there would kill him in order to take his beautiful wife, Sarah. Evidently, he thought that they would have been more concerned about committing adultery than committing murder. Of course, this was before Moses wrote the Ten Commandments. So, wanting to preserve his life, Abraham told the people at Mamre that Sarah was his sister. This statement was not full disclosure. Sarah was certainly his half-sister, but more importantly, she was his wife.

When the king of Gerar, Abimelech, heard of this new, beautiful, and supposedly available woman in town, he sent for her and proceeded to make her a part of his harem. She would make him an appealing wife, he probably thought. However, before Abimelech could consummate his "forced-upon, one-sided" marriage to Sarah, God visited him at night in a dream. God said to Abimelech, "Behold, thou art but a dead man, for the woman which thou art taken; for she is a man's wife" (Gen. 20:3). God was merciful to Abimelech because it was not totally his fault that he had taken Sarah. God could have killed him for taking the woman God had selected to be the mother of many nations—His special Hebrew people. God protected Sarah from Abimelech, and in so doing prevented Abimelech from dying. God is truly merciful and eager to forgive!

Even though God was merciful to Abimelech, he was not completely exonerated from all consequences relative to his behavior. God stepped in and prevented him from laying his hands on Sarah. In addition, God closed the wombs of all the women in Abimelech's household so that they were barren. God said to Abimelech, "Now therefore restore the man his wife; for he is a prophet, and he shall pray for thee and thou shalt live: and if thou restore her not, know thou that thou shall surely die, thou, and all that are thine" (Gen. 20:7). God intervened on behalf of Abraham and Sarah, and extended conditional mercy to Abimelech. Abimelech was required to comply with God's instruction of returning Sarah to Abraham so that he might live. This must have been an humbling experience for Abimelech. Undoubtedly, this must have been his first time restoring a wife involuntarily. But he obeyed God, even if he had to swallow his pride. The God of Abraham had spoken.

Abimelech restored Sarah to Abraham. "And Abimelech took sheep, and oxen, and men servants, and women servants, and gave them unto Abraham, and restored him Sarah his wife" (Gen. 20:14). Abimelech was extremely sorrowful and repentant for his unintentional error. He compensated Sarah by giving Abraham, her "brother," one thousand pieces of silver. "So Abraham prayed unto God [on behalf of Abimelech]: and God healed Abimelech, and his wife, and his maid servants; and they bare children" (Gen. 20:17). The Bible does not speak to the length of time that Sarah was in Abimelech's palace. However, regardless of the length of time Sarah was there, God protected her from Abimelech. She was safe under God's protective care.

The Bible does not speak to the deposition of Abraham while Sarah was in Abimelech's palace; perhaps he believed that God would take care of her. This begs the questions: Did Abraham know that God would protect him from the people of Gerar and that he did not need to tell a half-truth? Did he need to put his wife through what was undoubtedly a difficult and stressful situation? We have no answer to such questions; especially since God counted Abraham's faith in Him for righteousness.

God told Abimelech that Abraham was a prophet. This was probably the first time the word *prophet* is recorded in the Bible. To prove to Abimelech that Abraham was a prophet, God arranged for Abraham to pray for Abimelech and all the women in his household. God answered Abraham's prayer immediately. God spared Abimelech's life and removed bareness from the women of his household. Although Abraham was less than transparent with Abimelech, God protected Sarah for God's own sake and for the sake of Abraham, Sarah, and the future descendants of Abraham and Sarah. God showed that His fellowship with Abraham was completely intact despite the fact that Abraham was not completely transparent with the people of Gerar. This reminds us that God is ready to hear, and eager to respond to the sincere prayer of one who has strayed and one who return to God with a broken spirit and contrite heart.

Eliezer of Damascus Prays; God Answers!

When Abraham was old, and perhaps thought he would soon depart from the earth, he sent his trusted and long-time worker, Eliezer, to Mesopotamia, Abraham's home, to select and take back a wife for his son Isaac. He wanted a woman who, with Isaac, would be the ancestors of the children of Israel—the Jews/Hebrews. They would be the ancestors of Jesus Christ. What great confidence Abraham must have had in his servant—a worker, perhaps a Gentile from Damascus. Abraham gave Eliezer a quintessential assignment—the task of selecting a wife for Abraham's choice son, Isaac. This woman would share the role of the ancestors of the descendants of Abraham— descendants who would be as numerous as the stars in the skies, as numerous as the sand on all the ocean shores of the world.

What an assignment! What would you do if your boss gave you a similar assignment? Not only did Abraham give a quintessential assignment to Eliezer, but he also made him swear that he would do his best to carry out the assignment successfully.

Would you swear to do all you can to assist at least one person get to know Jesus Christ as his or her Lord and Savior? What would you do if you had Eliezer's assignment? This was perhaps the singularly most important assignment recorded in the Bible that was given to a man by another man. Eliezer of Damascus, did exactly what you would do as a Christian. He prayed. He had learned about the God of Abraham not from Abraham's preaching of words, rather from Abraham's lifestyle, by the demonstration of his faith—the depth of faith that would allow Abraham to sacrifice his son, Isaac on the altar as a burnt offering—death.

Eliezer of Damascus, Abraham's trusted servant, embarked on the most important mission that was ever assigned to a servant by a man—an assignment by the first patriarch. He took his assignment seriously. He gathered the best gifts available, and off he went on the mission of his life. He knew that failure was not an option.

When Eliezer reached Haran, he disembarked by a particular well, as though by divine revelation. He looked around and prayed a powerful, fervent, and sincere prayer with confident expectation that the God of Abraham would hear and answer his prayer. He had undoubtedly heard Abraham pray and had seen the results of Abraham's prayer.

The Prayer of Eliezer of Damascus

Moses records Eliezer's most passionate prayer: "O LORD God of my master Abraham, I pray thee send me good speed this day, and show kindness unto my master Abraham. . . . And let it shall come to pass, that the damsel to whom I shall say, let down thy pitcher, I pray thee, that I may drink; and she shall say, Drink, and I will give thy camels drink also: let the same be she that thou hast appointed for thy servant Isaac; and thereby shall I know that thou hast shewed kindness unto my master" (Gen. 24:12, 14). What a powerful, unselfish, specific, and trusting-in-God prayer, coming from a Gentile servant on behalf of, perhaps, the greatest man that lived on the earth at that time—the Patriarch Abraham.

Not until Moses prayed for the children of Israel in the wilderness when God threatened to annihilate them, and when Jesus Christ prayed for His disciples and for you and me, shortly before He was crucified, has there been such an intercessory prayer as was the prayer of Eliezer.

What can we learn from elements of Eliezer's prayer? He recognized that the God to whom he prayed is the God of Abraham his master. He asked God to act quickly on his specific request of God, not for himself, rather for his master. The request was that God would send him a specific damsel who would show a specific kindness toward him. He prayed that the damsel would give him water from her pitcher when he made the request of her. And not only would the young lady offer him water, but she would also provide water for his ten thirsty and water-consuming camels as well.

How do you think God responded to that prayer? Of course, you are correct. To Eliezer's great delight, deep appreciation, and exuberance, God gave him exactly what he had requested with confident expectation. What an affirmation of the efficacy of prayer when combined with faith and confident expectation!

God Answered Eliezer's Prayer in Every Detail

A Gentile man, from Damascus, who lived with and observed Abraham's relationship and fellowship with the Almighty God learned how to pray to Abraham's God. More importantly, he knew that his almost impossible assignment required

God's intervention for optimal success. And he succeeded in a magnificent way. Through the guidance of God, he selected a wife for Isaac, the miraculous son God gave to Abraham and his wife Sarah.

It is reasonable to conclude that Eliezer's prayer and God's immediate manifestation of God's response resulted in the selection of the wife for the man who was destined to be ancestor of the children of Israel and ultimately the ancestor of Jesus the Christ, the Messiah.

It is noteworthy that the young lady Rebekah who conducted herself in the manner in which Eliezer prayed demonstrated that she possessed the characteristics which made her worthy to be the wife of the man who would carry out the legacy of Abraham. She exhibited the qualities of beauty, humility, kindness, obedience, dedication, compassion, attention to detail, stamina, and hard work.

Rebekah would need all those foregoing qualities in order to satisfy the expectations of Abraham and his wife Sarah—her prospective father-in-law and mother-in-law, respectively. She would be able to carry out the responsibilities of her husband, Isaac—heir to Abraham, and ancestor to the Jews, including Jesus Christ.

Eliezer was on his return journey to Beersheba, Canaan, with his prize bride for Isaac. He was almost home. Isaac, during his daily walks, spotted the camels with Rebekah riding on one. Rebekah spotted Isaac as well and dismounted the camel. When Isaac met the lovely Rebekah, it was love at first sight. Isaac took Rebekah to meet Sarah, his mother. Rebekah, Isaac's soon-to-become wife, met Sarah's approval. Isaac and Rebekah got married right away (Gen. 24:61–67). God had answered the prayer of Eliezer of Damascus, and guided him in the selection of a wife for Isaac. Isaac, Rebekah, Sarah, and, presumably, Abraham were all well pleased with Eliezer's choice of the wife for Isaac. Of course, God orchestrated the outcomes for His glory, because Eliezer prayed.

This young lady would have the awesome responsibility of comforting Isaac at the death of Sarah, shortly after Isaac married her. Rebekah was now a "mother" (a comforter) to Isaac and his wife. Later on, Isaac petitioned God on behalf of Rebekah to cure her bareness. This was similar to how Eliezer petitioned God when he was selecting a wife for Isaac.

I am deeply moved by the sincerity of this servant, Eliezer, by his faithfulness to his master Abraham, by his trust in God, and by his willingness to take on the greatest assignment that was ever given by one man to another. He understood the importance of prayer, and most importantly, he accepted God's response to his prayer and obeyed God.

What will you and I do with the assignment that Jesus gives us? Will we accept it, pray about it, and then take it on with enthusiasm? Or will we simply ignore it, or worse reject it? I trust that you and I will follow the example of Eliezer of Damascus as he executed the assignment which Abraham gave to him.

I encourage you to read the entire incident as God relates it to Moses in Genesis 24. This incident will encourage you to pray before embarking on any major endeavor, or any endeavor at all. In addition, the incident teaches that believers should remember that others are observing them and may emulate them. Eliezer observed Abraham and accepted Abraham's God and prayed to Him. Who is observing and emulating your prayer life, perhaps without you even knowing it

Isaac Prays; God Answers!

Isaac was the miracle son God had promised to Abraham and his wife, Sarah when Sarah had already passed the normal childbearing age. He would be the heir to Abraham—a patriarch, ancestor of the children of Israel—and to Jesus Christ, the Messiah. God promised Abraham that his descendants would be through his miracle son with Sarah. Abraham's descendants, through Isaac, would be as many as the stars in the skies.

Abraham undoubtedly related God's promise to Isaac, that Isaac would be the ancestor of great nations. Isaac believed the promise. However, when Isaac was a grown man of sixty years of age and his half-brother, Ishmael, was having children and descendants, Isaac had no children. Isaac had been married to beautiful Rebekah, whom he loved dearly, for twenty years and they had no children.

Eliezer had selected Rebekah for Isaac's wife, and she was affirmed by Abraham and Sarah and presumably approved by God., yet Isaac and Rebekah had no children. Isaac was now sixty years old and had been married for twenty years, yet they had no children.

Unfortunately, or perhaps, fortunately, Rebekah was barren. Peradventure God wanted Isaac and Rebekah to know that just as Isaac was a miracle baby, their children would be by a miracle as well. Perhaps God wanted Isaac and Rebekah to understand and appreciate that they could depend on God to supply their needs.

Isaac did exactly what Eliezer of Damascus had done some sixty years earlier. Isaac did the right thing. He prayed.

Isaac Prays for Rebekah's Conception

In the same manner that Eliezer observed Abraham pray, Isaac also observed his father pray. When Isaac needed to find a solution to a twenty-year impossible situation, he went to the source of all possibilities—the God of Abraham. Isaac loved his wife, Rebekah, dearly and knew that she felt guilty that she had not been able to bear him a son. How could Isaac carry out the legacy of Abraham and be the ancestor of many nations if Rebekah could not bear a child, they probably thought! Isaac's love for Rebekah and his compassion for her compelled him to seek God's assistance in this singularly important matter.

God already knew the needs of Isaac and Rebekah; however, God wanted them to humble themselves and come to him in faith. Isaac knew that he was a miracle baby of Sarah's old age and he knew that his wife, Rebekah was selected for him by God. So after twenty years of trying to have a child by their own effort, Isaac decided to petition God on behalf of his wife, Rebekah.

Isaac offered a most passionate prayer on behalf of his barren wife. While the details of Isaac's prayer are not disclosed in the Bible, the Bible states, "And Isaac intreated the LORD for his wife, because she was barren: and the LORD was intreated of him, and Rebekah his wife conceived." (Gen. 25:21). What a beautiful thing Isaac did. He prayed. He did not play the blame game of accusing his wife of their childless state.

Neither did Rebekah demand that Isaac give her children. Neither did Rebekah ask Isaac to go in with her maid, as Sarah did to Abraham (which resulted in Ishmael). Rather, Isaac petitioned God on behalf of Rebekah and perhaps himself that God would open the womb of Rebekah that she would conceive. He pleaded with God. It appears that Isaac was more motivated by the love for his wife and for her happiness, rather than a desire to please himself—to have descendants.

I have not read where Abraham petitioned God on behalf of Sarah when she was barren. In any case, Isaac was a miracle child, He had a God-sent wife, Rebekah. Isaac was aware of the unselfish and passionate prayer of Eliezer of Damascus, the trusted servant of Abraham his father.

Eliezer prayed on behalf of Abraham that God would select a wife for Isaac. Now Isaac emulated Eliezer and prayed to God to open the womb of his barren wife, Rebekah so that she might conceive. As previously stated, we are not privileged to any additional details of Isaac's prayer. He might have reminded God that he was the ancestor of the children of Israel and the Messiah and that he needed to have a child. After all, he was sixty years of age and had been married for twenty years. Or his prayer might just have been as Moses implied in the quotation above: "Please, God, help my wife to conceive."

We do know that Isaac was humble and obedient even to death. God answered Isaac's prayer immediately and in a spectacular way. God opened the womb of the barren, Rebekah, not only for her to have one child, but rather for her to have a set of twin boys. These two boys would grow up to become the head ancestors of two different types of great and rival nations—Israel and Edom.

You and I should follow the example of the great patriarch, Isaac who was not envious of his brother, Ishmael's children; neither did he play the blame game of blaming Rebekah for not having children. Rather, he went to God who is able to make all things possible in accordance with His divine will. You and I should emulate Isaac by always going to God in prayer— praying without ceasing for what we need, even though God already knows our needs. Prayer works and works best when we work it, and trust God, with confident expectation, to answer according to His will.

Jacob Prays; God Answers!

Jacob had conspired with his mother, Rebekah to deprive his brother Esau, of his birthright—right to be the head of his family and privileges appertained thereto. In addition, they deprived (stole) Esau of special blessings that were normally bestowed on the firstborn son in the family. When Esau found out that Jacob had tricked Isaac, his father, in stealing his birthright blessings, Esau vowed to kill Jacob as soon as Isaac, their father died.

Rebekah did not want to lose both of her sons—one by being murdered and the other by the consequences of being a murderer. So she obtained Isaac's consent to send Jacob to Padanaram to stay with Rebekah's brother, Laban. She thought that Esau would eventually cool off and Jacob would be able to return home. Of course, Isaac did not know the real reason for which Rebekah was sending Jacob away. Rebekah's reasoning that after a while Esau would cool off and would no longer want to kill his brother was correct. However, undoubtedly, she did not know that she would not live to see Jacob again or to witness Esau's forgiving Jacob and the reunion of Jacob and Esau.

When Jacob left home for Padanaram he was really afraid of losing his life. His mother packed his bag, and he immediately left. With much haste, Jacob was on his way to Padanaram. After traveling for a while, it began to get dark; the sun was going down. Jacob got tired and sleepy and decided to select a comfortable place on the ground for his bed. He selected stones as his pillows.

During his sleep on the holy ground, with God watching over him, Jacob had a dream. In this dream he saw a ladder stretching from earth to heaven and God standing above the ladder. He saw angels descending and ascending the ladder. No doubt God was sending a symbolic message to Jacob that God was the source of all he needed and would need.

Angels take messages and requests to God and deliver blessings and all good things to those who make their needs known unto God. This was probably the first time that Jacob had a personal encounter with the God of Abraham and Isaac—and later his God.

When Jacob awoke in the morning, he made a vow, a prayer, to God in this manner: "And Jacob vowed a vow saying, If God will be with me, and will keep me in this way that I go, and will give me bread to eat, and raiment to put on, So that I come again to my father's house in peace, then shall the LORD be my God" (Gen. 28:20–21). The specificity of Jacob's prayer is noteworthy in many ways. Firstly, he asked God to be with him and protect him on his journey. Secondly, he asked God to give him bread during the journey. He was a mom's boy and had not learned how to fend for himself, so he definitely needed God's assistance so that he would not starve to death before reaching his uncle's home at Padanaram. Thirdly, Jacob asked God to provide him with clothing to protect him from the elements until he got to his uncle's home. And fourthly, and perhaps most importantly, he asked God to bring him safely back to his father's (Isaac's) house in peace. He definitely needed peace with Esau from whom he was running.

Jacob's prayer was so specific that Jacob would have no difficulty in knowing when God answered each element of the prayer. Did God answer Jacob's passionate prayer? Yes, God did. God guided and protected Jacob on his journey to Padanaram. He kept him safe at Padanaram for twenty years and blessed him with enormous prosperity. And God gave him more than he had requested in his vocal prayer—two lovely wives, two concubines, eleven sons, and one daughter while he was in Padanaram, and one son (Benjamin) when he returned to Beersheba.

Jacob was a wise and successful man and was now ready and eager to return to his father's home at Beersheba. Twenty years earlier Jacob had asked God to bring him back to his father's house in peace. Along with that request, Jacob had made a vow to God in this manner, "So that I come again to my father's house in peace, then shall the LORD be my God" (Gen. 28:21). God had answered all aspects of Jacob's initial prayer, except his request for a peaceful return to his father's house. This was yet to come.

On his way home from Padanaram, Jacob prayed again that God would deliver him from his brother Esau. "And Jacob said, O God of my father Abraham, and God of my father Isaac, the LORD which sadist unto me, return unto thy country, and to thy kindred, and I will deal well with thee. Deliver me, I pray thee, from the hand of Esau: for I fear him, lest he will come and smite me, and the mother with the children (Gen. 32:9, 11). Despite his material accomplishments and wealth, Jacob was suffering from fear and anxiety as a consequence of what he had done forty and twenty years ago respectively.

Forty years earlier, Jacob had tricked his brother, Esau out of his birthright in exchange for a bowl of stew, and twenty years earlier, he had conspired with his mother, Rebekah to steal Esau's special blessings which Isaac intended to bestow on Esau.

Is there any wonder that Jacob felt compelled to pray again for peace with his brother Esau as he contemplated to return home? Under normal circumstances, Jacob should be proud and happy to return home as a successful businessman, but instead he was scared because he was aware of the wrongs he had done to his brother and to his father.

Again, Jacob's prayer for safety and peace at home, in Beersheba, was specific. Jacob declared that he was praying to the God of his father Abraham (his grandfather) and the God of his father Isaac. This is important since it is likely that people in Padanaram worshipped multiple idol gods. He was calling on the true and only God: "Hear, O Israel: The LORD our God is one LORD" (Deut. 6:4). He asserted that it was God who had told him that the time had come for him to leave Padanaram and return to Beersheba to be with his family and that God would deal well with him (Genesis 32:9).

Jacob was obeying God's instruction and needed God's assistance. Now Jacob was concerned with the just and natural consequence for his unjust treatment to his brother, Esau. He needed God's reassurance that He would intervene on his behalf and deliver him from the wrath of Esau. In addition to fearing for his own life, he was fearing for the lives of his wives and children and his animals.

We give credit to Jacob for acknowledging that his safety, security, and protection were not assured by his physical or material possessions and his craftiness; rather, he sought God's assistance through prayer. God answered Jacob's prayer for protection from his brother Esau in an amazing manner.

Instead of Esau attacking Jacob and killing him as he had vowed some twenty years earlier, he welcomed Jacob with open arms. When Esau saw Jacob approaching in the distance, he ran to meet Jacob. Moses puts their affectionate encounter in this manner: "And Esau ran to meet him, and embraced him, and fell on his neck, and kissed him: and they wept" (Gen. 33:4). This was undoubtedly the greatest forgiveness and most joyful reunion between human beings recorded in the Bible up to that point. This happened centuries before Joseph forgave and embraced his brothers who had sold him into slavery to the Ishmaelite merchants.

This type of genuine forgiveness could only have occurred through God's intervention in response to the sincere prayer of Jacob. This is an incident of love and forgiveness which is worth emulating. Esau might have anticipated the prayer which Jesus taught his disciples, "And forgive us our debts, as we forgive our debtors" (Matt. 6:12).

You may ask, "Of what sins were Esau guilty?" And one may answer, "For claiming he was starving to death because he was a little hungry and for using the hyperbole of starvation to forfeit his birthright—leadership role of his family. But most importantly, he had committed virtual murder because he had vowed in his heart to kill Jacob as soon as their father Isaac died."

Esau had not committed physical murder; however, the Apostle John states later, "Whosoever hateth his brother is a murderer" (1 John 3:15). There is no doubt that Esau hated Jacob. After all, Jacob had done him wrongfully, and he probably felt that his hatred of Jacob was justified. However, through God's intervention, Esau's vow to kill his brother was transformed into forgiveness and love for his brother, Jacob. So Esau demonstrated his forgiveness of and love for Jacob by embracing him during their reunion.

You should be inspired, by Jacob, to pray when a situation seems insurmountable, as well as to pray at all time. Pray with confident expectation that God will answer your prayer. Esau demonstrated a spirit of forgiveness motivated, evidently, by his changed heart and his new love for his brother. We can infer from the love that Esau demonstrated toward Jacob that Jacob's prayers played an important role in the change of the heart of Esau. This change of Esau's heart inspired him to forgive Jacob. Esau's hate and vow to kill Jacob were transformed into love and compassion. However, it is important to remember that it was God's intervention which changed Esau's heart. In addition, Jacob deserves credit for recognizing his error and praying for God's intervention.

CHAPTER TWO

GOD SENDS DELIVERANCE FOR
THE CHILDREN OF ISRAEL

What must have been the intensity of the prayers of the children of Israel when they were in slavery in Egypt as they appealed to God for deliverance? God had promised Abraham, "Know of surety that thy seed [his descendants] shall be a stranger in a land that is not theirs, and shall serve them; and they shall afflict them four hundred years" (Gen. 15:13). In addition, God said to Abraham, "And also that nation, whom they shall serve, will I judge: and afterward shall they come out with great substance" (Gen. 15:14).

The children of Israel were not always slaves during their sojourn in Egypt. In fact, Jacob and eleven of his twelve sons (Joseph was already there) went to Egypt on their own volition. They went there because there was famine in Canaan. Joseph, Jacob's eleventh son, was governor in Egypt, second in command only to Pharaoh. At the time, Jacob and his family went to live in Egypt.

The children of Israel were prosperous in Egypt during the time Joseph was alive and for some years after his death. Then a new Pharaoh was appointed over Egypt. The new Pharaoh and the Egyptians became envious and perhaps scared of the prosperous children of Israel. The new Pharaoh and his administration enslaved the children of Israel for no valid reason at all.

The Egyptians became extremely cruel to the children of Israel. The cruelty escalated to the murdering of male Hebrews at the time of their birth.

Moses, who escaped death by the brutal Pharaoh regime, through the intervention of God, years later records the terror this way: "And the king of Egypt spake to the Hebrew midwives, of which the name of the one was Shiphrah, and the name of the other Puah: and said, When ye do the office of midwife to the Hebrew women, and see them upon the stools; if it be a son, then ye shall kill him: but if it be a daughter, then she shall live" (Exod. 1:15–16). It is unimaginable what pains Hebrew midwives must have endured as they were forced to murder their own Hebrew little, infant boys; as they were being delivered from their mothers' wombs!

The Bible does not specifically record when the children of Israel started to cry out to God for deliverance from Egyptian slavery and other atrocities; however, by extrapolation, it appears that their cries began shortly after the death of Joseph. Joseph was born in 1910 BC and died at 110 years old in 1800 BC. God called Moses in 14400 BC to deliver the Hebrews out of slavery in Egypt. This was exactly four hundred years after the death of Joseph and eighty years after the birth of Moses. These four hundred years would have fulfilled God's promise to Abraham as cited from Genesis 15:13–15 above.

What pains and sufferings were the Hebrews in Egypt enduring when God said "enough is enough" and appeared to Moses on the mountain of God—Horeb? God said unto Moses, "I am the God of thy father, the God of Abraham, the God of Isaac, the God of Jacob . . . And the LORD said, I have surely seen the affliction of my people which are in Egypt, and have heard their cry by reason of their taskmasters; for I know their sorrows; And I am come down to deliver them out of the hand of the Egyptians, and to bring them out of that land unto a good land and a large, unto a land flowing with milk and honey; unto the place of the Canaanites . . ." (Exod. 3:6–8). God heard the cries for help which the Hebrews sent up to Him in prayers and supplications.

It is conceivable that many of the Hebrews were aware of God's promise to Abraham that He would deliver His people from the strange land after they had been in bondage for four hundred years. The children of Israel were now ready to take God at His promise. The cries and prayers of the children of Israel had reached up to God in a manner that they got God's attention and God was ready to take action. The time had come for God to fulfill His promise to Abraham. The children of Israel had done their part; they prayed for deliverance.

We know that the sincere and urgent prayers borne out of pains, griefs, and sufferings receive God's immediate response.

This is not to say that you will necessarily experience God's answer to your prayer right away, even though God has answered your prayer. God heard the prayers of the Hebrews for deliverance and decided that it was time to fulfill His promise to Abraham that He would deliver Abraham's descendants from slavery in a strange land.

God came down from heaven at the moaning, groaning, praying, and crying of the Hebrews. He appointed the best suitable human being leader on earth at the time—Moses—to deliver the children of Israel from the most powerful, vicious and evil nation on the earth, at that time.

Yes, when God's people pray together for God's intervention, God will hear and answer. Four hundred years had passed since the death of Joseph—the Hebrew governor of Egypt—until the time God sent Moses to deliver the Hebrews from slavery in Egypt. God's plan for the Hebrews in Egypt was fulfilled and He answered their prayers for deliverance!

We might think that God is slow to respond to our requests. And we might even think that He is late, but God is always on time, and He does not forget his promises. As the children of Israel in slavery in Egypt did, we must pray always and not faint, as Jesus commands, "And he spake a parable unto them to this end, that men ought always to pray, and not faint" (Luke 18:1). Presumably, the children of Israel started to pray for deliverance from Egypt soon after the death of Joseph. Undoubtedly, their prayers got more persistent and passionate as the Egyptians executed harsher and more severe cruelty on them.

Even though the manifestation of God's answer to your prayers may not be immediately evident to you, do not give up on your prayers. You probably will not have to pray for four hundred years or any time close to that to experience the manifestation of God's answer to your prayer.

CHAPTER THREE

MOSES PRAYS FOR THE CHILDREN OF ISRAEL

Moses was arguably the greatest human leader the world has ever seen. He led about two million Hebrew children out of Egypt and crossed the Red Sea into the wilderness heading toward the Promised Land—Canaan.

If anyone had a reason to pray, Moses did. He probably prayed a lot while he was on the Hillsides of Hebron shepherding his father-in-law's sheep. He did not record that in the Book of Genesis; however, he records many of his prayers as he walked closely with God, leading the Hebrew children from Egypt toward the Promised Land. I will mention just a couple of his prayers.

Moses Prays for Deliverance from Pharaoh at the Bank of the Red Sea

When Moses and the approximately two million children of Israel were leaving Egypt, after traveling for three days, they reached the Red Sea. Pharaoh reconsidered his decision to allow the children of Israel—his ex-slaves—to leave Egypt and changed his mind about that decision.

Pharaoh and his armies decided to pursue and re-enslave the children of Israel. They overtook Moses and the children of Israel at the bank of the Red Sea. The former Hebrew slaves panicked; Pharaoh and his armies were closing in on them, and they had nowhere to go. They probably saw their alternatives as either throwing themselves into the Red Sea with the likelihood of drowning or submitting themselves to Pharaoh and be taken back into the harsh cruelty of Egyptian slavery. Not good alternatives at all.

It was at this point that Moses proclaimed a prayer and affirmation, demonstrating his trust in God to protect the children of Israel from existential destruction by Pharaoh and the Egyptians. Moses prayed and assured the people that God would answer his prayer. He said, "Fear not, stand still, and see the salvation of the LORD, which he shall shew to you today: for the Egyptians whom ye have seen today, ye shall see them again no more forever. The LORD shall fight for you, and ye shall hold your peace" (Exod. 14:13–15). What a prayer with confident expectation! What an affirmation! What a deep and sincere trust in God to deliver on His promise of protection immediately! There was no time to wait; the manifestation God's response was needed right away. Moses expected God to fight for the children of Israel immediately!

Are you able to speak with similar confidence when you are trusting God to deliver on a promise or to see you through an assignment? You should always trust God to give the right answer and to determine the outcome in every situation. I have relied on Moses's exhortation recorded in Exodus 14:14 on many occasions. I have that verse framed and it is hanging on the wall in a bedroom of my house.

Moses was absolutely sure that the God, who had sent him to deliver the children of Israel out of slavery in Egypt, would deliver them out of the hands of Pharaoh and the Egyptians at the bank of the Red Sea. In addition, he recognized that the God who had sent ten plagues on the Egyptians and had broken the heart of Pharaoh was ready to fight the battle for the children of Israel.

What level of confidence Moses displayed in the power of the omnipotent God when he declared, "The LORD shall fight for you, and ye shall hold your peace" (Exod. 14:14). Moses had ongoing relationship and fellowship with God and did not wait until he was on the brink of annihilation at the bank of the Red Sea before he called on God. Praying should not be reserved only for times of problems and emergencies. It should be always and without ceasing.

It is difficult for me to select two or three prayers from the many powerful prayers of Moses to include in this book; however, I have thoughtfully selected two. Moses walked closely with God. He prayed a lot during the forty years while leading the stiffed-neck children of Israel from Egypt toward Canaan. At one point, the children of Israel were just about to revolt against Moses because they had no water to drink. Moses was frustrated with them; nevertheless, he did not give up. Instead, he prayed.

Moses Prays for Water

Moses could not provide the grumbling children of Israel with water which they desperately needed. So Moses cried out to God for help in this manner, "And Moses cried [prayed] unto the LORD, What shall I do unto this people? They be almost ready to stone me" (Exod. 17:4). This was an urgent prayer that requires immediate affirmative response in order to prevent the children of Israel from revolting and to satisfy a basic physiological need.

Moses needed a rapid response from God. Where would Moses find water for the children of Israel who thought they and their animals were about to die of thirst and dehydration?

The same God who had made a highway through the Red Sea when Pharaoh was pursuing and closing in on the children of Israel was on time again. He was there to provide water for these murmuring, always complaining, and often ungrateful children of Israel. Moses did not need to wait a long time for God's answer to his SOS prayer for water.

God answered by giving Moses a command, "And the Lord said unto Moses, Go on before the people, and take with thee of the elders of Israel; and thy rod. Behold, I will stand before thee there upon the rock, thou shall strike the rock, and there shall come water out of it that the people may drink. And Moses did so in the sight of the elders of Israel" (Exod. 17:5–6). Needless to say, that God provided the water for the children of Israel in the wilderness. By providing water, God prevented a physical revolt against Moses and against God, in that incident.

Moses prayed, and God answered his prayer. The children of Israel should now know that God is their provider; however, they continued to be rebellious against Moses and against God.

Have you ever felt that you were at the end of the rope and there was nothing left for you to do? You have done all you can and no one seems to appreciate your yeoman efforts. It may be for the family, at church, or at work. What do you then? You do what Moses did without malice toward anyone—you pray! Why do I say that he had malice toward none? Even though at times Moses was very disappointed, upset, and even grieved, he continued to petition God on behalf of the children of Israel throughout his forty years leadership of them.

Moses Prays that God Would Forgive and Spare the Children of Israel

Despite God's protection and Moses's leadership, the children of Israel continued to be unappreciative, ungrateful, and downright rebellious. At one point, God remarked to Moses that He would destroy the disobedient children of Israel. God spoke unto Moses saying, "I have seen this people, and, behold, it is a stiff-necked people. Let me alone, that I may destroy them, and blot out their name from under heaven: and I will make thee a nation mightier and greater than they." (Deut. 9:13–14).

Moses really had a great challenge on his hand. Dealing with Pharaoh and the stiff-necked children of Israel was simply nothing compared with going up in intercession with the Jehovah God who declared that He wanted to destroy His own people.

God had lifted the heavy load of dealing with Pharaoh and now He wanted to deal with His rebellious children of Israel. So why should Moses intercede, with God, on behalf of God's own children of Israel? In addition, if God was not simply testing Moses's faithfulness to God's promises to Abraham, Isaac and Israel, then the children of Israel could be called the children of Moses, or some other name which God chooses to call them.

How would Moses respond to the challenge and opportunity? Would he accept God's offer to destroy the children of Israel and start a new nation in the name of Moses? Of course not. Moses wanted God to keep His promises to Abraham, Isaac, and Jacob (Israel).

Moses did as you as a Christian would have done or you will do in a (very unlikely) similar situation. He prayed an intercessory prayer on behalf of the children of Israel and their predecessors—Abraham, Isaac, and Jacob—the great patriarchs. Other than the prayer of Jesus for his disciples, which I discussed in a subsequent section of this book, Moses's prayer might be the most the most intense and powerful intercessory prayer in the entire Bible.

Moses recounted to the children how he pleaded with God not to destroy them in the wilderness. Moses said, "I fell down before the LORD forty days and forty nights" (Deut. 9:25). Moses prayed, appealed, interceded to God asking Him not to destroy the children of Israel in the wilderness.

A portion of Moses's earnest, urgent, and persistent prayer to the LORD, Jehovah, Almighty God, is as follows: "O LORD

God, destroy not thy people and thine inheritance, which thou hast redeemed through thy greatness, which thou hast brought forth out of Egypt with a mighty hand. Remember thy servant Abraham, Isaac, and Jacob; look not unto the stubbornness of this people, nor their wickedness, nor their sin. Yet they are thy people and thine inheritance, which thou broughtest out by thy mighty power and by thy stretched out arm" (Deut. 9:26, 27, 29).

Not since the prayer of Eliezer of Damascus, approximately six hundred years earlier, was there such a passionate, unselfish, and intercessory prayer recorded in the Bible. Abraham had pleaded with God to save Sodom; however, Abraham's appeal although persistent was not as passionate as the prayer of Moses.

How do you think God responded to such a prayer from His appointed and greatest human leader? Of course, you are correct! God said yes to Moses. Moses proved that he had every desire to honor God's covenant with Abraham, Isaac, and Jacob, and he was willing to humble himself before God and fast and pray for forty days to demonstrate to God and to the children of Israel that He was sincere.

I wonder how the children of Israel acted after they knew all Moses did and endured to spare their lives from the wrath of God! Are you intervening of behalf of a family member, a friend, a colleague, a neighbor, an elected official, or others?

Are you committed to continuing to intervening until you get an answer and/or see results of your intervention? Moses walked daily with God, yet he humbled himself and prayed for forty days to save the nation of Israel and to honor God's Covenant with Abraham, Isaac, and Jacob (Israel).

You may have a cause or a person who needs your effectual fervent prayer. If so, pray for the person or the situation. If no, just pray that God's kingdom will come in earth as in heaven.

Moses Prays to Know the Time of His Death

I will mention just one more of Moses's prayers. It's perhaps the best known and most frequently read and recited prayers of Moses. This is Psalm 90. It is frequently read at funeral services. The Psalm renders praises and thanks to the everlasting God. It addresses the transiency and brevity of life. Moses prayed, "So teach us to number our days, that we may apply our hearts unto wisdom. And let the beauty of the LORD our God be upon us: and establish thou the work of our hands up on us; yea, the work of our hands establish thou it" (Psa. 90:12, 17).

There is really no need for me to make comment regarding this beautiful prayer. It speaks for itself. It is believed that Moses wrote this prayer probably close to end of his forty-year walk in close relationship and fellowship with God. I encourage you to read and study the prayer in its entirety. It will bless your soul.

So how did God answer this passionate prayer of Moses? Moses records God's answer in the Deuteronomy as follows: "And the LORD said unto Moses, Behold, thou shalt sleep with thy fathers; and this people will rise up, and go a whoring after the gods of the strangers of the land, whither they go to be among them, and will forsake me, and break my covenant which I made with them" (Deut. 31:16). God knew and revealed to Moses that His unfaithful, rebellious, and ungrateful would turn away from Him as soon as Moses was no longer with them.

After all, they had rebelled against God several times when Moses was leading them and their rebellious hearts had not changed. Yet the faithful and merciful God would spare them from total annihilation because Moses had interceded on their behalf.

Moses had now completed the mission which God had assigned him. He had delivered the children out of slavery in Egypt—mission accomplished. The children of Israel had not yet reached the Promised Land. They were in close proximity; however, it was not the responsibility of Moses to lead them across the River Jordan into the Promised Land—Canaan. Joshua, son of Nun, would succeed Moses and provide that leadership that would take the children of Israel into the Promised Land.

So God summoned Moses to Mount Nebo for his reward for his forty-year excellent leadership award. "And Moses went up from the plains of Moab unto the mountain of Nebo, to the top of Pisgah that is over against Jericho. And the LORD shewed him all the land of Gilead, unto Dan. And the LORD said unto him, This is the land which I sware unto Abraham, unto Isaac, and unto Jacob, saying, I will give it unto thy seed: I have caused thee to see it with thine eyes, but thou shalt not go over thither" (Deut. 31:16; 34:1, 4). Moses saw the physical Promised Land; however, he did not travel to it. God had a better plan for him.

God was kind and generous to His faithful servant, Moses. God answered Moses's prayer that God would let him know, beforehand, the time of his death. God allowed Moses to view the Promised Land but told Moses that he would not go there. In fact, God told Moses that he would sleep with his fathers when he dies.

The Bible states, "So Moses the servant of the LORD died there in the land of Moab, according to the word of the LORD" (Deut. 34:5). God granted Moses his request to know the days of his life and undoubtedly, Moses was ready for the rest which he had earned after forty years of dedicated service to God and to the children of Israel.

There was much work and fighting ahead for the children of Israel before they would be able to occupy the Promised Land. God wanted His faithful servant, Moses, to rest from all toil and worry and so He called him home and provided the children of Israel with a familiar man to lead them!

CHAPTER FOUR

JOSHUA PRAYS AND GOD ANSWERS

Joshua, the son of Nun, was the devoted and loyal assistant leader to Moses. He succeeded Moses and led the children of Israel across the River Jordon into the Promised Land–Canaan. He picked up where Moses left off to fulfill God's Covenant with Abraham, Isaac, and Israel. Joshua divided the land they captured, in Canaan, among the eligible tribes of Israel.

Before I present two of Joshua's powerful prayers, I want to relate a significant incident in the life of Joshua. You and other members of your family might be familiar with this significant incident.

The Men of Gibeon Asked for Help

Joshua received an urgent plea for help—"save our souls" (SOS)—from the men of Gibeon, with whom he had earlier signed a non-aggression contract/covenant. Even though the men of Gibeon were deceptive in causing Joshua's men to sign the contract with Gibeon, Joshua decided to honor the contract. The men of Gibeon needed help badly because the Amorites were going to destroy them. So Joshua and his small band of warriors left their base at Gilgal and headed for Gibeon.

The LORD assured Joshua that he would be victorious. As Joshua and his warriors, with God's help, battled the Amorites, Joshua needed a little more daylight from the sun.

Joshua Prayed for Sunlight and Moonlight

As Joshua and his small band of warriors were raging war against the Amorites, sunset was imminent and the war was still in progress. So in the hearing of the children of Israel, Joshua prayed and made this audacious declaration, "Sun, stand thou still upon Gibeon; and thou, Moon, in the valley of Ajalon. And the sun stood still, and the moon stayed, until the people had avenged themselves upon their enemies" (Joshua 10:12–13).

Joshua needed the extended period of daylight to complete the battle he was waging against the aggressive Amorites. He had no electric light or flashlight. He had no torch bright enough to illuminate the battlefield and he could not put the battle on hold until the next day.

What had to be done that day had to be done that day! Joshua and his warriors needed light to complete the task at hand: defeat the aggressive Amorites. So he commanded the sun and moon to stand still. Joshua of himself had no power over the sun and the moon; therefore, he was appealing to Jehovah God to answer his prayer and command the sun and moon to stand still.

God answered Joshua's prayer in the affirmative right away and the manifestation of the affirmative answer was immediately evident. Joshua continued to fight and won the battle because God answered his prayer and commanded the sun and moon to obey Joshua!

Joshua had seen what God had done in Egypt and how Moses had divided the Red Sea through the empowerment of God. He himself had divided the River Jordan, with God's help. So he was sure that with the power of God, he could command the sun and moon to stand still while he completed the battle on behalf of the people of Gibeon—the same people of Gibeon who tricked the leaders of the children of Israel into signing a non-aggressive covenant with them.

Is there someone, some community, some issue that you feel strongly about who or which God wants you to defend? Sometimes we must stand up for issues, concern, or challenges, and/or opportunities, which are larger than ourselves, knowing that we can address them with God's help.

What a powerful and impactful prayer with confident expectation Joshua uttered! God answered immediately, and the Amorites were soundly defeated.

God used Moses and Joshua to fulfill His promise to Abraham, Isaac, and Israel to give the Promised Land to their descendants. Moses did his part in leading the children of Israel from Egypt to the border of the Promised Land. Joshua succeeded Moses and led the children of Israel across the Jordan River into the Promised Land.

Sometimes God calls His people to carry out specific assignments and no more. May you listen to and do what God wants you to do for Him and no more.

CHAPTER FIVE

OLD TESTAMENT PRAYERS IN PALESTINE

Hannah Prays; God Answers!

Hannah was an ordinary housewife who was married to a highly religious man by the name of Elkanah. Hannah's husband really loved her, even more than he loved his other wife. He had two wives. The problem was that the other wife had children, and Hannah was barren. To be barren in Israel during those days was considered a curse.

In addition, Hannah might have noticed that the existing priest in Israel, Eli, was getting old, and his sons were just not right to succeed him. Hannah decided to do something about her barrenness for her own sake and for the sake of Israel. For her sake, to remove the curse of being barren, and for Israel's sake, to have a replacement for Eli as the judge, prophet, and priest in Israel. Hannah mentioned her desire for a child to her husband. She even cried for being childless, especially since her husband's other wife had sons and daughters.

Elkanah did not blame her for not having children. He could have justifiably done that because she was barren. Instead, he empathized with her situation. He was very considerate, telling her that he was better to her than ten sons could ever be and that she should not worry herself.

Those were nice comforting words by Elkanah, and he had a great attitude toward Hannah; however, his kind and thoughtful words did not diminish her desire for a child. Lady Hannah went to the temple at Shiloh to speak directly with God regarding her situation and her desire. There was a general belief that if God could not be found anywhere else, He could always be found in the synagogue-place of worship. So there Hannah went with nothing but praying in her heart and on her mind and positive expectation for an affirmative answer from the God of Abraham, Isaac, and Israel.

Samuel records, "And she was in bitterness of soul, and prayed unto the LORD, and wept sore. And she vowed a vow and said, O LORD of hosts, if thou wilt indeed look on the affliction of thy handmaid, and remember me, and do not forget thine handmaid, but will give unto thine handmaid a man child, then I will give him unto the LORD all the days of His life, and there shall no razor come upon his head" (1 Sam. 1:10–11). Hannah continued to pray silently with only her lips moving. The priest Eli observed her moving lips and thought she was intoxicated with wine and admonished her to sober up herself.

When Hannah explained her barrenness to Priest Eli and her desire to have a son, he empathized with her and pronounced a blessing on her, "Go in peace: and may the God of Israel grant thee thy petition that thou hast asked of him" (1 Sam. 1: 17). You already know the end of this incident. Hannah prayed fervently and vowed to give the child to the service of God, if God would remove her barrenness or the curse. She vowed to give the child back to God to serve in the temple.

Priest Eli conferred God's blessing on Hannah that she would conceive and have a male child. So God responded with a big yes. The child she bore was Samuel who became one of the greatest judges, prophets, and priests in the Bible. He was the last judge of Israel and anointed Saul as the first king of Israel and later anointed David as the second King of Israel.

In addition, Samuel defeated Israel's archenemy, the Philistines, and recaptured the Ark of the Covenant.

Hannah was an ordinary woman with an extraordinary prayer request to God and a sincere vow to back up her bold request. God responded to her prayer and gave her more than she requested because her motive was pure and her trust in God was unshakable.

God wants us to ask Him to do the impossible in our lives. We can do the small things by ourselves. You must have the right motive and the willingness to do your part when you ask God to lift the heavy load.

Hannah Dedicates Samuel to God for Lifetime Service

Hannah did not just pray to conceive and have a child. She gave great thanks to God. When Samuel was just an infant, Hannah took him to Eli to fulfill her vow of giving the child for service in the house of God. Samuel records, "And when she [Hannah] had weaned him [Samuel], she took him up with her . . ., and brought him unto the house of the LORD in Shiloh [to Eli]: and the child was young" (1 Samuel 1:24). Hannah had just weaned Samuel, but she was ready to deliver on her promise to God.

Hannah did not want to make any excuse for not carrying out her vow to God; neither did she ask for a delay. The child was probably between two and four years of age, which was the customary age of weaning babies, in the Jewish culture, at that time.

When Hannah got to Shiloh to deliver Samuel to the care of Priest Eli, she quickly reminded Eli that she was the woman who was praying with only her lips moving, who he thought was intoxicated. He had blessed her. She conceived, gave birth to a son, and was there to dedicate the young boy to the service of God and to assist Eli in the house of God.

Samuel records the incident in this manner: "And she said, Oh my lord, as thy soul liveth, my lord, I am the woman that stood by thee here, praying unto the LORD. For this child I prayed; and the LORD hath given me my petition which I asked of him" (1 Sam. 1:26–27). Hannah was very appreciative of what God had done for her. She brought Samuel to Eli as she had promised God. She dedicated Samuel to the service of God, not for a few weeks, or months, or years. Rather for the rest of his life (1 Samuel 1:28).

Hannah's Prayer of Thanksgiving!

Hannah appreciated how God had opened her womb and enabled her to conceive. She uttered to God the following prayer of thanksgiving and praise, "My heart rejoices in the LORD, mine horn is exalted in the LORD: my mouth is enlarged over mine enemies; because I rejoice in thy salvation. There is none holy as the LORD: for there is none beside thee: neither is there is any rock like our God" (1 Sam. 2:1–2). Hannah had no selfish motive in praying that God would grant her a male child. She promised that she would dedicate the child to the service of God. She rejoiced when God granted her request. She acknowledged that God was the source of her blessing—her conception and birth of a son.

Hannah thanked God, not only with her lips, as she did when she prayed for her conception; rather, she thanked God with her voice and her deed—dedicating the child to God as well. She turned over the child to Eli the priest.

We can learn much from the prayers and attitude of Hannah. She knew that prayers change circumstance and people. She saw a need in the house of the LORD and had a desire to cooperate with God and Eli to fill that need. Hannah understood that nothing is too hard for God to do. We too just need to ask God. Pray, trust Him, and wait patiently for Him to answer.

Samuel's Prayer at Mizpeh for Protection from Philistines

The young Samuel now squarely had the full weight on his shoulders as judge, prophet and priest of Israel. He summoned Israel to Mizpeh to pray and repent for their sins. The Philistines learned that the children of Israel were at Mizpeh and decided to declare war against them. The children of Israel were terrified of the Philistines. "And the children of Israel said to Samuel, "Cease not to cry unto the LORD for us, that he will save us out of the hands of the Philistines" (1 Samuel 7:7–8). The children of Israel had strayed from the true God of Abraham, Isaac, and Israel.

The rebellious children of Israel were worshipping idol gods—Baalim and Ashtoreth. They were very much aware of the proclamation of the true God, "Hear O Israel: The LORD thy God is one LORD" (Deuteronomy 6:4). They knew that only the God of Israel could save them from the ferocious Philistines. So they beseeched Samuel to pray to Jehovah God of Israel to defend them. The children of Israel realized that the Philistines were an existential threat to their very existence.

Now Samuel had a perfect teachable moment to demonstrate and affirm the efficacy of prayer and the power of the omnipotent God of Israel; the God of all nations, for that matter. Samuel responded to the appeal of the children of Israel in this manner, "And Samuel took a sucking lamb, and offered it for a burnt offering wholly unto the LORD; and Samuel cried unto the LORD for Israel: and the LORD heard him" (1 Samuel 7:9). The God of Israel heard and responded to Samuel's prayer immediately.

While Samuel was still offering the burnt offering, the Philistines advanced their armies toward Mizpeh, ready to attack the man of God and the children of Israel. Then out of nowhere, really out of heaven His dwelling place, God acted decisively with power. The Bible records God fight against the Philistines in this manner, "And as Samuel was offering up the burnt offering, the Philistines drew near to battle against Israel: but the LORD thundered with a great thunder on that day upon the Philistines, and discomforted them: and they were smitten before Israel. And the men of Israel went out of Mizpeh, and pursued the Philistines and smote them, until they came unto Bethcar" (1 Sam. 7:10–11).

The children of Israel listened to God as God spoke through the Samuel. They got rid of their idols and turned to God, at least for a time.

God heard and answered the prayer of Samuel and destroyed the Philistines who had poised to attack the children of Israel at Mizpeh. The Almighty God of Israel still answers effectual, fervent prayers of His people today!

You can trust God to answer your prayers when you believe in Him, obey Him, and pray in the name of Jesus. Are you fighting battles that are difficult or even impossible for you to win? God will fight them with you, if you will ask, trust, obey, and wait patiently on Him.

The manifestation of God's response to your prayers may be as instantaneous as in the case of Samuel or may take a longer time; that's God's decision.

Hezekiah Prays; God Helps Defeat Sennacherib, King of Assyria

Sennacherib, king of Assyria—the most powerful nation in the vicinity of Judah at the time—sent an army to besiege Jerusalem and a threatening message to Hezekiah, king of Judah. The letter essentially demanded that King Hezekiah surrender to King Sennacherib. And to add insult to injury, Sennacherib's messenger shouted to the Jews of Judah that Hezekiah was deceiving them by asking them to trust in the LORD, who could not protect or defend them.

Sennacherib's message said, "Thus saith the king, Let not Hezekiah deceive you: for he shall not be able to deliver you.

Neither let Hezekiah make you trust in the LORD, saying, The LORD will surely deliver us: the city will not be delivered in the hand of the king of Assyria" (Isa. 36:14–15).

Not only was the king of Assyria threatening Hezekiah and the people of Judah, but he was disrespectful of the true Almighty God of Israel. In addition, he was sowing seeds of doubt in the hearts of the people of Judah regarding the ability of God to defend them against the wicked Assyrian army.

This was an extremely difficult situation for King Hezekiah. He thought that the army of Judah was no match for the ferocious Assyrian army. He needed assistance. What would be his response to the message from Sennacherib?

King Hezekiah was quite upset when he received the disrespectful message from Sennacherib. "And it came to pass, when King Hezekiah heard it, that he rent-ripped his clothes, and covered himself with sackcloth, and he went into the house of the LORD. And Hezekiah prayed unto the LORD, . . ." (Isa. 37:1, 15). So he did the right thing—he prayed. He petitioned the help of God!

Hezekiah knew that he and the army of Judah by themselves were no match for Sennacherib and the Assyrian army, so he went to Solomon's Temple to solicit God's intervention in this threat by Sennacherib. He humbled himself before God and demonstrated his humility physically and remorse so that the people of Judah could see. He took off his royal garments and replaced them with rags, which is symbolic of humility and repentance. Then he petitioned God's intervention.

He could have prayed in his palace; however, he wanted his people to know that he trusted in God and it is God who would deliver them from the fierce Assyrian army. He wanted to leave no doubt regarding the efficacy of prayer and the faithfulness of God in delivering His people who call up on him. No doubt, he was also sending a message to Sennacherib and the Assyrians that the LORD of Abraham, Isaac, and Jacob has the awesome power to deliver Judah from the Assyrians.

The Bible describes Hezekiah's prayer for protection from the Assyrians in this manner: "O LORD of hosts, God of Israel . . . thou hast made heaven and earth. Incline thy ear, O LORD, and hear; open thine eyes, O LORD, and see: and hear all the words of Sennacherib, which hath sent to reproach the living God. Now therefore, O LORD our God, save us from his hand, that all the kingdoms of earth may know that thou art the LORD, even thou only" (Isa. 37:16–17, 20). Before Hezekiah could even complete his prayer (please read the entire prayer), God responded. He gave the Prophet Isaiah a message for Hezekiah that He would defend Judah from King Sennacherib and the Assyrians.

God sent the Prophet Isaiah immediately to deliver His answer to Hezekiah's prayer: "Thus saith the LORD God of Israel, Whereas thou hast prayed to me against Sennacherib king of Assyria: This is the word which the LORD hath spoken concerning him; The virgin, the daughter of Zion, hath despised thee, and laughed thee to scorn; the daughter of Jerusalem hath shaken her head at thee" (Isa. 37:21–22). God heard and answered Hezekiah's prayer.

Firstly, God acknowledges the significance of Hezekiah's prayer. For those who believe in and trust God, prayer should precede every task or mission. Hezekiah did not wait until he was involved in battle with the Assyrians before he sought God's assistance. He did not ask the Prophet Isaiah to pray to God for him; he prayed himself.

Secondly, most likely, God was offended by the arrogance of Sennacherib and his lack of reverence for God and lack of respect for King Hezekiah and the people of Judah.

Thirdly, Sennacherib failed to recognize the awesome power of the only true God. Consequently, God heard the prayer of Hezekiah and executed judgement on Sennacherib and the Assyrians. They were utterly destroyed.

Furthermore, God defended the city of Jerusalem and the nation of Judah for His own sake. God's proclamation to

Hezekiah was clear and precise: "For I will defend this city to save it for my own sake, and for my servant David's sake. Then the angel of the LORD went forth, and smote the camp of the Assyrians a hundred and four score and five thousand: and when they arose early in the morning, behold, they were all dead corpses" (Isa. 37:35–36). God answered the prayer of Hezekiah right away. It was sincere, unselfish, and Hezekiah had confident expectation.

In addition, God showed Sennacherib and the Assyrians that the only true God is the God of the people of Judah; the Assyrian's gods are nothing but idols. Furthermore, God declared that He would save the city (Jerusalem) for His own sake and for the sake of the man of His own heart—David.

Hezekiah was one king of Judah who humbled himself before God and prayed. God answered his prayer immediately.

The same God who answered Hezekiah's emergency call is available to answer your prayer and my prayer if we "Seek ye the LORD while he may be found, call ye upon him while he is near" (Isa. 55: 6). It is a good thing to maintain fellowship with God so that you will be near Him when you have an emergency or an urgency!

Hezekiah Prays and Weeps for Extension of His Life

King Hezekiah was gravely ill. God instructed the prophet Isaiah to inform Hezekiah to get his house in order because he would not recover from his illness and his death was imminent. Isaiah delivered the sad message to King Hezekiah. Isaiah delivered God's message to King Hezekiah just as bluntly as God had given it to him: "Thus saith the LORD, Set thine house in order: for thou shalt die, and not live" (Isa. 38:1). Hezekiah knew that he had unfinished work that he was doing on behalf of God. He had not yet completed the work and asked God for a little more time, longer life.

He had good fellowship with God. It was the same God of Israel who had assisted him in destroying the ferocious Assyrian army some time ago. More accurately stated, rather, it was the same God who had responded to his prayer for urgent assistance and destroyed the Assyrians who warred against Israel.

What would you have done or what would you do if you receive a message from God notifying you of your imminent death as Hezekiah did? How would you react, especially if you had been doing God's work and you know that God's Word does not return void? Would you have said or would you say, "He is God. Let Him do what seems good. *Ita est fati* (it is my fate)"? Would you then pray for forgiveness for any wrongs you have done so you would be with God when you die? Or yet, would you tell God that you are not quite ready to die and ask for a little more time on earth?

Well, Hezekiah prayed arguably one of the most profound prayer recorded in the Bible which a human being prayed on his own behalf. Moses had prayed for the children of Israel, Solomon asked for understanding so that he would be a good ruler or judge, Jacob prayed for protection from Esau, but none asked for extension of his life. Now Hezekiah is asking for an extension of his life. He was not in defiance of God's message that his death was imminent; rather in humility and with sincerity, he prayed for a little more time. His prayer was effectual and fervent with confident expectation for a positive response.

The Bible records, "Hezekiah turned his face to the wall, and prayed unto the LORD" (Isa. 38:2). Hezekiah prayed out his heart to God in this manner: "And remember me now, O LORD, I beseech thee, how I have walked before thee in truth and with a perfect heart, and have done that which is good in thy sight. And Hezekiah wept sore" (Isa. 35:3). Hezekiah knew that the God of Abraham, Isaac, and Jacob, who had answered his prayer and defended Judah from the Assyrians, would answer his prayer again.

Some might say that Hezekiah seemed a bit immodest in his prayer; however, at least he could say that he did what was right in the sight of God and walked in truth. And he wept in humility. God did not chide Hezekiah for his self-assurance.

Hezekiah's prayer received God's immediate attention and action. God responded with grace, and mercy. He dispatched the Prophet Isaiah to Hezekiah with good news for Hezekiah. The same prophet who had proclaimed a dismal future (imminent death for Hezekiah) was now instructed to deliver exciting, positive news. His prayer has been answered and his request has been granted.

God's instruction to the greatest prophet of Judah was succinct, clear, and life extending "Go, and say to Hezekiah, Thus saith the LORD, the God of David thy father, I have heard thy prayer, I have seen thy tears: behold will add to thy days fifteen years" (Isa. 38:5). It is evident from God's immediate responses to the two incidents of Hezekiah's prayers that Hezekiah had close fellowship with God. Hezekiah recounted that he had been obedient to God. He even seems to proclaim to God that he was a righteous man.

Perhaps God wanted Hezekiah to appreciate that it was God's grace and mercy which would save him; rather than his imperfect righteousness. He needed to humble himself before God and not to rely on his righteousness. Nevertheless, Hezekiah had a history of seeking God's assistance when he was in need. He knew that he could depend on the faithful God of his father David for grace and mercy. Perhaps the basis of his righteousness was similar to that of Abraham—his belief in God.

What type of relationship and fellowship do you have with God? Do you feel comfortable to call on God when you face impossible situations? Do you have confident expectation that God will hear and answer your prayer every time?

May the faith, prayers, and confident expectation of positive outcomes exemplified by Hezekiah inspire you to pray always with the expectation that God will answer your prayers!

Jabez Prays; God Hears and Answers!

More than likely you are familiar with the character and incident recorded in the Bible about a man named Jabez. He appeared to be of no particular outstanding stature or family lineage; however, when he prayed, something marvelous happened to him. The only distinguishing attribute he had compared to his brothers, according to First Chronicles, was that his mother bore him with sorrows, "And Jabez was more honourable than his brethren: and his mother called his name Jabez, saying, Because I bare him with sorrow" (1 Chron. 4:9). The Bible does not speak of the type of sorrows Jabez's mother might have gone through during her pregnancy with Jabez; however, it must have been quite severe for her to name her son, not to memorialize the joy of having a son, rather to remember her sorrows.

Could the name Jabez reminded Jabez of his mother's sorrow and cause him to want to do something that would make his mother proud of him and be joyful? The answer to both questions is a plausible yes. However, I will not be presumptuous to say what motivated Jabez to be more honourable than his brothers. Quite likely, it did not take a lot for Jabez to be more honorable than his brothers.

One thing that stood out about Jabez other than his name, and undoubtedly his most important attribute, was that he knew God.

Perhaps we need to commend Jabez's mother for introducing Jabez to God. Incidentally, no father is mentioned. Whatever the circumstance, Jabez did the absolutely best thing that he could have done, he prayed. Preachers have preached sermons on Jabez's prayer. Bible scholars have written about this prayer, and religious teachers have taught about this prayer. What makes this prayer so meaningful? Let me write the short prayer in its entirety and then offer suggestions regarding the prayer.

Jabez's prayer follows the statement of Jabez's mother, "Because I bare him with sorrow" (1Chron. 4:9). We do not know how much time had elapsed between the statement of Jabez's mother and Jabez's prayer. However, what is evident is that she did not make the statement just in the hearing of Jabez. And perhaps Jabez was not even there when she made the statement. The length of time that she was carrying the feeling of sorrow is not explicit in the Bible.

Regardless, Jabez uttered this prayer, "And Jabez called on the God of Israel, saying, Oh that thou wouldest bless me indeed, and enlarge my coast [border], and that thine hand might be with me, and that thou wouldest keep me from evil that it may not grieve me! And God granted him that which he requested" (1 Chron. 4: 10). Some Bible scholars and pastors have done detailed analyses of every aspect of this straight forward, specific request, and intentional prayer. No doubt, Jabez prayed with confident expectation.

I will not attempt to engage in any detailed analyses of this succinct prayer. Nevertheless, I offer a few suggestions regarding the impact of this prayer when it was prayed and its continuing impact in our time. Firstly, Jabez knew the God of Israel, and probably was concerned about how far Israel had strayed from God. Knowing God and His omnipotence, omniscience, omnipresent, infallibility, and the on-time nature is extremely important. Jabez knew God and believed that God would answer his prayer. He trusted the faithful God who had delivered the children of Israel out of slavery in Egypt, through many miraculous acts, and brought them to the Promised Land.

Secondly, Jabez saw a problem throughout Israel that needed fixing, and he wanted to be a part of the solution. Perhaps, even to defend Israel.

Thirdly, Jabez's prayer was an unselfish prayer. He wanted to use his blessing to assist Israel.

Fourthly, he was humble, he knew that he could not do what he sought to do without God's blessings, continuing protection, and empowerment. We do not know if Jabez had a desire to please his mother and console her of her sorrow or even if she was still alive. In any case, his mother would have been proud of his accomplishments. In addition, Jabez might have wanted his brothers to see that one who was honorable could be successful.

God Answers Jabez's Prayer

God gave Jabez exactly what he requested. "And God granted him that which he requested" (1 Chron. 4:10). Jabez wanted greater opportunities to do good deeds for Israel so that God would be glorified. Undoubtedly, he wanted to be a positive role model for his brothers and even all of Israel. His motive was consistent with God's will, and God granted him expanded opportunities.

We do not know all that Jabez did with the authorization, empowerment, and protection which God granted him. However, what is noteworthy is that an ordinary man saw a need that he wanted to meet and he prayed passionately to God for the opportunity and capability to meet the need. God essentially responded, "Your request is granted, as made, with no strings attached." What's more, it appears that the manifestation of God's response was immediate.

One ordinary man, whose name represented his mother's sorrow during her pregnancy and at his birth, saw a need and wanted to meet it, saw a problem and wanted to solve it and sought God's assistance. In humility and with confident expectation, Jabez asked God to give him more responsibility and God gave him all that he needed to get the job done.

Isn't it interesting that someone is praying to God, not for more help to do the work or for rest form the current work? Rather, Jabez asked God to expand his territory—to give him greater assignments. Have you ever felt that you are not doing enough for God in your church, in your community, in the nation, in the world? I have felt that way. What if I had done a little more? Perhaps things might have been different.

If Jabez's mother was still alive at the time God answered his prayer, I wonder what she might have done! Would she have asked him to change his name to reflect her great pride in him and her new joy in his accomplishments?

What challenges are you facing in your family, in your church, or in your community as a result of your name, your family name, as a result of past events in your life, or because of the history of your family? God already knows your situation and is ready to assist you in meeting and solving the challenges. However, like Jabez, you need only to humble yourself and seek God's assistance. Will you?

CHAPTER SIX

PRAYERS OF DAVID

David Prays; God Hears and Answers!

The Bible says that David was a man after God's own heart. David demonstrated the teaching of his ultimate descendant—Jesus Christ—who is quoted as follows: "And spake a parable unto them to this end, that men always ought to pray, and not faint" (Luke 18:1). David is credited for writing at least 73 of the 150 Psalms in the Bible, most of which are some of prayers. Among the most popular and best known Psalms of David are Psalm 23, Psalm 51, and Psalm 27.

Two of my favorite prayers of David are found in Psalms 34 and 37. For this book on prayers, I have selected a few of David's prayers which I have arbitrarily included. They include prayers found in 1 Chronicles 17:16–27; 2 Samuel 7:18–29 (God denies David's desire to build a temple); Psalm 23, which I call a prayer for protection and assurance; Psalm 51, a prayer of regrets and repentance; Psalm 143, a prayer for help; Psalm 55, a prayer that God will hear and answer; and Psalm 64, a prayer for the poor and needy.

David's Prayer for Forgiveness

David was king of Israel. He was a "man after God's own heart" (1 Sam. 13:14). He could have chosen any available woman he wanted for his wife, and God probably would have permitted him to have that woman. He only needed to ask God.

Yet when he went on the roof of his palace, he saw the beautiful Beersheba, Uriah's wife, taking a bath. His desire and lust for her were uncontrollable. He failed to exercise self-discipline. The devil might have tempted him, but the devil did not make him do what he did. Centuries later, the Apostle Paul, writing to the Corinthians, said, "There hath no temptation taken you but such as is common to man: but God is faithful, who will not suffer you to be tempted above that ye are able; but will with the temptation also make a way to escape, that ye may be able to bear it" (1 Cor. 10:13). David's response to the temptation brought about by what he saw reminds us of how Eve saw the forbidden fruit in the Garden of Eden and had to have it, of course, with Satan's urging. She might have resisted.

In his time of weakness, David succumbed to his temptation, he just had to get Uriah's wife to be his lover and wife. David used his positional authority, as the king of Israel, to summon this beautiful woman to his palace. Interestingly, her husband, Uriah, was a faithful captain in David's army, who at the time was leading a battle against the Ammonites.

David slept with Beersheba and she conceived. He had violated one of God's sacred commandments: "Thou shalt not commit adultery" (Exod. 20:14). David was well aware that God knew what he had done. Nevertheless, he tried to cover up his role in the pregnancy of Beersheba by trying to arrange for Uriah to sleep with his wife. That scheme did not work because Uriah refused the luxury of sleeping with his wife while his soldiers were in the battlefield fighting.

So David took a more aggressive and vicious approach. He connived with soldiers under the control of Uriah to have Uriah killed in battle by not protecting him in the battle. The soldiers conspired with David and withdrew protection of Uriah, so the Ammonites, killed him in battle.

David now felt he had gotten away with this trick—aided and abetted in the premeditated execution of Uriah. He could now marry Beersheba because she was now a widow, who was pregnant with his child. However, David had violated another of God's strict commandments, "Thou shalt not kill" (Exod. 20:13).

While David was taking his proverbial victory lap, in a way of speaking, proud of his accomplishment on gaining this beautiful woman, God was watching the drama. David had gained Beersheba by premeditated murder, but the Prophet Nathan showed up. God had given the Prophet Nathan a parable to deliver to David.

Essentially, Nathan told David, "That there was a man who had one sheep which he and his family had raised from it was a lamb. It was now like a member of his family. A rich many who had a large herd of sheep had a friend from out of town visiting him. The man who had many sheep wanted to have a feast for his visiting friend. Instead of taking a sheep from his herd, this rich man took the one sheep that this poor man had and used it for the feast".

When David heard this atrocity he was disgusted and furious. This was unconscionable he thought. He said to Nathan, "As the LORD liveth, the man that hath done this thing shall surely die. And he shall restore the lamb fourfold, because he did this thing, and because he had no pity" (2 Sam. 12:5–6). David rightly proclaimed that the wicked rich man must restore the poor man's sheep fourfold. In addition, he must be executed. That would have been justice. But God chose to exercise mercy toward the man of his own heart.

Imagine how King David must have felt when Nathan said to David, "Thou art the man, Thus saith the LORD God of Israel, I anointed thee king over Israel, and I delivered thee out of the hand of Saul. Wherefore hast thou despised the commandment of the LORD, to do evil in his sight? thou hast killed Uriah the Hittite with the sword, and hast taken his wife to be thy wife, and has slain him with the sword of the children of Ammon" (2 Sam. 12:7, 9).

My heart trembles within me as I read and sensed God's rebuke of David. Nathan continued to rebuke King David. He did not try to be politically correct; rather he delivered God's proclamation to David with the seriousness fitting for such an egregious crime. David himself had declared that such a wicked man must restore the poor man's sheep and be executed.

Nathan continued God's admonition of David in this manner: "Thus saith the LORD, Behold, I shall raise up evil against thee out of thine own house, and I will take thine wives before thine eyes, and give them unto thy neighbour, and he shall lie with thy wives in the sight of this sun. For thou didst it in secret: but I will do this thing before all Israel, and before the sun" (2 Sam. 12:11–12). God strongly chastised David, who God had appointed king of Israel. However, instead of executing justice on David, God granted him mercy. God's reprimand of David reminds us of His reprimand of Adam and Eve in the Garden of Eden.

Often God reprimands and chastises His special people to get them back on track. So how did David respond to God's reprimand? He had been caught with his hand in the proverbial cookie jar—guilty as charged. There was no denying of his guilt. David, the warrior, the man after God's own heart, had two qualities that all Christians should emulate. He was humble, and he was the epitome of a man with a repentant heart.

David Repents and Prays for Forgiveness; God Spares His Life!

Nathan had barely concluded his rebuke of the great King David when David in in sincere humility prayed one of his shortest and most impactful prayers recorded in the Bible. "And David said unto Nathan, I have sinned against the LORD" (2 Sam. 12:13). David took full responsibility for what he had done. He did not play the blame game as Adam and Eve did in the Garden of Eden. Adam blamed Eve for making him eat the forbidden fruit, and Eve blamed the serpent for tempting her.

David did not say that he was on the roof of his house minding his own business when the beautiful woman exposed herself to him, and he just could not resist her. Neither did he say that Beersheba knew that he would have been on the rooftop and she intentionally and deliberately induced and seduced him. Rather, he held himself accountable and exclaimed that he had sinned. It was his fault, and his alone. He was not a victim but the perpetrator of rebellion against God's commandments—lust, covetousness, adultery, and murder. He was guilty as charged. But that was not the end for David.

Almost before David could finish confessing his sin, God answered. The normal consequence of that sin is death. This was a consequential sin. God granted grace and mercy to David immediately. "And Nathan said unto David, The LORD also hath put away thy sin; thou shalt not die" (2 Sam. 12:12). David, no doubt realized how closely he had gotten to receiving the consequence of his indiscretion—death? God spared him because he was remorseful and quick to confess his sin and repented immediately.

A longer version of David's prayer of confession and his seeking forgiveness is recorded in Psalm 51. David prayed, "Have mercy upon me, O God, according to thy lovingkindness: according unto the multitude of thy tender mercies blot out my transgressions. Create in me a clean heart, O God; and renew a right spirit within me. Cast me not away from thy presence; and take not thy holy spirit from me" (Psa. 51:1, 10–11). Psalm 51 is model prayer for those who have transgressed against God and are seeking God's forgiveness.

In this prayer, David poured out his soul to God. You can feel David's sorrow and remorse as you read the prayer. While we regret David's error which necessitated this passionate, heartfelt, and sincere prayer, we give thanks to God that David shares his misdeed and this wonderful prayer with us!

There is no doubt that God inspired Samuel to record the action of David—his indiscretion, his repentance, and his remorsefulness—in order to remind us that even a man after God's own heart is just a man who is capable of sinning. And perhaps more importantly, reminds us that God uses imperfect persons to carry out His perfect will and mission.

What would you have done or what would you do if you did something that was wrong and you were confronted by a higher authority? You thought that you had gotten away with your misdeed and you were safe, then out of nowhere someone of higher authority confronted you about your misdeed. Would you deny what you did, justify what you did, blame someone or circumstances for what you did, or confess and seek forgiveness? How you deal with your recognized errors or revealed wrongs speaks volume about your character and your relationship with God.

God granted grace and mercy to David and he continued to be the greatest king of Israel.

May you be eager to forgive others and to seek God's forgiveness at all times!

David's Prayer When God Denied His Desire to Build the Temple

David had built an impressive palace for himself. He had subdued the Philistines and other enemies of Israel. He now wanted to build a temple to accommodate the ark and establish a permanent place where God could meet the children of Israel and they could corporately worship God.

With great enthusiasm, David mentioned his desire to build a temple to the Prophet Nathan. Nathan gave David the affirmation that it was quite appropriate for Him to build a temple. In fact, Nathan said to David, "Go, do all that is in thine heart; for the LORD is with thee" (2 Sam. 7:3). David felt good. No doubt he started to work overtime to design the temple in his mind. He had received affirmation from the great Prophet Nathan, who had replaced Samuel. However, God said, "Not so fast, David." Nathan had not asked God for His plan regarding the temple.

The very night Nathan had given David approval and affirmation to build the temple, God reversed Nathan's approval. Nathan had not consulted God about the building of a temple before he gave David his approval.

God instructed Nathan to tell David that He did not ask him to build a temple for Him and did not want him to build a temple. However, God would assign the building of the temple to one of David's descendants. In addition, God declared that He would build a permanent kingdom, and David's descendant would sit on the throne forever.

God softened the blow inflicted on David's ego by adding to the message, "But my mercy shall not depart away him, as I took it away from Saul, whom I put away before thee. And thy house and thy kingdom shall be established for ever before thee: thy throne shall be established for ever" (2 Sam. 7:15–16). It was not all bad news for King David; in fact, it was good news—the faithful God consoled David and made him a wonderful promise.

The faithful Almighty God shared detailed plans with David through Nathan. However, the message was clear: David's good intention was not consistent with God's plan. David and Nathan should have consulted with God and seek His approval before making their assumption that God would be pleased with the temple that David wanted to build.

When Nathaniel delivered God's message to David, perhaps David had a feeling of ambivalence—sorrowful that he would not build the temple, joyful that God had a more elaborate plan for the building of a physical temporary temple as well as a plan for a permanent and everlasting kingdom. Furthermore, David's descendant would build the temple and another descendant would sit forever on the throne built by God.

David went into the tabernacle and sat before the Ark of the Covenant and uttered a prayer of thanksgiving with passion and sincerity. He talked with God from the depth of his heart. David prayed, "Who am I, O Lord God? and what is my house, that thou hast brought me hitherto? (2 Sam. 7:18). David confessed that that he did not deserve what God had already done for him, yet God was planning to do more for his family.

In thanksgiving and humility, David recounted all the great and merciful things God had done for the people of Israel—from delivering them from slavery in Egypt to fighting and driving out other nations, enemies in Canaan, and giving the Promised Land to the children of Israel. In addition, God had now promised to establish an everlasting throne on which a descendant of David would sit forever. God's goodness to David was more than David could comprehend. Nevertheless, David asked God to fulfill all His promises to him.

King David, the man after God's own heart, ended his heart-to-heart, passionate prayer with confident expectation in this manner, "Therefore now let it please thee to bless this house of thy servant, that it may continue for ever before thee: for thou, O Lord God, hast spoken it: and with thy blessing let the house of thy servant be blessed for ever" (2 Sam. 7:29). David knew that God's promises were a done deal—they would be fulfilled.

There was no need for David to try to negotiate with God to reconsider His decision. What God had proclaimed was significantly more superior to what King David had in his finite mind. Therefore, David cooperated with God and thanked God in advance as though God's proclamation had already been fulfilled.

The interesting thing about the two promises God made to David is they were not fulfilled while David was alive. One promise was that a descendant of David would build the temple. The second promise (new covenant) was that David's descendant (Jesus Christ) would sit on the throne forever. Although the promises had not yet come to fruition, David had confident expectation that God would fulfill His promises.

David uttered a prayer of thanksgiving in joyful submission to the infinite wisdom and will of God. David knew, as I mentioned previously, that God had fulfilled promises which He made to Abraham centuries earlier to deliver the children of Israel out of slavery in a strange land (Egypt) and to give the Promised Land to his descendants. He knew that he could count on God to fulfill His promises to him. He had that unwavering trust in God. He was a man after God's own heart!

How much do you trust God and how long will you wait for the fulfillment of God's promises to you? Do you thank God for answering your prayer even though you have not yet seen the manifestation of His answer? David did! Your trust in God will grow as you practice trusting Him day by day.

I encourage you to read and study David's prayer in its entirety as recorded in 1 Samuel 7:18–29. It will provide you with a glimpse into the heart of David and the faithfulness of God to fulfill His promises. The prayer will be uplifting to you. In addition, it will provide you with the assurance that you can trust God for the right answer for your situation because He is on our side and knows what is best for you.

God completely fulfilled His promise to David regarding the temple by permitting Solomon, David's son, to build the magnificent Solomon's Temple within a few years after David died. The second promise has not been completely fulfilled. God sent His son Jesus Christ into the world to redeem human beings from their sins and provide them (us) a pathway to everlasting life.

When Jesus was crucified, He rose from the dead and ascended to Heaven where He sits on the spiritual throne at the right hand of God. However, that second promise has not been completely fulfilled. God will establish the everlasting throne on which David's descendant, Jesus Christ, will reign forever. This will occur when Jesus returns to earth on His second advent, as King of kings and Lord of lords. No doubt, David is patiently waiting for the complete fulfilment of that marvelous new covenant.

CHAPTER SEVEN

PRAYERS OF THE WISEST MAN AND GOD'S INSTRUCTIONS ON PRAYER

Prayer for Understanding; God Gives Solomon More Than He Requested!

The Bible records that Solomon loved God. The writer of First Kings puts it this way, "And Solomon loved the LORD, walking in the statues of David his father: only he sacrificed and burnt incense in high places" (1 Kings 3:3). Solomon went to Gibeon to sacrifice unto God at the great high place (altar). The Bible records that Solomon offered one thousand burnt offerings.

There was no question regarding the extent to which Solomon loved God at that time. While Solomon was at Gibeon, God appeared to him in a dream by night, and "God said, Ask what I shall give thee" (1 Kings 3:5). Imagine God gave King Solomon the opportunity to ask Him for anything he wanted. God owns everything and could have given Solomon anything his heart desired, as long as the request was consistent with God's will or plan for him.

If you were in a similar situation as Solomon, what would be your request? Do you have any unfulfilled burning desire? Solomon's request was right in line with God's plan for him.

Solomon had already learned to delight himself in God in order to receive the desire of his heart.

More than likely, Solomon knew the Psalm his father David had written years earlier, "Delight thyself also in the LORD; and he shall give thee the desires of thine heart" (Psa. 37:4). Without giving God's "all you can ask for" opportunity a second thought, Solomon made his request.

Solomon's request shows that he had proper motive. In fact, Solomon's response to God was in the form of a beautiful and sincere prayer. He recounted how good God had been to his father David, and how God had enabled Solomon to succeed his father David as king of Israel. He then acknowledged that he was but a little child, who had no experience in leading the great nation of Israel, whose people could not be counted. Solomon then made an amazingly wise and unselfish request of God.

Solomon prayed, "Give therefore thy servant an understanding heart to judge thy people that I may discern between good and bad: for who is able to judge this thy great people?" (1 Kings 3:9). What a selfless request! It was not about Solomon; rather it was about what he needed in order to be a king in the stature of his father, the great King David.

Yes, when God gives you an assignment, it's reasonable for you to ask for the provision to carry out the assignment. It is said that God will not give you an assignment without providing the wherewithal necessary for you to be successful. Nevertheless, God wants you to ask. When you ask-pray, you are saying to God that you are not self-sufficient and independent of Him. Rather, you need and desire His help.

Solomon was well aware of challenges his father David faced as he ruled Israel. In addition, David had given him specific instructions on a number of matters. It is noteworthy that when David was on his dying bed, he asked Solomon to punish Joab for what Joab had done to him.

David admonished Solomon regarding Joab in this manner, "Do therefore according to thy wisdom, and let not his hoar head go down to the grave in peace (don't let him die a natural death)" (1 Kings 2:6). It's apparent that David knew that Solomon would be a wise king who would deal appropriately with Joab. Perhaps David had observed traits of wisdom and understanding in Solomon; therefore, there was no need to tell Solomon exactly what to do with or to Joab. In addition, he knew that God would have commissioned Solomon to build the temple; therefore, Solomon had to be a wise king!

Since Solomon's request of God was such a wise choice, you may logically conclude that Solomon had some level of wisdom before God enhanced his wisdom and made him the wisest man on earth. No doubt, God gave Solomon spiritual gifts of wisdom and understanding.

The significant point I am making here is that Solomon had the right motive when he asked God for an understanding heart so that he would be effective in judging the people correctly. God responded immediately to Solomon's prayer. These gifts would remain active in Solomon's life and behavior as long as he continued to humble himself before God, trust God, and obey Him.

The Bible records God's response to Solomon's prayer in this manner, "And the speech pleased the LORD, that Solomon asked this thing. And God said unto him, Because thou hast asked this thing, and hast not asked for thyself long life; neither hast asked riches for thyself, nor hast asked the life of thine enemies; but hast asked for thyself understanding to discern judgment; Behold, I have done according to thy word: lo, I have given thee a wise and understanding heart; so that there was none like thee before thee, neither after thee shall any arise like unto thee" (1 King 3:10–11). God was pleased with Solomon's request and rewarded him with more than he requested. He had a desire to please God by judging His people with justice and integrity. God gave him wisdom, understanding, and riches!

Solomon's Prayer at the Dedication of the temple

Solomon had done what God did not permit his father, King David, a man after God's own heart to do—to build the temple. He had built the first permanent, stationary Temple for God. He completed the building project in seven years (1 Kings 6:38). It was the most magnificent and spectacular building in that part of the world.

King Solomon had every reason to be proud and humble simultaneously. Proud because he had completed this God-approved, God-inspired, made-by-hands wonder of Israel—the magnificent temple which was pleasing and acceptable to God. Humble because God gave him the privilege to build the temple, a privilege his father, David, did not receive. In addition, he was humble because of the help he received from his, now deceased, father. David did significant preliminary work in gathering materials in preparation for the construction of the temple. And perhaps, most importantly, Solomon was humble because it was God who gave him guidance in every phase of this monumental temple construction endeavor (2 Chron. 6:12–21).

Praying in Sincerity with the Right Motives

There is no surprise that when this extraordinary house of God, the temple, was finally completed, after seven years, Solomon wanted a massive celebration. He planned and executed an elaborate dedication ceremony! Solomon wanted to make sure that He and the children of Israel paid proper homage to God.

So Solomon orchestrated the building of a fairly elaborate stage-platform, "Five cubits long, and five cubits broad, and three cubits high, and set in the midst of the court: and upon it he stood, and kneeled down upon his knees before all the congregation of Israel, and spread forth his hands towards heaven" (2 Chron. 6: 13). It is on this platform-stage (pulpit), where Solomon, the wisest and richest king of Israel, humbled himself before God and the people of Israel and offered a most solemn prayer of dedication to God.

Evidently, Solomon wanted to be on the stage, where the people could see and hear him well, and give full attention to the ceremony. Review the passage above and note again and reflect on the posture of the great king as he modeled humility and obeisance to God for the people of Israel to emulate.

It was at this dedication of the temple-House of God, when Solomon bent on his knees, with his hands spread towards heaven, in sincerity and with the right motives, prayed, "And said, O LORD God of Israel, there is no God like thee in the heaven, nor in the earth: which keepest covenant, and shewest mercy unto thy servants, that walk before thee with all their hearts" (2 Chron. 6:14). Solomon gave recognition to the true God, the God of Abraham, Isaac, Jacob, David, and his other ancestors. How fitting!

Solomon continued the long solemn prayer recorded in 2 Chronicles 6:14–42. He ended the dedicatory prayer in this manner, "Now my God, let, I beseech thee, thine eyes be open and let thy ears be attent unto the prayer that is made in this place. . . . O LORD God, turn not away the face of thine anointed: remember the mercies of David thy servant" (2 Chron. 6:40, 42). Solomon's passionate prayer thanked God for past mercies and perhaps more importantly sought God's mercies in the future. Of great importance is Solomon's request that God would answer the prayer that is made in the temple. There must be something special about two or three or more sincere people gathering in a place of worship to pray.

God responded immediately to Solomon's passionate and sincere dedicatory prayer. The Prophet Samuel records God's immediate affirmative response: "Now when Solomon had made an end of praying, the fire came down from heaven, and consumed the burnt offering and the sacrifices; and the glory of the LORD filled the house" (2 Chron. 7:1). The manifestation of God's answer to Solomon's prayer was immediately evident to all at the dedicatory ceremony. There was no doubt that God was pleased with Solomon and his work and prayer!

Wouldn't it be great, for you, if each time you pray, God gives you an immediate answer which you can understand? It does not always work that way. Even though God might answer your prayer immediately, it does not mean that the manifestation of His answer will be immediately evident to you.

The Prophet Isaiah reminds us of God's promise: "And it shall come to pass, that before they (we) call, I will answer; and while they (we) are yet speaking, I will hear" (Isa. 65:24). God decides when and how He reveals to us His answers to our prayers. King David reminds us to "Wait on the LORD: be of good courage, and he shall strengthen thine heart: wait, I say, on the LORD" (Psa. 27:14). David's admonition is so applicable to those who pray to the Almighty God!

In another section of this book, I discussed how the Prophet Daniel waited twenty-one days to receive a message which God gave to an angel to deliver to him.

Although God might respond immediately to your prayer, it does not necessarily mean that the manifestation of His answer immediately evident to you. So be patient as David admonishes in the quotation cited above.

In the incident of Solomon, at the dedication of the new (first) temple, it was important for the children of Israel to know that God had approved the temple and had approved Solomon to be His representative. The important message here is that God can respond to a request or a situation faster than any first responder on earth; in fact, faster than the request can be made. However, He chooses how and when He responds.

God Reaffirms His Acceptance of the temple and Solomon's Prayer

The writer of Chronicles records, "And the LORD appeared to Solomon by night, and said unto him, I have heard thy prayer, and have chosen this place to myself for an house of sacrifice" (2 Chron. 7: 12). God had already shown His acceptance of the temple and Solomon's prayer when He dispatched fire to consume the burnt offerings and sacrifices. Nevertheless, He wanted to assure Solomon that his prayer was answered.

You can imagine how pleased and even elated and joyous Solomon must have been at this point in his great accomplishment and, more importantly, his fellowship with God. But then God made a proclamation that perhaps Solomon, the wisest man on earth, might not have fully comprehended at the time. God already knew the future, which Solomon did not know—He knew that Israel would rebel and sin.

God's Instruction for an Effective Prayer for Forgiveness

Solomon had prayed and asked God that if the children of Israel repent after they sinned against Him that God would forgive them. Solomon listed numerous actions that God might use to punish the people. Solomon asked God that if the people sin and God closed the heaven and there is no rain on the land and there is famine, epidemic, or other calamities, if the people look toward the temple, humble themselves, repent, and pray that God would hear their prayers, He will forgive their sins and heal their land (1 Kings 8:35–37; 2 Chron. 7:12–14).

God responded to Solomon's prayer by proclaiming to Solomon, "If I shut up heaven that there be no rain, or if I command the locusts to devour the land, or if I send pestilence among my people" (2 Chron. 7:13). This prelude to God's instruction for His healing of the land is rarely quoted; while the verse which follows, 2 Chronicles 7:14 often is frequently quoted, especially in times of national calamities. It is conceivable that God wanted Solomon to know that He already knew that Solomon and the children of Israel would sin.

It is God's decision to execute the chastisement in 2 Chronicles 7:13 and His decision to exercise grace and mercy as He chooses. Surely the children would need God's grace and mercy.

God knows that the human heart is fickle, and God wanted to give Solomon and the children of Israel the message that God will chastise them; however, He provides a way for them to repent. God assured Solomon that He will provide grace and mercy and forgiveness to the children of Israel for their sins, which they certainly will commit. And He provide healing for the nation, if the people follow God's instruction in seeking healing of the land.

The merciful and gracious God, does not take pleasure in chastising or punishing His people, even when it is for their good. However, God demands remorsefulness and repentance of those who sin. God gave Solomon the requirements (formula) that he and the children of Israel must apply in order for God to remove future chastisements, which are mentioned above, and heal the land. The instructions that God gave to Solomon are applicable for God's people of our time.

Understanding God's Instruction to Solomon on Prayer for Healing of the Land

One of the most misunderstood and often quoted instruction which God gave to Solomon is found in 1 Kings 8 and 2 Chronicles 7. As discussed above, after Solomon had completed the temple, according to God's specifications, and had dedicated it to God, God was pleased with the temple and with Solomon's dedicatory ceremony. However, Solomon thought and God knew that it would be just a matter of time before His people would disobey God and stray from Him. So Solomon prayed in advance for the people.

I am devoting a little extra time in discussing God's instructions, as recorded in 2 Chronicles 7:13–14 because they are so relevant in our time. God gave the instructions to Solomon and the children of Israel about 960 BC. The instructions are consequential and applicable to God's people and our nation as they were to Israel.

God knows that disobedience and straying away of His people from God often result in their disillusionment, a feeling of guilt, and even depression. The loving God knows that He will chastise and correct His people as He chooses. As previously discussed, Solomon asked God to be merciful to the children of Israel when they stray away from God and repent and return to God. He made it clear to Solomon that there is a way out. God extends grace and mercy to His people, so even when He chastises them, they do not bear the full consequences of their misdeeds.

The writer of Proverbs—probably Solomon, in this instance—says, "Though hand join in hand, the wicked shall not be unpunished: but the seed of the righteous shall be delivered" (Prov. 11: 21). God placed Solomon on notice that there is a way that he and the children of Israel can receive relief from God's corrections. God continues the proclamation referenced in 2 Chronicles 7:13 above.

In 2 Chronicles 7:14, which I refer to as God's requirements for the relief of chastisement of the people of Israel and the healing of the land, God Himself puts it this way: "If my people, which are called by my name, shall humble themselves, and pray, and seek my face, and turn from their wicked ways; then I will hear from heaven, and I will forgive their sins, and will heal their lands" (2 Chron. 7:14).

You may have heard, as I have heard many times, preachers declaring that if the President of the United States of America, or the governor of a state, or the mayor of a city, or some other elected official would humble themselves and pray, God would heal the nation, the state, or the city respectively. Well, I do not know whether the president, governor, and/or mayor is among God's people, who are called by God's name. However, I do believe that God's people today are those who have accepted Jesus Christ as their Lord and Savior and are called Christians.

That being the case, it should be the preachers, evangelists, deacons, and all followers of Christ who should be doing what God told Solomon to do in 2 Chronicles 7:14—to humble ourselves and pray and carry out God's instructions.

It is the church—the body of Christ, the Christians, the believers—who constitute God's people in our time. God's original audience for the instructions were the children of Israel, descendants of Abraham. Those who believe in Jesus Christ are descendants of Abraham, not by physical lineage; rather by adoption by God through accepting Jesus Christ as Lord and Savior.

Consequently, all who accept Jesus Christ as Lord and Savior are called by God's name and have the responsibility to carry out God's instructions as recorded in 2 Chronicles 7:14, regardless of title, position, ethnicity, place of origin, gender, age, socio-economic condition, and so forth. In this context, it is the acceptance of Jesus Christ as Lord and savior which makes you and me among God's people, who are called by His name.

There is no doubt that there have been, and there might be, Christian presidents, governors, mayors, and other government leaders throughout the world; however, God expects the church to be His people on earth and to carry out Christian ministry, including serving as His representatives on earth—proclaiming His Word and seeking healing of the land.

The church cannot relegate such an important responsibility of calling on God for the healing of the land to secular leaders. Rather, they must call on God and then work with secular leaders as necessary and appropriate, including praying for leaders—spiritual and secular.

In the time of Solomon, the children of Israel were God's chosen people, who were under the leadership of God, with Solomon being the representative of God. When things were working well in Israel, the king (government) and the prophets and priests worked in harmony. Each office had its designated responsibilities and duties; nevertheless they worked together.

In many nations today, there is strict legal separation of the state (government) from the church (religious organizations); therefore, many secular leaders are prohibited from publicly proclaiming their religious beliefs or religious preference. Many are prohibited from bringing their governments and people to the acknowledgement and worship of God Almighty.

Some churches and Christians are expecting too much when they assert that our political leaders, governmental officials and other secular leaders should lead our nations to God. God delegates that responsibility to His people, who are called by His name, to Christians, who adopted our name from Christ, our Lord and Savior. This is a responsibility that is uniquely ours, similar to our responsibility for the great commission (Matthew 28:19–20; Acts 1:8)!

You should feel good in knowing that, as a Christian, you have a vital role in praying for the nation. If you are a leader in your church, you have an added responsibility to harness and engage your membership and the community in praying for the nation. God has already said that He will respond, and God's Word does not return void. It delivers intended results.

You are just one person, and you cannot do all the praying and humbling of self and seeking God's face for the entire city, state, or nation; however, you can do what you can do. Perhaps you are the one who God is calling to start to organize your church to do what only God's people, who are called by His name are specifically instructed by God to do.

I am very much aware that there are religions which do not give primacy to Jesus Christ as the Son of God, the Messiah, and Savior; however, it is my unwavering belief that Jesus is the Son of God, the Messiah. I do not purposefully intend to offend any religion which does not accept Jesus Christ as the Son of God, Messiah, and Savior; however, that is my fundamental and unchanging belief.

As I conclude this chapter of the book, I am reminded of the Apostle Peter's mini-sermon to the Sanhedrin Council when the apostles were brought before the Council for teaching about the resurrected Jesus Christ. In his declaration about the risen Jesus Christ, Peter boldly declared, "Neither is there salvation in any other: for there is none other name under heaven given among men, whereby we must be saved" (Acts 4:12). I firmly agree with the teaching of Peter in the context cited, just as I firmly believe that Christians have the quintessential obligation to pray for our nation and all nations!

CHAPTER EIGHT

PRAYERS OF ELIJAH AND ELISHA

Elijah Prays and God Answers

Elijah was one of the twelve great Major Prophets in the Old Testament. He was on the level of such great prophets as Isaiah and Jeremiah. Some Bible scholars even consider him the greatest of the prophets, since when he completed his assignment on earth, God took him alive into heaven. He did not experience death.

The Prophet Elijah came on the scene when Israel was at its absolute worse in its relationship with God. The kingdom of Israel, which consisted of twelve tribes, over which Saul, David, Solomon reigned was now divided into two kingdoms. Ten northern tribes had now broken away and constituted the Northern Kingdom called Israel. Only two southern tribes remained loyal to David—the tribes of Judah and Ephraim, known as Judah, the Southern Kingdom.

Elijah's Righteous Indignation and Proclamation Against King Ahab and Israel

When Elijah became a prophet of Israel or was announced with a brief introduction, Ahab was King of the Northern Kingdom, Israel, consisting of ten tribes. Elijah is introduced in the Bible as follows, "And Elijah the Tishbite, who was of the inhabitants of Gilead, said unto Ahab, As the LORD God of Israel liveth, before whom I stand, there shall not be dew nor rain these years, but according to my word" (1 Kings 17:1). What bold and audacious manner in which Elijah introduced himself to Ahab, the evil king of Israel!

The Bible described Ahab in this manner: "And Ahab the son of Omri did evil in the sight of the LORD above all that were before him" (1 Kings 16:30). To add proverbial insult to injury, Ahab's wife, Jezebel, aided and abetted Ahab in his evil and rebellious ways. She was perhaps the most infamous, wicked woman in the Bible. Jezebel's only close rival in wickedness would probably be Delilah, the wife of Samson.

King Ahab served the idol god Baal, worshipped him, and built altars on which he offered sacrifices to Baal. Ahab's idolatry was described in in this manner: "Ahab did more to provoke the LORD God of Israel to anger than all the kings before him" (1 Kings 16:33). This was the situation in Israel when the Prophet Elijah was introduced to Israel as a prophet. Elijah had righteous indignation toward King Ahab and confronted him in this manner: "And Elijah the Tishbite, who was of the inhabitants of Gilead, said unto Ahab, As the LORD liveth, before whom I stand, there shall not be dew nor rain these three years, but according to my word" (1 Kings 17:1). Was this a confrontation or not!

We have not seen such a man's confrontation against evil with such righteous indignation since Moses confronted Pharaoh. Even so, Moses had God's rod in his hand and the assurance of God's protection.

What was Elijah thinking? He spoke to Ahab as a man with authority from God! The interesting thing is that the Bible does not say that God instructed Elijah to make that pronouncement to Ahab. Later it is shown that Elijah had a special relationship and fellowship with God.

Sometimes evil is so glaring that it must be confronted. It is advisable to pray about it first, even if it is a short silent prayer, and confront it. Elijah confronted Ahab. His boldness and apparent certainty of the outcome clearly indicate that he was making the proclamation with the power of the God of Israel.

It is conceivable that Elijah might have uttered a silent urgent prayer with confident expectation. And there again, he might have prayed out loudly to God, who hears and responds to spoken and silent prayers.

Elijah evoked God's name and put God's reputation on the line. He undoubtedly expected God to deliver for him. Ahab needed to be reminded that there is a true God in Israel. Not since Joshua commanded the sun and moon to stand still had a man interfere with the natural process of nature.

What great trust Elijah had in the faithfulness of God to respond to an urgent, nature-changing matter! Well, God did respond. He told Elijah to get out of the way of the wrath of Ahab and Jezebel. This was a clear indication that God had answered Elijah's prayer. However, God did not completely shield Elijah from the consequences of his righteous rebuke of Ahab. He had to go in hiding for a while. But God would take care of his physical needs. He would be sheltered and fed during the three-year drought that he had pronounced on Ahab and Israel.

Have you ever had to deliver bad news, such as terminating an employee? What about disapproving a loan application or telling a student that he or has earned a failing grade in the last course required for graduation?

What did you do after delivering the sad news?

Elijah followed God's instructions and took cover while the answer to his prayer played out. God made sure that Elijah was well fed during the three-year period of drought and famine. Meanwhile, Ahab and Jezebel got the message quite clearly that God had answered Elijah's prayer and that there is a true and living God in Israel. No doubt, Ahab and Jezebel and all the false prophets of Baal appealed to Baal to send rain, but to no avail.

Sometimes God makes assignments to us which require spiritual empowerment and the application of intelligence and common sense in order for their accomplishment. For example, I am gifted to teach Sunday school and Bible study classes. However, there have been times when the weather was so bad with snow-covered highways, street, and church grounds. In such an instance, it would be foolhardy and downright unwise for me to travel forty miles to the church building and to ask others to risk the possibility having accidents due to icy highways, streets, and/or church grounds to attend the classes. God is able to protect His servants; however, He expects His servants to apply faith, intelligence, knowledge, understanding, and wisdom in their daily lives.

So even with the empowerment of God, Elijah stayed away from Ahab until it was time for the rains.

Elijah Prays for Reviving the Widow's Son

Elijah was on the run—in hiding from the evil King Ahab and his wicked wife, Jezebel. He was staying by a brook, and a raven brought him meat twice per day. Unfortunately, due to the prolong drought, which he had proclaimed, the brook ran dry.

The faithful God of Israel prepared a widow, at Zarephath, to provide lodging and meals for Elijah during the remainder of the three-year drought and famine in Israel. There was a symbiotic relationship between Elijah and this kind widow. She provided meals and lodging for Elijah and Elijah ensured that she had an adequate supply of meal and oil.

The mutually beneficial relationship between Elijah and the widow went well until tragedy struck. The widow's only son, living with her, died. In the twinkling of an eye, the widow's joy and happiness were transformed into grief, bitterness, sadness, and perhaps resentment toward Elijah.

The widow assumed that Elijah was punishing her, for some wrong which she had done, by causing the death of her son. You can imagine the pain in her heart and the sadness on her face as she tearfully talked with Elijah. What the widow did not realize was that Elijah was as surprised and sad with the death of her son as she was. The only difference was that Elijah knew the source of all life. He knew that the death of this child was not by chance. It was an opportunity for him to confirm to the widow that the God of Israel is able to do all things, including restoring life to the physical and spiritual dead.

Elijah grasped the dead boy in his arms and took the lifeless child to the room where he was staying. He placed the dead child on his bed, and there Elijah had his most intimate and fervent intercessory prayer with God. Elijah lifted up his voice and in desperation, and with empathy for this widow, grieving mother who had lost her only son, he cried out to God in a profound manner: "O LORD my God, hast thou also brought evil upon the widow with whom I sojourn, by slaying her son?" (1 Kings 17:20). Then Elijah took action with faith. He understood that prayer should precede action and that faith demands work to achieve desired outcomes.

As James the apostle teaches, "Even so faith, if it hath not works, is dead, being alone" (James 2:17). So Elijah, with his faith in the efficacy of prayer and the importance of working with faith, began to work. "And he stretched himself upon the child three times, and cried unto the LORD and said O LORD my God. I pray thee, let this child's soul come into him again" (1 Kings 17:21). Elijah prayed in faith. He worked—did what he could do. He prayed again with confident expectation that God would answer his prayer and restore life to the boy. Then he waited to see the answer.

This prayer was urgent—SOS. It requires God's immediate discernable response. There was a widow who was mourning for the loss of her son. She is probably blaming herself for doing something wrong or for not doing something that she should have done. She thought that the man of God had cursed her, hence the death of her only son. And there was a dead body lying on the bed which the kind widow had provided for Elijah without cost to him.

There was certainly an emergency for the widow and, to some extent, for Elijah, but not for God; He already knew the outcome. For the sake of the widow, Elijah wanted God to respond as though it were an emergency, although it was not an emergency for God. It was just a teachable moment for Elijah.

Nevertheless, the manifestation of God's answer was quite prompt, "And the LORD heard the voice of Elijah; and the soul of the child came into him again, and he revived" (1 Kings 17:22). God, again granted grace to the widow. It was God's grace in the first place which had allowed her and the child to survive thus far during the drought and famine. And now God had restored life to the boy. More importantly, God reaffirmed the faith of Elijah that he could depend on the faithful God to answer his prayers and supply his needs!

Can you imagine the joy which filled the heart of the widow when she received her son alive! No, she had not done anything wrong which resulted in the death of her son; no, she was not accursed. Yes, the man of God appreciated her kind hospitality; yes, the God of Israel and of Elijah is the true God who can do all things. Yes, God deserves the praise and glory for restoring life to the widow's son.

And there was joy in the heart of the man of God as well—joy because the widow was joyful; joy because God had responded to his prayer immediately and in such a profound manner, raising a dead boy to life and assuring the widow that the God of Israel is an awesome God.

Do you believe that God does miracles today? Yes, he does!

Elijah Prays for Rain in Israel

The three-year period of no rain in Israel was concluding soon. The faithful, merciful, and gracious God instructed Elijah to get out of hiding and show himself to Ahab. Elijah obeyed God. He asked Ahab to gather the people of Israel and the prophets of Baal on Mount Carmel. Then Elijah challenged the people of Israel, telling them that it was time for them to decide who they will serve—the LORD God of Israel or the idol Baal. The people did not respond. He gave them a second challenge.

Elijah asked to have the false prophets offer a sacrifice to the idol god Baal, and he would offer a sacrifice to the LORD God of Israel, and if Baal accepts the sacrifice by consuming it with fire, Baal would be God. However, if Baal did not accept and consume the sacrifice and the LORD God of Israel did, then the LORD God is the true God. Of course, the idol god Baal did not and could not accept and consume the sacrifice despite the all-day pleading of the false prophets.

When it was time for Elijah to offer sacrifice to the LORD God of Israel, he prepared an altar. Then Elijah prayed, "LORD God of Abraham, Isaac, and Israel, let it be known this day that thou art God in Israel, and that I am thy servant, and that I have done all these things at thy word. Hear me, O LORD, hear me, that this people may know that thou art the LORD God, and that thou hast turned their hearts back again. Then the fire fell [from heaven] and consumed the burnt sacrifice, and the wood, and the stones . . ." (1 Kings 18:36–38). God responded immediately to Elijah's prayer by sending fire to consume the offering, the wood, and even the stones which were used for the improvised altar.

God demonstrated that He is the LORD God of Israel. Elijah did not need to pray all day in order for the true and only God to hear and answer his prayer. Baal was just an idol without any power; therefore, it could not respond the pleading of the false prophets. The children of Israel now realized that Baal was just a powerless idol and that King Ahab was leading them down a path of destruction. They responded positively to God and to Elijah.

The Bible records the response of the people of Israel to God's answer to Elijah's prayer in this manner: "And when the people saw it (the complete consumption of the sacrifice) they fell on their faces: and they said, The LORD. He is the God" (1 Kings 18:39). Was it worth three years of Elijah risking his life, hiding from Ahab in order to bring the people of Israel back to the LORD God of Israel? Of course, you will say a big yes!

It is important that prayers should be of such that answers to them glorify God. When God answered the prayer of Elijah, the people of Israel humbled themselves before God, repented of their sins, and glorified Him.

What sacrifices are you willing to make to bring your family, your church, your community, and or the nation in closer relationship and closer fellowship with God? What small steps are you willing to take in the immediate future? Are you willing to start with sincere and fervent prayers with confident expectation that God will answer your prayer according to His will and His timeframe? I pray that you answer each question with unwavering "yes, I will."

The Rain Came Pouring Down

Elijah ordered that all the false prophets of Baal be destroyed on Mount Carmel. He assured Ahab that abundant rains were imminent, and encouraged him to eat and drink. Ahab did as Elijah suggested.

Elijah and his servant went further up the top of the mountain. Elijah had confident expectation that there would be rain shortly. The same LORD God of Israel who had prevented rain in Israel for three years and had recently dispatched fire to consume the burnt sacrifice would cause it to rain shortly.

When Elijah and his servant reached the summit of Mount Carmel, Elijah assumed a praying position. "He cast himself up on the earth, and put his face between his knees" (1 Kings 18:42). He told his servant to keep going back looking at the clouds towards the sea. The servant looked six times and there was nothing for the servant to report to Elijah. Then the servant looked the seventh time and saw something different.

With his face toward the ground in absolute humility to God, Elijah was undoubtedly petitioning God for another miracle: rain.

There had been no rain or dew in Israel in three long years. Elijah already knew that seven is the symbol of perfection (completeness). So he was not surprised when on the seventh look, the servant rushed back to Elijah full of excitement, "Behold there ariseth a little cloud out of the sea, like a man's hand" (1 Kings 18:44). That was the symbol, the signal Elijah was waiting to show up. He immediately dispatched the servant to tell King Ahab to head for home because rain, abundance of rain was imminent.

The Bible records, "That the heaven was black with clouds and wind, and there was a great rain. And the hand of the LORD was on Elijah; and he girded up his loins and ran before Ahab to Jezreel [the city where Ahab lived]" (1 Kings 18:46). God had now done the fourth public miracle in response to prayers of Elijah: God prevented rain and dew from falling in Israel for three years; He restored life to the widow's son; He dispatched fire to consume the burnt offering on Mount Carmel; and now, He is sending abundance of rain all over drought-stricken Israel.

The Bible tells us that God will answer our prayers even before we ask. This might have happened in the case of Elijah when he declared that there would be no rain in Israel for three years. It is important to have ongoing relationship and fellowship with God so that we can hear His still, small voice speaking to us all the time. In addition, we can sense the presence of the Holy Spirit guiding us.

Elijah was an ordinary man who cooperated with God and through the power of God, did extraordinary things, including restoring the children to God and restoring the life of a widow's son!

God will do miracles in you and through you in proportion to His plan for you, and your faith, trust in Him, and your obedience in and patience with Him.

Do you believe that God can use you to do small and great things?

Sometimes the faith wavers a bit—not the faith that God is able to do what He promises; rather, sometimes, you may have a feeling of uncertainty or doubt as to whether you are doing what God wants you to do. That is when prayer is particularly essential. I have experienced uncertainty in my own life at times, never about God's faithfulness and His awesome power to deliver on His promises. Rather about my faithfulness to God and the extent to which I know that I am pursuing God's plan for me. This is when I pray most fervently.

Even Elijah got weary and tired, so much so that God relieved him of his earthly responsibilities and provided an appropriate successor in the person of Elisha. Elijah definitely teaches us that God responds to prayers. Sometimes the manifestation of His answer is immediate, and sometimes the manifestation is revealed through a gradual process. God's answers are always on His own timeframe and in His own way, and are always on time.

The important message for you and me is that you and I must believe in the efficacy of prayer and that we must have an active prayer life and positive fellowship with God—Jesus through the Holy Spirit.

Elisha Prays: God Opens the Eyes of His Servant

Elisha succeeded Elijah as the lead prophet of the prophets of Israel about 851 B. C. He had asked Elijah to grant him a double portion of his power. Elijah promised Elisha that if he saw him when he was leaving earth his request would be granted. On his last day on earth, Elijah journeyed to the Jordan River with Elisha at his side. Elijah used his mantle to strike the Jordan River and it divided so both crossed on dry ground.

As Elijah and Elisha were walking on the other side of the Jordan River, a chariot of fire came down from heaven and swooped up Elijah. As Elijah was ascending, he dropped his mantle. Elisha picked it up. His request was granted; he received a double portion of Elijah's power. His first use of this power, God's power, was to use the mantle to strike the Jordan River so it divided and he went across through a dry pathway.

Elisha used is prophetic power to warn King Jehoram of Israel on numerous occasions when the king of Syria was plotting to trap and capture him.

The king of Syria learned that it was the prophet Elisha who was disclosing his evil intention to the king of Israel. The king of Syria plotted to capture Elisha and take him to Syria. Elisha and his servant were at the city of Dothan. Early one morning, the servant of Elisha noticed that Dothan was besieged by Syrian army, chariots, and horses. He was petrified and panicked. He rushed to Elisha being afraid, and in an alarming voice, he cried out to Elisha, "Alas, my master! how shall we do?" (2 Kings 6:15).

Elisha had no fear at all. The situation provided him with a teachable moment. He could demonstrate the power of God to his servant without preaching a long sermon to him. In fact, he could demonstrate the efficacy of prayer, when it is uttered to the Almighty God of Israel.

With a sense of calm certainty, Elisha responded to frightened servant with a reassuring, and confident voice, "Fear not: for they that be with us are more than they that be with them" (2 Kings 6:16). Elisha was confident that the same God whose power had allowed him to use the mantle, he inherited from Elijah, to divide Jordan River, so he could cross through a dry pathway, would protect him. In addition, a short while earlier, through the power of God, he was able to cause the iron head of an axe to float in the Jordan River.

Certainly, God would protect him from the Syrian army. Elisha called on God on behalf of his servant, "And Elisha prayed and said, LORD, I pray thee, open his [servant's] eyes that he may see. And the LORD opened the eyes of the young man: and he saw: and behold the mountain was full of horses and chariots of fire round Elisha" (2 Kings 6:17). God's answer to Elisha's prayer was manifested immediate to Elisha's servant.

God responded to Elisha's prayer immediately. Elisha knew all along that God had his back; however, he did not want his servant to have an anxiety attack and mental break-down. Elijah prayed aloud so that the young man would know that the Almighty God was the source of his and Elisha's protection. God answered Elisha's prayer right away and the manifestation of His answer was instantaneous. God opened the young man's his eyes so he could see what Elisha saw all along—the mountain full of horses and chariots of fire ready to protect Elisha and the servant

You may find ourselves in the company of others who do not see what you see or who have not received the vision which you have received. Perhaps they have not yet attained our level of spiritual growth and maturity you have attained. In such instances, rather than trying to convince others of what you see and your vision, probably you should pray that God would open their eyes and their minds that they might see and perceive.

Jesus puts it this way: "But blessed are your eyes, for they see: and your ears, for they hear" (Matt. 13:16). God blessed Elisha's servant so that he could immediately see and hear the horses and chariot of fire which God provided to protect Elisha and him.

Elisha's praying did not end with God opening the eyes of his servant so that he could see the horses and chariots of fire surrounding and protecting them at Dothan. Rather, when the Syrian armies advanced toward Elisha, thinking they had trapped him, ". . . Elisha prayed unto the LORD, and said, Smite this people, I pray thee, with blindness. And he smote them with blindness according to the word of Elisha" (2 Kings 6:18). Elisha prayed to God with confident expectation. He expected that God would answer his prayer and God did. Elijah did not want to destroy the Syrian armies; in fact, he intended to render kindness to them.

I have said on numerous occasions that prayers should be specific, that is asking God for specific outcomes. However, since we can only see a situation partly, we should ask God that His will be done in every situation.

It is worthy to note the specific requests which Elisha made to God.

Firstly, he asked God to open the eyes of his servant that he may see. He did not ask God to give his servant eyes, he already had eyes. Often, we assume that because a person is in our company or in class with us, he or she sees what we are seeing or hearing what we are hearing or saying or agreeing to what we are saying.

Understanding what one sees or hears is quite a different matter than just the casual or superficial seeing and hearing. Hearing and seeing things from a spiritual perspective adds another dimension.

Secondly, Elisha specifically asked God to smite members of the Syrian armies with blindness that they would not be able to see. Because Elisha made such specific requests of God, there would be no doubt that God had answered his prayer.

In addition, it worth noting that Elisha did not ask God to destroy the Syrians who had besieged Dothan with the intention of capturing him and taking him to the king of Syria. In fact, Elisha was most merciful toward the Syrian armies.

He led the men to Samaria and instructed the King of Israel to feed them and send them home to the king of Syria without harm. Elisha executed what the writer of Proverbs admonished more than one hundred years earlier, "If thine enemy be hungry, give him bread to eat; and if he be thirsty, give him water to drink: for thou shalt heap coals of fire upon his head, and the LORD shall reward thee" (Prov. 25:21–22). Is there any wonder that Elisha was such a great prophet! He trusted God, he prayed, and he rendered good to the Syrians who meant him evil. And God answered his prayers and rewarded him mightily. Yes, prayer works, because God answers prayers!

Elisha is certainly a role model for those who desire to have fellowship with God. He was a prophet who prayed for the benefit of others and extended kindness to those who sought to hurt him.

Are you prepared to pray for your enemies and to show kindness to those who seek to hurt you? If your answer is yes to these questions, it is likely that the Spirit of God dwells in you. If you are a Christian and you are unable to truly answer the questions in the affirmative, then you need to pray for the activation of the Holy Spirit in you.

I discussed activation of the Holy Spirit, at length, in another book, *Becoming a Joy Fulfilled Christian in the Twenty-First Century and Beyond*. I strongly recommend that book for your reading, if you have not already read it. If you are not yet a Christian or a believer, please pray that God will open your ears, your eyes, and your heart that you see, hear and believe in Jesus, and be ready to accept Jesus as your Lord and savior. I am praying with and for you.

CHAPTER NINE

THE MAN WHO TRIED TO DEFY GOD AND LIVED TO TELL ABOUT IT

Jonah Prays for His Life; God Hears and Saves Him!

Sometime during the reign of Jeroboam II, King of Israel (786 BC and 746 BC), God called and commissioned Jonah to deliver a message to the king and people of Nineveh, capital of Assyria, demanding that they repent and turn from their evil ways or suffer imminent destruction. While the exact date of God's instruction to Jonah is not recorded in the Bible, many Bible scholars calculated the date to be around 751 BC.

The message that God instructed Jonah to deliver to the city of Nineveh was clear, unambiguous, and succinct: the people of the great city of Nineveh must repent, stop their evil ways, and turn to God or suffer imminent annihilation.

Jonah, a minor prophet, tried to defy God's direct instruction to preach to the people of Nineveh. Perhaps Jonah thought that the wicked Gentiles, people of Nineveh, deserve to suffer the consequences of their evil ways. Therefore, he did not want to preach to that great city of 120,000 people. He did not want them to repent and be saved.

There are at least two important principles which Jonah did not understand about the God of Israel. Firstly, he did not understand that God is merciful, forgiving, and extends grace and mercy as He chooses. Secondly, he did not understand that he could not run away or hide from the omnipresent God.

Perhaps he had not read David's declaration that no one can hide from God. Some suggest that Jonah was arrogant, acting as though he were God; he was deciding who deserved to be saved and who should suffer the negative consequences of their evil ways.

So Jonah—in his self-righteous indignation, leaning on his own understanding, and desiring to see the city of Nineveh destroyed—decided to disobey God's instruction.

Instead of heading for Nineveh, Jonah went to Joppa and boarded a ship going in the opposite direction to Tarshish. He went below the deck of the ship and fell asleep. Perhaps Jonah thought he was now out of the sight and reach of God so he could get some rest and relaxation.

It is interesting to note that even this prophet of God had such limited understanding of the omnipotent, omniscience, and omnipresent of the awesome God. Jonah was fortunate that God had called him, an ordinary man, to carry out an extraordinary mission. All he had to do to complete this quintessential mission was to trust and obey God.

Jonah's problem was not lack of ability; rather it was his arrogance and unforgiving heart. He must have felt relieved and safe, thinking that he would not need to go to Nineveh. His comfort was short lived. He discovered to his great discomfort that he could not run or hide or defy God.

While Jonah was asleep below the deck of the ship, God sent a great storm upon the sea which was causing the ship to be in danger of being destroyed. Jonah, with much humiliation, confessed that he was the cause of the precarious situation and difficulty the ship and crew were experiencing. He suggested that the only solution to the problem was to throw him overboard.

With great trepidation and reluctance, the crew members finally complied with Jonah's suggestion and threw him from the ship into the raging sea. The storm and sea calmed immediately.

God would not permit Jonah to defy His instruction by drowning. The same God who orchestrated the storm and the throwing of Jonah into the sea wanted the people of Nineveh to have another opportunity to repent and avoid destruction.

So God made provision to save the disobedient Jonah from death in the sea. God provided a large fish to swallow Jonah without hurting him. The fish was more obedient to God at that time than was Jonah.

It was while Jonah was in the belly of the fish that he prayed passionately to God vowing to offer sacrifices to God and thanking God for sparing his life. He had now learned that even when he is in the belly of a fish God sees him and could hear and answer his prayer.

Jonah lifted up his voice and prayed a lifesaving prayer. It appears that in the Book of Jonah chapter 2, Jonah recounted his experience as he thought he was facing imminent death in the belly of the fish.

He recounted his prayer in this manner: "I cried by reason of my afflictions unto the LORD, and he heard me; out of the belly of hell cried I, and thou heardest my voice" (Jon. 2:2). He continues to recount the prayer from the belly of the fish: "I went down to the bottom of the mountains; the earth with her bars was about me for ever: yet hath thou brought up my life from corruption O LORD my God" (Jon. 2:6). Jonah continued his prayer.

He acknowledged that when he was losing his life in the belly of the fish, he turned his face to the Holy Temple and prayed earnestly. He remarked that those who worship false gods turned away from the true God. Then he pledged to offer sacrifices to God with songs of praise and will keep whatever vows he makes to God (Jon. 2:7–9).

Jonah ended recounting his experience and prayer from the belly of the fish in this way, "And the LORD spake unto the fish, and it vomited out Jonah upon the dry ground" (Jon. 2:10). God extended grace and mercy toward Jonah, answered his prayer when he prayed from the belly of the fish, and saved him from certain death by drowning or by being devoured by some creature in the sea.

The incident of Jonah reminds us that God answers prayers regardless of circumstances or physical situations, provided such prayers are sincere and accompanied with remorse, repentance, and trust in God to hear and answer.

God called Jonah a second time and gave him the same mission to preach to the people of Nineveh. The message was clear, the people must repent or be destroyed. Jonah obeyed God. He preached in Nineveh for three days, the number of days it took him to preach throughout the city. The king and the people repented, fasted, and prayed. God spared the city and its 120,000 people and the animals.

The previously defiant Jonah, and perhaps still reluctant, was perhaps the most effective short-term prophet recorded in the Bible. Consider he preached only one—the same sermon for three days, in the great city of Nineveh, and the king and 120,000 people repented.

In contrast, Noah preached for one hundred years and only eight persons were saved in the ark. The great major prophet Jeremiah preached for forty or so years, and the kings of Judah refused to repent. In fact, in 586 BC, Nebuchadnezzar and the Babylonians captured Jerusalem and destroyed that city including the beautiful Solomon's Temple, plucked out the eyes of the last king of Judah, Zedekiah, and took him along with people of Judah into captivity in Babylon.

Jonah prayed from the belly of a fish, and God heard his prayer and saved his life. The king and the people of the great city of Nineveh heard Jonah's sermon. They repented and prayed. God heard and answered their prayers and spared the city from destruction.

God still hears and answers prayers and grants grace and mercy to His people. He still calls His people to repentance. And He still uses humans to deliver His messages in and outside places of worship-His house. Is God calling you or has He called you to deliver a message or messages? If you are not sure of the answers, pray with positive expectation for god's answer and discernment!

CHAPTER TEN

PRAYERS OF A HEBREW IN CAPTIVITY

Daniel Prays For The Deliverance of the Babylonian Captives!

The name Daniel in Hebrew means "God is my judge." When Nebuchadnezzar invaded Jerusalem in 605 BC, initiating the Babylonian captivity, the Babylonians took the wisest and most handsome men and beautiful women to Babylon. Daniel was among the captives Nebuchadnezzar took to Babylon at that time. Daniel must have been a young man or even a child when Nebuchadnezzar carried him from Jerusalem to Babylon.

In addition to Daniel (Belteshazzar), Nebuchadnezzar took other young men to Babylon as well, including Hananiah (Shadrach), Mishael (Meshach), and Azariah (Abednego). The names in the parentheses are the Chaldean (Babylonian) names which Nebuchadnezzar gave to the four young men.

Even if you are only somewhat familiar with the Old Testament of the Bible, you are likely to have heard or read about how God delivered Daniel from the lion's den in Babylon. You are likely to have read or heard of the incident when God delivered Shadrach, Meshach, and Abednego from the burning fiery furnace in Babylon. However, you may not be familiar with Daniel's passionate plea (prayer) to God on behalf of

Jerusalem, Judah, and Israel. I am presenting Daniel's prayer in some details, although not in totality.

During the first year when Darius was King of Babylon, Daniel, who served in the king's court, read and recalled the prophecy of Jeremiah that the people of Judah would be in captivity for seventy years. Daniel himself had been in Babylon since 607 BC, since he was a boy. He realized that the seventy-year period would be coming to an end soon.

The complete invasion and destruction of Jerusalem and Judah, including the destruction of Solomon's Temple and the wall around Jerusalem occurred in 586 BC. The initial invasion of Jerusalem and Judah and deportation of the people of Judah to Babylon began in 607 BC. Jeremiah had prophesied that Jerusalem would be in ruin and desolation for seventy years.

Once Daniel realized the ending of the seventy-year period of God's chastisement of the people of Judah by the Babylonians (allowing the Babylonian to take the people of Judah into captivity) was coming to an end soon, he decided to petition God for His intervention.

Daniel records a narration of his petition to God on behalf of Judah. Sometimes it seems that Daniel is recounting and sharing his prayer; while at other times he seems to be making his petition to God. Daniel begins by sharing his disposition, frame of mind, attitude, thusly, "And I set my face unto the Lord God, to seek by prayer and supplication, with fasting, and sack cloth and ashes" (Dan. 9:3).

It is conceivable that Daniel turned his face toward the direction of site where Solomon's Temple once stood at Jerusalem. The temple was already destroyed by the Babylonians in 586 BC. Centuries earlier, when Solomon dedicated the temple, he asked God that if His people sinned, and then look toward the temple, and repent, that God would hear their prayers, forgive their sins, and heal their land (1 Kings 8:33–39, 50–51).

Apparently, Daniel was aware of Solomon's prayer. In any case, Daniel, demonstrated sincere humility, sorrow, repentance, and a need to be close to and have fellowship with God.

Daniel, evidently, had a broken spirit and a contrite heart. He provides details of his approach to God for the benefit of the readers of his time as well as our time. It is clear that Daniel wants readers of the prayer to have an insight of his attitude as he petitions God on behalf of Jerusalem, Judah, and all Israel.

So Daniel prays, "O Lord the great and dreadful God, keeping the covenant and mercy of them that love him, and to them that love his commandments. We have sinned and have committed iniquity, and have done wickedly, and have rebelled, even by departing from thy precepts and from thy judgements" Daniel 9:4–5). It is of interest to note that Daniel was just a child when he was deported (taken from Judah to Babylon in 607 BC) almost twenty years before final Babylonian captivity. Yet he was a righteous man, as shown by how God protected him in the lion's den. However, he did not exclude himself from the sins of his ancestors.

Daniel's Prayer of Confession and Ownership

Daniel confessed, "We have sinned and committed iniquity, and have done wickedly, and have rebelled, even by departing from thy precepts and from thy judgements" (Dan. 9:5). Daniel recognizes that God is awesome—powerful yet forgiving. God's people had departed from God. They had rightly deserved God's judgement—captivity in Babylon and the destruction of Jerusalem and Solomon's Temple.

Continuing his intercession, Daniel notes that God is righteous, but the people are confused—those at Jerusalem, Judah, and all Israel who are in Babylon as well as those scattered among other nations. He confessed that they-we are all guilty. They have all trespassed against God. Daniel confessed that all the people have sinned—our kings, our princess, and our fathers. He acknowledges that only God can execute mercy and forgiveness to the rebellious people.

Daniel recounted that God had delivered the children of Israel out of slavery in Egypt, and Moses gave them the Law; however, they continued to transgress against the Law of God, and elicited God's judgement upon themselves. Thus, God allowed them suffer just consequences of their evil hearts and behavior. Daniel knew that the people of Judah received what they deserved. However, the period of punishment was coming to ending. So Daniel made this passionate appeal unto God, "O Lord, according to thy righteousness, I beseech thee, let thine anger and thy fury be turned away from thy city of Jerusalem, thy holy mountain: because for our sins, and for the iniquities of our fathers, Jerusalem and thy people are become a reproach to all that are about us" (Dan. 9:16). Daniel now confessed the sins of the people and appealed to God for grace and mercy, asking God to remove His anger from Jerusalem and the holy mountain (Zion).

It was the people who had sinned, including religious leaders; however, the city of Jerusalem and Mount Zion had suffered as well. The city of Jerusalem was in desolation, the city and the people had become a laughing stock and an embarrassment. Daniel needed God's intervention in restoring Jerusalem and in returning the Jewish captives, who were in Babylon, to Jerusalem.

As in the weeping of a hurting man, who is in desperate need for urgent assistance, Daniel cried out, "Now therefore, O God, hear the prayer of thy servant, and his supplication, and cause thy face to shine upon thy sanctuary, that is desolate, for the Lord's sake. O Lord, hear: O Lord forgive; O Lord, Hearken and do: defer not, for thine own sake, O my God: for thy city, and thy people are called by thy name" (Dan. 9:17, 19). Daniel understood that often times God does things for His own sake, that his name is glorified.

Daniel knew that the people of Israel and Judah had ignored God's Word, which was delivered to them, over the years, by His prophets. They did not deserve God's intervention—help. However, he appealed for God's grace and mercy that God would intervene on behalf of His people who are called by His name and for the sake of the city of Jerusalem, and to honor God's own name.

God made a promise to Solomon about 420 years earlier when the people of Israel—the Kingdom of twelve tribes—turned from God and were under punishment and distress: "If my people, which are called by my name, shall humble themselves, and pray, and seek my face, and turn from their wicked ways; then will I hear from heaven, and will forgive their sin, and will heal their land" (2 Chron. 7:14). Daniel had done exactly what God had told Solomon that His people must do when they have sinned and were experiencing the consequences of their sins. Daniel humbled himself, confessed his sins and the sins of Israel and Judah and sought God's forgiveness on behalf of the people.

In addition, as stated earlier, although Daniel was in Babylon, some 1678 miles from Jerusalem, he turned his face toward the site of Solomon's Temple at Jerusalem and poured out his soul to God. Daniel understood that often God answers prayer for His own sake, so he asked God to answer his prayer for God's own sake. Daniel had done what God had prescribed; therefore, he could wait patiently on God, with confident expectation, for a positive response, and surely, God responded in a mighty way!

The Babylonians thought that they were invincible. The nation was on top of its war-game. Although some Jewish people were occupying important positions in the government of Babylon, the Babylonians had punished and were punishing the captives—God's special people more than was necessary.

Daniel had prayed for God's intervention. It was time for God to act and He did. God raised up Persia under the leadership of King Cyrus. The Persians defeated Babylon in 538 BC. One of Cyrus's first proclamations, in 537 BC, was to free the people of Judah from captivity in Babylon. He enacted a decree which permitted Jewish people to migrate or return to Judah, if they so desire.

God answered Daniel's prayer. Seventy years after Daniel was taken as a captive to Babylon in 607 BC. The Babylonian captivity had ended. God can use whoever He chooses to do whatever He chooses. He used the Persians to defeat the Babylonians for His own sake—so that the people of Judah were freed from Babylonian captivity.

Is God using you for any special work or service? Have you prayed or praying about the assignment? Have you said, "Yes God, I will go or do whatever you want me to do"?

CHAPTER ELEVEN

PRAYERS AND DEEDS OF NEHEMIAH

Nehemiah Prays and Works in Faith

Nehemiah was a Jewish cupbearer for King Artaxerxes—a Persian—at his palace at Shushan (Susa) in Persia. In 446 BC, approximately one hundred years (ninety-one years) after the Babylonian captivity ended, Nehemiah's brother, Hanani, returned to Susa after visiting Jerusalem.

Nehemiah inquired about Jerusalem. Hanani informed Nehemiah of the deplorable conditions of Jerusalem and Judah. He told Nehemiah that city was in ruin. The wall around the city of Jerusalem was broken down during the Babylonian invasion and had not been rebuilt. The Babylonians had destroyed Solomon's Temple during the invasion in 586 BC.

The construction of a replacement for Solomon's Temple, which was referred to as Zerubbabel's Temple, was completed in 516 BC. This was done under the leadership of Zerubbabel. However as late as 446 BC, the wall around Jerusalem was not rebuilt. Hanani told Nehemiah that the remnant of Jews in Jerusalem and Judah "are in affliction and reproach: the wall of Jerusalem also is broken down and the gates thereof are burned with fire" (Neh. 1:3). This news was extremely distressing for Nehemiah. He had to do something.

When Nehemiah thought about the sad condition of his fellow Jews in Judah, his response was in this manner, "I sat down and wept, and mourned certain days, and fasted, and prayed before the God of heaven" (Neh. 1:4). Nehemiah recounted how he prayed fasted before the God of heaven, "And said, I beseech thee LORD God of heaven, the great and terrible God, that keepeth covenant and mercy for them that love him and observe his commandments. Let thine ear now be attentive, and thine eyes now open, that thou mayest hear the prayer of thy servant, which I pray before thee now, day and night, for the children of Israel thy servants, and confess the sins of the children of Israel, which we have sinned against thee: both I and my fathers have sinned" (Neh. 1:5–6). Nehemiah continued his prayer of remorse, repentance. He took ownership of the sins of the children of Israel.

Nehemiah recounted God's promise of what He will do if His people disobey Him and He scatters them abroad, among many nations, "But if you turn unto me, and keep my commandments and do them;...yet I will gather them from thence, and will bring them unto the place that I have chosen to set my name there" (Neh. 1:8–9). Nehemiah was quite familiar with God's promises to King Solomon and the children of Israel. He was now asking God to fulfil the promise of fully restoring Judah, presumably, including rebuilding the wall around Jerusalem.

Nehemiah concluded this prayer by asking God to help him to have favor in the sight of King Artaxerxes to whom he served as cupbearer. He was getting ready to ask a very big favor of the King. He wanted permission from King Artaxerxes to go to Jerusalem to rebuild the wall around Jerusalem and do other needed repairs there.

You can feel the intensity of the ending of Nehemiah's monumental prayer, which he recounted, thusly, "O LORD, I beseech thee, let now thine ear be attentive to the prayer of thy servant . . . and prosper, I pray thee, thy servant this day, and grant him mercy in the sight of this man [King Artaxerxes]. For I was the king's cupbearer" (Neh. 1:11). Let now thine ear be attentive, Nehemiah prayed. He needed immediate assistance from God. This is one of the most powerful prayers recorded in the Bible. It was intentional with a specific request for immediate favor in the sight of King Artaxerxes.

Similar to the Daniel, whose prayer was discussed earlier, Nehemiah confessed his sins against God as well as the sins of his fathers—his ancestors. Even though the Bible does not record any specific sins, which Nehemiah committed, he sought God's forgiveness.

Nehemiah then rehearsed God's promise to gather His people who are scattered abroad among nations. Nehemiah was now prepared to make his bold request to King Artaxerxes.

He was confident that God had answered his prayer. He was ready to step out in faith.

In his usual manner, Nehemiah went to serve the king, but there was nothing usual about this normally pleasing cupbearer. Not only was he burdened in his heart by what he had learned regarding the deplorable conditions in Jerusalem and Judah, but his face was clearly disclosing that his heart was burdened.

The king noticed that Nehemiah was sad. His countenance was solemn and dull. The observant and concerned King asked Nehemiah, "Why is thy countenance sad, seeing that thou art not sick? this is nothing else but sorrow of heart" (Neh. 2:2). Think about this, a Persian, Gentile king had that level of concern for his Jewish servant! This reminds us that it was the Persian King Cyrus who some one hundred years earlier had freed the Jewish people from Babylonian captivity and authorized those who wanted to go home to Judah to do so.

Nehemiah records is initial reaction to the King's inquiry in this manner, "Then I was very sore afraid" (Neh. 2:2). The king had observed the sadness in Nehemiah's heart as was revealed by the expression on Nehemiah's face, but Nehemiah was afraid to share his plight with the Persian King. Even though he had prayed, Nehemiah was temporarily afraid to ask the king for leave of absence from his highly important and trusting cup bearing position.

Truly, Nehemiah had no reason to be afraid. He had already fasted and prayed that God would grant him mercy (favor) in the sight of the king. Nehemiah's discomfort in approaching the king with his big request reminds us that there may be some doubt and uncertainty in the heart of the best of Christian. Prayer is the answer to bring about calm in such time and situations, and to strengthen faith and trust in God's promises and the efficacy of prayer.

When King Artaxerxes inquired about Nehemiah's sadness of heart, he opened the window of opportunity authorizing Nehemiah to share what was so heavily burdening him down. Despite Nehemiah's initial cold feet, he opened up to the King.

Nehemiah recounted that he expressed customary homage to the King. Then he succinctly and profoundly stated his case to the king as follows: "And I said unto the king, Let the king live forever: why should not my countenance be sad, when the city, the place of my fathers' sepulchers, lieth waste, and the gates thereof are consumed with fire?" (Neh. 2:3). The king was empathetic toward Nehemiah. He inquired how he could be of assistance to him.

The king said to Nehemiah, "For what dost thou make request. So, I prayed to the God of heaven" (Neh. 2:4). Again, the king showed interest in Nehemiah's situation. He was genuinely concerned about the man who has been acting as a canary in a coal mine—the taster of his wine, his cupbearer—making sure his wine was safe for him to drink.

Nehemiah, perhaps, had the opportunity of his life to influence the one man, on earth, who could assist him to go to Jerusalem and rebuild the wall around the city. In addition, he could assist with other needed repairs. Nehemiah intended to optimize this opportunity the king presented.

So Nehemiah would leave no stone unturned. Before he answered the king, he turned once more to the one source which he knew could not fail. The source that had got him to the point of having favor in the sight of the king. As cited above, Nehemiah prayed to the God of heaven. This was undoubtedly a short silent prayer; perhaps, he simply gave God thanks. He had already fasted and prayed. There was no need for another long prayer while he was have a conversation with the King.

Believing that his prayer was already answered, Nehemiah, explained the situation to the king and asked for leave from his job to journey to Jerusalem to build the wall around Jerusalem and do other needed repairs.

The king wanted to know the duration of Nehemiah's leave of absence and when he would return! Nehemiah provided the king with the information he needed. Nehemiah records, "And the king granted me, according to the good hand of my God upon me" (Neh. 2:8). Certainly, Nehemiah was quite pleased and appreciative of the positive response of the king to his request; however, he knew that the praise belongs to the God of Abraham, Isaac and Israel whose hand had guided him thus far as well as guided the King's response.

King Artaxerxes gave Nehemiah much more than leave of absence. In addition to the leave, the king gave Nehemiah letters to governors of various territories instructing them to provide Nehemiah assistance as necessary and available. For example, the king instructed Asaph, keeper of the king's forest to provide Nehemiah with timber for his building project at Jerusalem. In addition, the king sent soldiers and horses with Nehemiah to protect and assist him and his servants as needed.

Nehemiah had many challenges when he got to Jerusalem, including attempts by Sanballat, a provisional governor to sabotage, discredit, and conspire against Nehemiah and his volunteers. He even accused Nehemiah of building the wall so that he could revolt against the king of Persia. Then Sanballat and his conspirers tried to make Nehemiah and his helpers afraid and to weaken their hands so that they would cease from building the wall.

It was at this point that Nehemiah once again turned to the source of his strength and protection. He went to God and made this short and specific request (prayer), "Now therefore. O God strength my hands" (Neh. 6:9). What a powerful—save us from Sanballat prayer! Nehemiah was known for his long passionate prayers; however, this time, in his unwavering determination to complete the wall, he focused on one specific need—that God would strengthen the hands of the builders.

He did not want to be afraid of Sanballat and his conspirers and he did not want to be discouraged. More importantly, he needed God to strengthen their hands so that they could complete the building of the wall.

God had answered Nehemiah's prayers in the past, God had directed Artaxerxes to treat Nehemiah with great favor and kindness. And God was enabling Jewish leaders in Jerusalem to collaborate with Nehemiah on the wall-building project. Nehemiah was certain that God would assist him against Sanballat at this crucial point in his work.

In fact, at one point when Sanballat wanted to fight against Nehemiah and those building the wall, Nehemiah encouraged and exhorted his workers in this manner, "In what place therefore ye hear the sound of the trumpet, resort ye thither unto us: our God shall fight for us" (Neh. 4:20). What a relief if must have been to the builders when Nehemiah reassured them that God was on their side fighting with them.

God did fight with Nehemiah and his volunteers. Not only did Nehemiah prayed for God's protection; rather, he armed his volunteers with weapons so that they could fight the enemies with God's assistance. Nehemiah exemplified the effectiveness of combining faith with deeds.

Nehemiah was certainly a man of prayer, but he was also a man of deeds who took precaution. He armed his builders and prayed. He used a smart, split-shift team approach in the building project. Half of the workers would be building on one team, while the other half guarded and protected the team which was building at the time.

The teams of builders and guards alternated. Interestingly, those who were building shift would have their spears or swords strapped to their sides even when they were members of the building team. Not to mention that team which was guarding had their weapons ready at all times.

The Bible records that Sanballat, Tobiah, the Arabians, the Ammonites, and the Ashdodites heard of the building of the wall. They conspired to come and fight against Jerusalem to hinder the wall building process. However, Nehemiah went to his source of strength and protection. He recounts his appeal to God in this manner, "Nevertheless, we made our prayer unto our God, and set watch against them day and night, because of them" (Neh. 4:9). Nehemiah demonstrated that obstacles and objections do not prevent the completion of a project, when God is in agreement with the project and His assistance is solicited.

Nehemiah understood that prayer should precede any project, especially very important projects. He applied his understanding of the efficacy of prayer and God responded to his prayers and assisted him from the beginning to the end of his endeavor in Jerusalem.

It is worth mentioning one more of Nehemiah's prayers. When Tobiah and Sanballat continued their effort to try to hinder Nehemiah's unwavering determination to complete the wall, Nehemiah prayed in this manner: "My God, think thou upon Tobiah and Sanballat according to these their works, and on the prophetess Noadiah, and the rest of the prophets, that would have put me in fear (Neh. 6:14). This was not a prayer of blessing. Rather, Nehemiah asked God to take a look at the aforementioned persons in light on how they tried so hard to hinder him from building the wall around Jerusalem.

Nehemiah understood that God knows best how to deal with the enemies who hurt or try to hurt His servants. No doubt, Nehemiah was well familiar with the admonition of God, "To me belongeth vengeance and recompence; their foot shall slide in due time: for the day of their calamity is at hand and the things that shall come upon them make haste" (Deut. 32:35). Nehemiah was comfortable in leaving his enemies in God's hand for God to deal with them as it pleases Him.

God heard and answered Nehemiah's prayers. "So, the wall was finished in the twenty and fifth day of the month Elul, in fifty and two days" (Neh. 6:15). Yes, prayers work! Nehemiah saw an unmet need—a need to rebuild a wall around Jerusalem—he volunteered and collaborated with God and other volunteers and built it.

The wall remained in ruin for approximately seventy years after the building of the new temple—Zerubbabel's Temple—was completed. Nehemiah's first step was to seek God's forgiveness for Israel and to seek God's assistance before embarking on the rebuilding project. He sought God's protection during the building of the wall. He received God's immediate, positive responses to his prayers for assistance and protection.

Throughout his mission, Nehemiah stayed in close relationship with God. He was a praying man. He prayed for forgiveness and protection. However, at no time did he ask God to build the wall; that was his job and the job of his volunteers.

By the application of faith and work, Nehemiah and his helpers completed the building of the wall around Jerusalem in fifty-two days in spite of the hindrance of Sanballat and his conspirers.

For believers in God, Nehemiah is often held up as a model person, a person who saw an unmet need and took the initiative to harness resources to meet that need.

I encourage you to read the relatively short, Book of Nehemiah in its totality, if you have not already done so. Please note of his passionate prayers and how he combined faith with work and applied leadership, determination, and exhortation for his extraordinary accomplishment in a relatively short period of time. His prayers are worth emulating as appropriate.

Conclusion on Old Testament Prayers in the Book

There are numerous other prayers in the Old Testament that are not included in this book. I simply selected a few which had great impact on human lives. Many of these prayers continue to impact lives and the world in our time. I have not treated the selected prayers with detailed analyses as a theologian or a Bible scholar might. Rather, I present them in a clear and concise manner with some commentary.

My prayer is that you will find the prayers and commentaries beneficial as you embrace on or continue your active prayer life. Hopefully you will take time to read the prayers again and again and benefit more from them as you meditate on them. You might find it helpful to read the prayers in different versions of the Bible for additional clarity or explanation. I hope that the prayers and comments might pique your interest in identifying other relevant prayers in the Bible as you study it. You should find the prayers as relevant and inspiring as they were when they were written.

Perhaps, you will even write one or more prayer of your own!

CHAPTER TWELVE

SELECTED PRAYERS OF HUMANS
IN THE NEW TESTAMENT

This chapter of the book includes selected prayers in the New Testament uttered by humans. In some cases, God's answers to the prayers were manifested immediately, while in others cases His answers were not immediately known. Often the prayers were uttered out of desperation and were consequential to the person praying or to the person or persons for whom the prayers were offered.

The prayers are arranged in chronological order as they appear in King James Version of the Bible. Again, these are just my selection of prayers for inclusion. Another writer might have selected some, none, or all of these prayers. These prayers are inspirational to me, and I believe that they will inspire you as well.

Prayer of Zacharias and God's Answers

It is commonly accepted that God did not send a prophet to Judah or Israel for a period of four hundred years after the last Old Testament Prophet Malachi. In fact, it is said that God had not spoken to Israel or Judah during that time. It was after the four hundred years of silence that God sent the first New Testament prophet John the Baptist to Judah to prepare the way for the arrival of Jesus, the Messiah. (Israel, the Northern Kingdom, was lost, having been invaded by the Assyrians in 722 BC and has not been restored.)

Despite the fact that there was no known prophet in Judah since Malachi, people in Judah, continued to worship in the temple (Herod's Temple). The priests and other religious leaders worshipped God and conducted religious rituals, such as burning incense in the temple.

Luke records the account of a man named Zacharias. He was a priest in Judah who was of the priestly order of Abia. According to Luke, Zacharias was a righteous man who was married to a woman by the name of Elizabeth. According to the Gospel of Luke, Elizabeth was of the priestly line of Aaron.

Evidently, Zacharias and Elizabeth were a devoted couple. Despite their distinctive pedigree lineage, they had no children because Elizabeth was barren. Luke, a Gentile physician, who wrote about the incident some sixty years after it occurred must have heard great positive things about this special couple-servants of God. He describes them in a most complimentary manner, "And they were both righteous before God, walking in all the commandments and ordinances of the Lord blameless" (Luke 1:6). Considering that Luke was a physician—scientist and a Gentile, the accolade he bestowed on Zacharias and Elizabeth is authentic and beyond measure.

God's First Recorded Response to a Prayer in the New Testament: Prayer of Zacharias

The priestly duty of Zacharias was to burn incense in the temple at specific times. He carried out that duty with diligence and precision. Zacharias had been praying that God would open the womb of his barren wife, Elizabeth, so that she could bear them a child. Perhaps Zacharias was aware of how Isaac had prayed for his barren wife Rebekah some two thousand years earlier and how God responded by giving them the twin sons, Jacob and Esau.

Even though Zacharias and Elizabeth were beyond child bearing age, he might have still been praying for a miracle child. He probably knew the incident of how the barren Hannah prayed and how God opened her womb and she conceived and bore Samuel.

This day of burning incense in the temple began just as another day for burning incense until it became quite different day for Zacharias. Luke records that Zacharias had gone into the temple as usual to burn incense, "And a whole multitude of people were praying without [outside] at the time of the incense" (Luke 1:10). Luke does not indicate whether or not praying outside the temple at the time of the burning of incense was a customary. Neither did he record the reason the people were praying. Nevertheless, as Zacharias was performing his priestly duty of burning incense, an angel of the Lord appeared unto Zacharias.

When Zacharias saw the angel, he was afraid, perhaps terrified. Luke said, "He was troubled and fear (being afraid) fell up on him" (Luke 1:12). Suddenly, the priest, the man of God, was worried. Perhaps he started to wonder what he had done wrongfully or what he had inadvertently failed to do! Fortunately, he did not need to wait very long to learn that the angel had brought him good news.

The angel delivered an astounding, perhaps unexpected good news. This is the type of news that one human would say to another, "Sit, I have something I want to tell you." The angel broke the news, "But the angel said unto him, Fear not Zacharias: for thy prayer is heard; and thy wife Elizabeth shall bear thee a son, ad thou shalt call his name John. And thou shalt have joy and gladness; and many shall rejoice at his birth" (Luke 1:13–14). The angel went on to describe how John would be great in the sight of the Lord. In addition, he mentioned the qualities that John would possess and the great things that he would do.

Luke does not include any details about Zacharias' prayer. He simply said that God had heard his prayer and Elizabeth would bear him a son. It is reasonable that Zacharias had been praying that Elizabeth would bear him a son.

Zacharias was astonished by the good news and wanted a sign—assurance from the angel that his proclamation would materialize. Zacharias should not have been that surprised because he had been praying for that outcome. The angel disclosed that he was Gabriel who was sent by God. Gabriel gave Zacharias a sign, perhaps not the one he wanted—he would remain mute until baby John was born.

As the angel had told Zacharias, Elizabeth conceived. With the passing of time, she was ready to give birth to her baby. "Now Elizabeth's full time came that she should be delivered; and she brought forth a son" (Luke 1:57). Elizabeth's neighbors shared her excitement at the birth of the baby boy. They wanted to follow Jewish traditions and named the boy Zacharias after his father. However, that would not be. "And the mother answered and said, Not so; but he shall be called John" (Luke 1:60). Luke does not record whether or not Zacharias had told Elizabeth about his encounter with Gabriel and the naming of their son.

Regardless, after the birth of the child, Zacharias regained his ability to speak. He had already confirmed, in wring, that the boy's name was John; now he could reaffirm the name orally. In addition to regaining his ability to speak, he was filled with the Holy Spirit and prophesied.

Zacharias was not first person mentioned in the New Testament who prophesied. Elizabeth had already prophesied some three months earlier about the blessed Mary carrying the Messiah in her womb. Some thirty years later, John the Baptist— the son of Zacharias and Elizabeth, for whom Zacharias had prayed—prophesied and preached, in the wilderness, about the imminent appearance of Jesus the Messiah and Savior.

The Bible does not record how long Zacharias had been praying that God would heal the womb of his barren wife. However, it is reasonable to conclude that he had been praying for a long time because Zacharias and Elizabeth, his wife were, now old, and beyond child bearing age. Even though God might have answered his prayer when he first prayed, the manifestation of the answer was years later, in accordance with God's time frame.

It is conceivable that God wanted John, the forerunner of Jesus, to be born as a miracle baby, similarly to Jesus Christ. Of course, in the case of Jesus, no man was involved; Mary's conception was through the Holy Spirit, and she was still a virgin at the time Jesus was born.

Zacharias could not tell God when and how to answer his prayer. He might have been surprised at what he may have considered the lateness to the answer of his prayer. He might have even expressed some doubt when the answer finally came, hence his request for a sign. God answered his prayer at the right time and gave him the son that he needed. And that son John the Baptist was the great witness who prepared the people in the wilderness to receive Jesus the Messiah!

Do you ever give up on praying because you have not received an answer from God by your deadline and you are not sure if God is even hearing your prayer?

Remember the incident of Zacharias. God may be testing your patience or just waiting for the right time to reveal His answer to you!

Have you ever received a blessing years after you have prayed for it and thought that God had forgotten about it? Have you ever received a blessing when you have forgotten all about asking for it? Have you ever received a blessing, good news, to which you responded, "I just can't believe it"? The good news is that God does not forget and He answers or don't answers requests and prayers as He chooses!

Your responsibility is to always pray and not faint, as Jesus instructs His followers. And as Paul reminds us, we must pray without ceasing!

CHAPTER THIRTEEN

PRAYERS OF THANKSGIVING, REQUEST FOR DEATH AND FOR HEALING

This chapter of the book focuses on three types of prayers. In the first prayer, Mary humbly accepted God's assignment and expressed great thanks to God. In the next prayer, Simeon blessed baby Jesus and asked God to call him home; he wanted to die. In the third set of prayers, appeals are made for cleansing and wholeness.

Prayer of Mary the Mother of Jesus

Mary's prayer is unique and different from the other prayers which I discussed in this book. Mary had not initiated any request of God for a child. In fact she was not even married as yet. She was engaged to Joseph. One might say that Mary was busy minding, attending to, her own business, happily engaged to Joseph, and looking forward to the wedding day.

But Mary was about to experience a life-changing and transformational surprise for her, for Joseph, and ultimately for the world as well. God had found favor in Mary and had a unique and one of a kind assignment for her.

Elizabeth, Zacharias's wife, was in the six-month of her miraculous pregnancy. The same angel Gabriel, who had announced to Zacharias that Elizabeth would conceive and give birth to a boy baby, appeared to Mary. Mary was a young virgin woman who was engaged to Joseph and was living in the little village of Nazareth. The angel told Mary that she was highly favored by God and that she was blessed among women.

When Mary saw the angel, she was troubled (frightened and scared). However, Gabriel quickly calmed her troubled heart with the soothing words, "Fear not Mary: for thou has found favour with God. And thou shall conceive in thy womb, and bring forth a son, and shall call his name JESUS" (Luke 1:30). Gabriel's words were comforting, but mysterious to Mary. Gabriel went on to tell Mary that Jesus shall be great and He shall be called the Son of the Highest. In addition, God would give Him the throne of His father David forever.

Mary was no longer afraid, but was now perplexed. She inquired of Gabriel, "Then said Mary unto the angel, How shall this be, seeing I know not a man [have not slept with a man]?" (Luke 1:34). This was not a rhetorical question for Mary, she needed an answer and needed it quickly.

Undoubtedly, as a Jewish young lady, she knew about the miraculous conceptions of Sarah, Rebekah, and Hanna, but these women were married and presumably were sleeping with their husbands. In her case she was not yet married and she was a virgin. She needed an answer for the man she loved and to whom she was engaged. In addition, she probably had some level of confusion, which she needed to clear up.

Then Mary got her answer. The angel consoled her and told her, "The Holy Ghost shall come upon thee, and the power of the Highest shall overpower thee: therefore also that holy thing which shall be born of thee shall be called the Son of God" (Luke 1:35). The angel went on to tell Mary that her older cousin Elizabeth, who was barren, had conceived in her old age; she was six months pregnant and would give birth to a son.

Gabriel concluded his message to Mary, "For with God, nothing shall be impossible" (Luke 1:37). Mary could now see clearly, the mystery was solved. Mary was, more than likely, familiar with how the Holy Spirit overshadowed the first man, Adam and how God took one of his ribs and made the first woman, Eve. So she understood that it was possible for her to conceive without sleeping with a man.

How would young Mary respond to this mind-boggling revelation and proclamation of Gabriel, considering that she was looking forward to her marriage to Joseph? How would she explain her pregnancy to Joseph? What was this Jewish young lady to do with this news, and with herself? Mary was brought up as a devoted Jewish young lady and knew she had only one thing which she could do, she knew that she could pray, and that is exactly what she did. And her brief and exemplary prayer of faith is below.

Mary's Prayer of Humility and Obedience

Once Mary understood the message from God, delivered by the angel Gabriel, she burst out in a prayer of humility, acceptance, and submission to the will of God. Her prayer is powerful and succinct. "And Mary said, Behold the handmaid of the Lord; be it unto me according to thy word" (Luke 1:38). Mary was unwavering in her decision to accept God's plan for her life. She accepted God's plan with humility.

Mary did not need to ask Joseph's permission in order to accept the honor God had decided to bestow on her. Undoubtedly, she knew that she might have risked not marrying Joseph, whom she dearly loved. She was such a decisive young lady who was willing to accept potential consequences of her decision, even the ridicule of the people and the loss of the man she had expected to marry. She already knew that she ought to obey God rather than men.

Gabriel was delighted that Mary enthusiastically accepted the assignment which God had given her. And was ready to submit herself to the will and plan of God for her. So Gabriel departed for his next assignment, perhaps to give a praise report to God.

God was watching the entire scene all along and already knew how it would play out; nevertheless, he wanted to deliver the good news to God. Therefore, once Mary accepted the assignment, he departed for heaven.

Through her free will, Mary enthusiastically accepted God's assignment. She would be the mother of God's only begotten Son, and she and the world would be changed forever!

God granted Mary, perhaps, the greatest blessing that has been bestowed on a human being—mothering Jesus the Son of God, the Savior, the Messiah. Interestingly, the Bible does not record that Mary had prayed for that unspeakable honor. This clearly indicates that God decides those to whom He chooses to grant favor.

God Answers Mary's Prayer!

Mary graciously accepted God's assignment, and God fulfilled His promise to her. The Apostle Matthew tells us that Joseph and his pregnant fiancée, Mary, were married after God revealed to Joseph that Mary's pregnancy was done through the empowerment of the Holy Spirit, God's doing (Matt. 1:24).

While Mary was close to the time for delivering her baby, she accompanied Joseph up to the City of David, Bethlehem, to pay tax. While they were in Bethlehem the time had come for Mary to give birth to her son. "And she brought forth her first born son, and wrapped him in swaddling clothes, and laid him in a manger; because there was no room for them in the inn" (Luke 2:7). God chose a humble, young, virgin woman to be the mother of Jesus, His only begotten Son. And she gave birth to the Son of God, Jesus, in a lowly place, in a barn or stable, and she laid baby Jesus in feeding trough used for feeding animals.

Jesus, God's Son, would become the bread of life, not for animals which stay in barns. Rather for human beings who seek everlasting life through Jesus Christ. The same Jesus Christ now sits on the throne in heaven at the right hand of God His Father. Mary answered yes to God's plan to include her a central part of His plan of making salvation available to all through her Son, God's Son, Jesus Christ!

Have you ever received a blessing or assignment from God for which you had not asked or prayed? If so, what did you do, did you accept it with enthusiasm and appreciation? If it was a difficult, impossible assignment, did you ask "Why me?"

Pray that when God bestows a blessing on you or gives you an assignment, whether you ask for it or not, you might respond with the type of humility and obedience displayed by Mary. We give God thanks for Mary for her prayer of thanksgiving, her humble submission, and her enthusiastic acceptance of God's will for her. May we all strive to be more like Mary!

Prayer of Simeon, the Man of Faith and Patience

God had not sent prophets to Judah (Judea) for some four hundred years after He sent Malachi, the last Old Testament prophet. However, there were godly people in Judah, including priests. I previously discussed Zacharias a devoted priest.

Well, there was a man named Simeon, a righteous man, who was trusting in God's promise to him. He was dwelling in Jerusalem. Luke describes Simeon as "Just and devout, waiting for the consolation of Israel: and the Holy Ghost was up on him" (Luke 2:25). God had promised Simeon that he would not die until he saw Christ, the Messiah. "And it was revealed unto him by the Holy Ghost, that he should not see death, before he had seen the Lord's Christ" (Luke 2:26). Luke does not reveal whether or not Simeon had prayed, was praying to see the Messiah before his death, or God had decided to grant him that privilege through God's own plan.

Simeon Prays for His Death

Simeon was now old and ready to die; however, he was waiting for the fulfillment of God's promise to him to see the Messiah. The Holy Spirit led him into the temple. Joseph and Mary brought baby Jesus to the temple to dedicate Him unto God. God was working out His purpose.

Simeon, without a request, permission, or hesitation, took baby Jesus in his arms. He blessed the baby and offered to God a prayer of thanksgiving and a request for his death. Simeon prayed, "Lord, now lettest thou thy servant depart in peace, according to thy word: For mine eyes have seen thy salvation, Which thou hast prepared before the face of all people; A light to lighten the Gentiles, and the glory of thy people Israel" Luke 2:29–32). Simeon's short prayer was of thanksgiving and a transformational prophecy.

There have been a few times in the Old Testament when God's servants, out of frustration, disappointment or even arrogance, have asked God to take their lives. Moses in the wilderness, out of frustration with the rebellious children of Israel, asked God to take his life. Jonah, out of arrogance and an attitude of unforgiveness, asked God to take his life when God spared Nineveh. Jonah preached to the people of city of Nineveh and they repented so God spared them. Jonah was angry that God extended grace and mercy to Nineveh.

Simeon's prayer was different. God had fulfilled His promise to him. He had lived to see baby Jesus, the Messiah, the apex of his earthly desire. He blessed baby Jesus and was now ready to die. He prayed a wonderful prayer of thanksgiving and requested that God would fulfill His second promise to him—take him home.

What a great example of knowing when God's assignment is completed and bowing out gracefully or simply passing on the torch or baton

In addition, Simeon made one of the greatest prophecies of God's fulfillment of His promise to humanity. God had sent Jesus as "A light to lighten the Gentiles, and the glory of thy people Israel" (Luke 2:32). This acknowledgement of God's fulfillment of His promise to provide light, salvation, to Gentiles was particularly astounding.

The Jews always knew that they were God's special people, who God loves greatly. Now Simeon is announcing that Jesus was bringing light to the Gentiles so they would no longer need to live in darkness—without salvation. Simeon was truly grateful that God had allowed him to see the fulfillment of His promise to see the Messiah who brings salvation to Jews and Gentiles. He was ready to transition from this earth.

There are times when a Christian, a believer, completes the assignment which God gives and he or she wants to keep hanging on; rather than passing the torch or just find another assignment. May God help you to know when you have completed His particular assignment? May He help you to pass the torch or baton gracefully and seek and go to the next assignment according to His plan!

Prayer of a Leper and Jesus's Response!

Mark records the prayer of a leper which occurred early in Jesus's ministry. This is perhaps the first or close to the first prayer of a human being to Jesus during His ministry. Jesus had already turned water into wine at the marriage feast at Cana of Galilee, at the request of His mother Mary. However, I am not considering Mary's request as a prayer.

Jesus had been preaching in the synagogue at Capernaum and healing and casting out demons. He had healed Peter's mother-in-law of her fever. Jesus told His disciples that they were going to the next towns. They went to Galilee, and Jesus preached in synagogues throughout Galilee and cast out demons.

While in Galilee, a leper went to Jesus. Think about that. A leper could not have gone close to a high priest; however, he went close to the Son of God. He must have heard of or seen miracles Jesus had done and seen the love, compassion, empathy, and humility which Jesus had shown to others. For whatever reason, the leper felt comfortable in drawing in close proximity to Jesus.

The leper displayed humility and showed reverence and respect for Jesus, and trust in Jesus. Mark records, "And there came a leper to him, beseeching him, and kneeling down to him, and saying unto him, If thou wilt, thou canst make me clean" (Mark 1:40). It should be understood that the "if" in the leper's prayer was not an expression of doubt in the ability of Jesus to cleanse his leprosy. Rather, the "if" expressed the recognition of the leper's feeling of unworthiness to be cleansed by Jesus He believed that Jesus could cleanse him if Jesus wanted to do so. The leper felt unworthy because leprosy was considered as a curse pronounced on the parent(s) of the leper before birth of the leper or a curse on the leper himself or herself.

Jesus Answered the Leper's Prayer

Jesus was moved with empathy for the leper. No doubt, Jesus saw the sincerity of the leper's humility, reverence, and faith. Mark records, "And Jesus, moved with compassion, put forth his hand, and touched him, and saith unto him, I will: be thou clean" (Mark 1:41). It is quite interesting that although Jesus had healed others in Capernaum and Galilee before he cleansed the leper, the leper is the first person whose prayer Mark records.

The leper was an outcast, his disease was highly contagious, and he was considered unclean and could not come in close contact with religious leaders. However, he got close enough to Jesus for Jesus to touch him and cleansed him. His prayer was succinct with one request. He wanted to be cleansed, nothing less. He did not hedge his request.

He desired that Jesus would answer his prayer either with a yes or a no. He had no doubt that Jesus could cleanse him from leprosy, if Jesus wanted to do so. He would not need to wonder if Jesus answered his prayer because his request was specific, with one desired outcome—to be cleansed of leprosy. However, he left the final decision in the hand of the all-wise Jesus: "if You will do it." The outcome of his prayer would depend entirely on the will of Jesus. And Jesus said, "Yes, I will."

This incident demonstrates that Jesus is ready to answer sincere prayers from anyone regardless of his or her circumstances. Even the outcast of society, the marginalized, and the least among us may receive the empathy of Jesus and His answer to our prayers.

Mark records that as soon as Jesus answered the leper's prayer he was cleansed. Then Jesus asked him to do something that he could not do. Jesus told him to keep his cleansing as a secret and to show himself to the priest. "But he went out, and to publish it much and blaze abroad the matter" (Mark 1:45).

The once leper, now cleansed, could not hold his peace; he had to tell everybody how Jesus answered his prayer and made him whole. He was perhaps the first evangelist among those who believed in Jesus. It all started with a prayer of a leper and Jesus's response, respectively. The leper prayed, "If thou wilt, thou canst make me clean. And Jesus saith unto him, I will: be thou clean" (Mark 1:40–41).

What is your request of Jesus? Do you desire a specific outcome? Do you give God the type of reverence and obeisance as the leper gave to Jesus? Is your childlike faith as strong as that of the leper? Is your prayer intentional with specific request and desired outcomes? What do you do when God answers your prayer?

The Prayer of Ten Lepers

Jesus had been teaching in the region of Capernaum for quite a while. He decided to journey to Jerusalem. He and His disciples were traveling through Samaria and Galilee. They entered into a certain village; Luke does not record the name of the village. Nevertheless, as they entered that village. "There met him ten men that were lepers, which stood a far off: And they lifted up their voices, and said, Jesus, Master, have mercy on us" (Luke 17:12–13). There is such a striking contrast between the approach and the prayer of the one leper discussed previously, recorded in the Gospel according to Mark, and the approach and prayer of the ten lepers as recorded in the Gospel according to Luke cited above.

The ten lepers understood the established protocol of Jewish custom regarding lepers. They should not get close to anyone, especially someone they recognized as Master. So they stood a far off and shouted their prayer in unison. Note that their request lacks the specificity of the prayer of the one leper in the incident previously noted. It does not state what they were asking Jesus to do. They asked for mercy, they might have been asking for alms, a few coins to purchase food. Perhaps they thought that their immediate need was evident or they were hedging their request. That anything they receive would be better than nothing.

Notice that they did not show the reverence, respect, and humility of the one leper previous discussed earlier. However, the ten lepers complied with the customary Jewish Law of not getting too close to the Master. It is conceivable that the lepers were Samaritans, since Jesus was in Samaritan territory. This would be another explanation why they did not want to get too close to Jesus and His disciples who were Jews. Jews despised Samaritans; Jesus was an exception. Nevertheless, Jesus heard their desperate cries for help. He could look beyond their shortcomings, apparent lack of reverence and humility, and address their needs.

Jesus Answers the Lepers' Prayer and Cleanses Them

Luke does not indicate that the lepers knelt in humility and reverence to Jesus. Whether they knew it or not, Jesus could read their hearts and discern the extent of their sincerity and reverence. In addition, Jesus knew what was best for them. Jesus answered their prayer in a most unusual manner. He asked them to do something which would test their faith and obedience. He said, "Go shew yourselves unto the priests" (Luke 17:14). Jesus sent them to the priests because in the Jewish custom, the priests had to certify that lepers are cleansed in order for them to regain or gain acceptance into social gathering or places of worship.

The lepers demonstrated both faith and obedience. On their way to the priests they discovered that they were cleansed-healed. All ten were healed. "And one of them, when he saw that he was healed, turned back, and with a loud voice glorified God. And fell down on his face at his [Jesus's] feet, giving him thanks: and he was a Samaritan" (Luke 17:15–16). Notice how the ex-leper went close to Jesus and threw himself at Jesus's feet in appreciation.

Often it is the unexpected person who truly appreciates kindness. Those who are close associates, family members, and friends sometimes take generosity for granted. Sometimes Christians, believers, take God's blessings for granted.

Ten lepers were cleansed, but only one returned to give thanks to Jesus. And Luke indicates that he was a Samaritan, which suggests that one or more of the others might have been Jews. This caused Jesus to ask a rhetorical question, "Were not there ten cleansed, but where are the nine others?" (Luke 17:17). Jesus has never sought thanks for all the great works he did on earth; however, His question suggests that it is right to give thanks when appropriate. It is noteworthy that ten percent of the lepers went back to thank Jesus. This might well reflect the percentage of truly committed believers who are in many Christian congregations today. They are usually the ones who get the job done and are always expressing praises and thanks to God.

Jesus may ask you to do something that does not appear logical to you. Showing themselves to the priest might not have seen logical to the lepers since lepers could not be in the company of priests. But Jesus told them to do it, and they obeyed. Perhaps, they believed that they would have been cleansed on the way to the priests. They were cleansed. They understood that if Jesus responded to their prayer, He would determine the outcome of their request!

Do you have that positive and confident expectation in the outcome of your prayer? Are you more concern that God answers your prayer than with the answer He gives? You should!

Prayer of Bartimaeus

Jesus was on His way to Jerusalem for the last time. He and His disciples were traveling from Jericho to Jerusalem. A large number of people were traveling with them. Bartimaeus, a blind man, was sitting by the wayside begging. But this time, things seemed different. He heard a great amount of noise coming from the people and asked what was happening. Someone told him that Jesus of Nazareth was passing by. Quite likely, Bartimaeus had heard of Jesus before.

This was Bartimaeus's once-in-a-lifetime opportunity to ask for the one thing he desired over all other things. Jesus could give him more than a few coins. He wanted something special from Jesus. Blind Bartimaeus mustered every strength is his body and every bit of air in his lungs and cried at the top of his voice, "Jesus, thou son of David, have mercy on me"

(Mark 10:47). The people, perhaps even the disciples, scolded him and told him to control himself and keep quiet.

Bartimaeus would allow no one to block him from receiving his blessing; so he cried out louder, "Thou so of David, have mercy on me" (Mark 10:48). It is significant to note that although the people told the blind man that it was Jesus of Nazareth who was passing, he addressed Jesus as the son of David. Jesus of Nazareth was not just another ordinary man. He was the son of David whom Gabriel had proclaimed to Mary would sit on the throne of His father David. So Bartimaeus prayed to Jesus for a life transforming miracle—to receive his sight

The people, traveling with Jesus, would have learned much had they listened to the proclamation of the blind beggar—"Jesus thou son of David." There were twenty-eight generations between David and Jesus. Evidently, the blind man was aware of the Old Testament prophecies regarding Jesus sitting on the throne of David. He was convinced that the son of David could grant him a miracle—he had that much faith. Often, people with physical sight walk by sight and not by faith. This physically blind man was walking by faith.

Jesus Answers Bartimaeus's Prayer for Sight

Apparently, Jesus was impressed with this blind man's faith and determination to receive his sight. Jesus knew that His primary mission is to give sight to the spiritually blind. However, Jesus stopped, stood still, paused His journey and commanded them to bring the blind man to Him. Jesus already knew what Bartimaeus wanted, what he needed, and what He would give to him. Nevertheless, Jesus wanted him to make his request clearly and specifically.

Jesus had taught the disciples, "Ask, and it shall be given unto you: for everyone that asketh receiveth" (Matt. 7:7–8). Jesus wanted His disciples to be specific in their requests. Similarly, He wanted the blind man to be specific in his request of Jesus. So Jesus asked him, "What will thou that I should do unto thee?" (Mark 10:51). Jesus's question reminds us of the time God asked Solomon to ask God for what he wanted. Solomon requested wisdom and understanding for ruling the people of Israel wisely and fairly.

Would this blind man ask for silver and gold so that he would not need to beg again? Jesus could have given him anything he requested. The blind man, who recognized and acknowledged that Jesus is the son of David, responded to Jesus's question with a simple, short, direct, and specific request—a sincere prayer, "Lord, that I might receive my sight" (Mark 10:51). His greatest desire was to be able to see that he would be able to take care of his needs.

It is very likely that Bartimaeus was born blind. Notice, he did not ask Jesus to restore his sight. Rather, he asked that he would receive sight. He was tired of being known as the blind beggar. He had met the Man who is the Light of the World and gives light to all who seek it. He believed that the son of David could give him physical sight. Did he receive spiritual sight as well?

Jesus rewarded Bartimaeus for his faith. It was his faith which made him cry out to Jesus to have mercy on him. It was his faith which inspired him to ask Jesus to give him what he desired most—his physical sight. In addition, Bartimaeus had the right motive for wanting to see—he wanted to follow Jesus, the son of David.

Therefore, Jesus answered his prayer on the basis of his faith and motive. "Go thy way; thy faith hath made thee whole. And immediately he received his sight, and followed Jesus in the way" (Mark 10: 52). The fact that Jesus permitted him to follow Him—Jesus, perhaps suggest that he was seeking or had received spiritual sight as well.

No longer would Bartimaeus be referred to as blind Bartimaeus or the blind beggar. Once he was blind, but then he could see, because the Light of the World gave him sight.

He showed his appreciation to Jesus of Nazareth, son of David, who gave him sight and a new life, by following Jesus. He did not go his way. Rather he wanted to follow Jesus. And Jesus rewarded him by permitting him to follow Him on His way.

Jesus did not permit the man from whom He had cast out legion demons to follow Him. Therefore, it was an honor Jesus bestowed on the now-seeing Bartimaeus by permitting him to follow Him.

Have you been following Jesus since you found Him and He gave you spiritual sight? What have you done or are doing to show your appreciation to Jesus for finding you and for giving you sight? Are you praying for a specific outcome or for specific outcomes? How has the incident of Bartimaeus asking for and receiving sight impacted or impacting your prayer life?

I pray that you will reflect on Bartimaeus—his persistency, specificity of request, his faith, his appreciation and his commitment to follow Jesu—and how Jesus rewarded him. This might be a good time for you to assess your relationship with Jesus and your faith in the efficacy of prayers!

CHAPTER FOURTEEN

THE GREATEST PRAYER OF FORGIVENESS OF A HUMAN BEING FOR OTHERS

Two of the greatest incidents of forgiveness of humans for other humans are recorded in the Book of Genesis. The first incident is that of Esau forgiving Jacob, his brother, for tricking him out of his birthright and for downright stealing his special blessings. The second incident was that of Joseph who forgave his brothers for selling him into slavery in Egypt. In neither of the incidents referenced was the victim being murdered at the time he prayed for the forgiveness of his murderers. In this chapter of the book, I discuss one human being—Stephen— who prayed for the forgiveness of those who were stoning him to death.

Prayer of Stephen

Stephen was one of the seven deacons who the apostles appointed to take care of the physical needs of widows and poor, particularly the Grecians (Greek-speaking Jews), during the early church in Jerusalem. The Grecians complained that their widows were not treated with equity when compared to the Hebrew widows. The deacons were supposed to be men who were reported to be honest, full of the Holy Ghost and wisdom.

Deacon Stephen was a very special person. Luke records, "And Stephen, full of faith and power, did great wonders and miracles among the people" (Acts 6:8). It appears that Stephen, who might have been of Grecian origin, was doing great things even before he was appointed as a deacon. Apparently, Stephen had emerged as the leader of the deacons.

In addition to carrying out his ministry as a deacon, Stephen was an eloquent preacher. The religious leaders disputed with Stephen in the synagogue, but Steven confounded them. The religious leaders could not counter Stephen's Holy Spirit–inspired preaching and teaching. Therefore, they decided to conspire against Stephen to kill him. They accused Stephen of blaspheming against Moses and against God.

The religious leaders at Jerusalem brought Stephen before the Sanhedrin Council and bribed men to witness against him. The false, bribed witnesses that Stephen continually blasphemed against the holy place, the temple, and against the law (of Moses).

In addition, the bribed witnesses accused Stephen of saying that Jesus of Nazareth shall destroy the temple and shall change the customs which Moses gave the Jews. They hurled concocted, baseless, false accusation against Stephen, testifying, "For we have heard him say, that this Jesus of Nazareth shall destroy this place, and shall change the custom which Moses delivered us" (Acts 6:14). Yes, words matter and lying words are destructive. No wonder the wisest man who ever lived said, "Lying lips are an abomination to the LORD: but they that deal truly are his delight" (Prov. 12:22).

When the high priest heard the accusations leveled against Stephen, he asked Stephen, "Are these things so?" (Acts 7:1). The high priest opened the door for Stephen to respond forcibly to the high priest and other religious leaders and his false accusers.

Philip's response was the preaching of a long, passionate, and piercing sermon. In his sermon, Stephen posed a rhetorical question followed by a condemning truth, "Which of the prophet have not your fathers persecuted? and they have slain them which shewed before of the coming of the Just One; of whom ye have been now the betrayers and murderers" (Acts 7:52). Stephen was certainly bold, and his truth was piercing the hearts of the religious leaders at Jerusalem. He accused the high priest and other religious leaders of murdering the Just One, Jesus. Clearly, he was not concerned about his own life. Stephen continued his piercing preaching-indictment which really got to the hearts of the religious leaders. Luke records, "When they heard these things, they were cut to the heart, and they gnashed on him with their teeth" (Acts 7:54). The truth is like a two-edged sword. The writer of Hebrews reminds us, "For the word of God is quick and powerful, and sharper than any two-edged sword, piercing even to the dividing asunder of soul and spirit . . . and is a discerner of the thoughts and intents of the heart" (Hebrews 4:12). Stephen proclaimed the Word of truth and it pierced the hearts of the religious leaders. They really wanted Stephen dead—murdered.

What really got under the skin and heightened resentment of the high priests and other religious leaders toward Stephen and sealed his murder was when Stephen said, "Behold, I see the heavens open, and the Son of man standing on the right hand of God" (Acts 7:56). The religious leaders lost control of themselves. Their anger and self-righteousness took over any rationality they might have had.

They were driven to rage. "Then they cried with a loud voice, and stopped their ears, and ran upon him with one accord. And cast him out of the city and stoned him" (Acts 7:57–58). There was not even the pretense of a conviction of Stephen by the Sanhedrin Council before the mob took over and conducted the most egregious murder of Stephen—death by stoning.

The religious leaders and their surrogates rushed upon Stephen and dragged him out of the city and stoned Stephen, as a common criminal. This they did because they could not bear to hear the truth Stephen was preaching, especially that they had crucified the Son of God.

They could not wait for the pseudo-trial of Stephen to conclude, even though the Sanhedrin Council would have more than likely pronounced the guilty verdict they wanted. They just could not stand to hear any more of the truth which was so condemning. So they rushed up on Stephen and took him by force for execution by stoning.

And what did the high priest do? He could have stopped the mob. Rather he acted similarly to Pilate at the pseudo-trial of Jesus. He gave the people what they wanted—permission to murder an innocent, righteous man. However, similarly to how they could mot murder the truth when they murdered Jesus; neither could they murder the truth when they murdered Stephen.

Stephen Commits his Spirit to Jesus and Prays for his Murderers

It was at the final moment of Stephen's life when he did what was impossible for a natural-temporal man to do. Luke describes Stephen as full of faith and power. He was also full of love, compassion, and forgiveness. So while the religious leaders and their accomplices were stoning Stephen, Luke records his reaction in this manner, "Stephen calling up on God, and saying, Lord, Jesus receive my spirit. And he kneeled down, and cried with a loud voice. Lord lay not this sin to their charge. And when he had said this, he fell asleep" (Acts 7:59–60). Stephen did what was impossible for natural human being to do—forgave and prayed for his enemies.

He forgave his murders while they were in the process of murdering him in cold blood. He did what Jesus teaches His disciples—followers, "But I say unto you, love your enemies, bless them that curse you, do good to them that hurt you, and pray for them which despitefully, and persecute you" (Matt. 5:44). Stephen did not simply embraced the teaching of Jesus as academic and idealistic, pie in the sky notion. Rather, he exemplified and applied the spirit of the teaching.

Jesus had taught His disciples that what was impossible with men was possible with God.

The Spirit of God, Jesus, was in Stephen; therefore, he was able to forgive and to love those who a natural-temporal human being, could not love and forgive. Without the indwelling of the Holy Spirit in him, it would have been impossible for Stephen to forgive and to love those who were violently murdering him. Stephen prayed to the Father-God to forgive his murderers while they were in the very process of murdering him.

Certainly, Stephen modeled Jesus's prayer of forgiveness while He was on Calvary's Cross giving up His life-dying for the atonement of sins for humanity. Many Bible scholars consider Stephen as a prototype-type of Jesus Christ. On the one hand, Jesus cried out, "Father, forgive them: for they know not what they do" (Luke 23:34). On the other hand, Stephen cried out, "Lord, lay not this sin to their charge" (Acts 7:60). On the one hand, Jesus cried, "Father, into thy hands I commend my spirit" (Luke 23:46). On the other hand, Stephen cried, "Lord Jesus, receive my spirit" Acts 7:60). There is no doubt that Jesus accepted the spirit of Stephen.

In fact, as noted above, while Stephen was being stoned, God gave him glimpse into heaven, while he was still a man. He saw Jesus standing at the right hand of God perhaps to welcome his spirit into heaven.

As I reflect on Deacon Stephen and how he emulated Jesus Christ in his spirit of forgiveness and love, I am led to believe that no other human being in the Bible demonstrates the spirit of forgiveness as did Deacon Stephen. Not even Esau and Joseph. Those were honorable men; however, they were not being killed at the time they forgave their respective brothers.

Even David, a man of God's own heart, when he was on his death bed, asked Solomon to use his wisdom to take action against Joab who had wronged him and two captains of the hosts of Israel (1 Kings 2:5–7). Stephen did not seek justice for the religious leaders and their accomplices. Rather he prayed that God would forgive them for their crime against him. He is certainly a human model of forgiveness and love. Christians would do well to strive to emulate Stephen's attitude of love and compassion and his prayer of forgiveness for their enemies.

Can you forgive and pray for those who have hurt you or are hurting you as Jesus and Stephen did? When the Spirit of Jesus is in you, you are able forgive and love your enemies. Stephen's love for his enemies, which was manifested by his prayer of forgiveness, is certainly the type of divine unconditional love which inspire Christians and believers to do as Stephen prayed and did!

As I reflect on Stephen and his prayer and how God rewarded this righteous man with a glimpse into heaven, I wonder if Christians and believers give Stephen the recognition which he deserves! He is a role model of forgiveness and love. Of all the saints mentioned in the Bible none come as closely in modeling Jesus Christ in the manifestation of forgiveness and love as Stephen did.

I pray that as a Christian and a believer, you might strive to have a heart of praying always and forgiveness as Stephen, the man full of faith and power demonstrated, and for which he was greatly rewarded.

CHAPTER FIFTEEN

TRANSFORMING PRAYERS OF A GENTILE AND A JEW

Prayer of Cornelius, a Gentile

Cornelius was a Gentile, an Italian, and a captain in the Roman army. Luke describes Cornelius as "A devout [dedicated to God] man, and one that feared God with all his house, which gave much alms to people and prayed always [prayed regularly]" (Acts 10:2). God rewarded Cornelius for his continuous prayers, devotion, and generosity.

About 3:00 p.m. one day, Cornelius had a vision. He was probably praying or meditating (the Bible does not say). However, an angel appeared unto Cornelius and called him by name, ". . . Cornelius. And when he looked on him, he was afraid, and said, What is it Lord? And he said unto him, "Thy prayers and thine alms [good deeds] are come up as a memorial before God" (Acts 10:3–4). Luke does not disclose the details of Cornelius's prayers. Perhaps, Cornelius similarly to Hannah, who was previously discussed, was a silent prayer. Luke mentions that Cornelius gave generously to the poor and prayed frequently.

Based on positive outcomes that are noted later we can infer, at least in part, plausible impact of Cornelius's prayers,

God answered Cornelius's prayer by giving an angel instructions for Cornelius. The angel delivered the instruction, "And now send to Joppa and call for one Simon, whose surname is Peter: he shall tell thee what thou oughtest to do" (Acts 10:6). It is quite interesting that God instructed Cornelius, a Gentile, to send for Peter, a Jew, to tell him what he needed to do.

God could have given the instruction to the angel for Cornelius. As the incident unfolded it becomes clear that God had a message for Peter as well. Although Peter was a leading apostle, having been converted on the Day of Pentecost, he thought that his ministry was solely to the Jews. He was not yet convinced that that he should minister to Gentiles as well.

So what was Cornelius praying continuously about? What was praying for? Could it be that Cornelius was praying that God would open the mind and heart of Peter that he would understand that Jesus makes salvation available to people of all nations—Jews and Gentiles? Might his prayer be for better understanding of the way of salvation—the truth, the way, and life? Luke, the Gentile writer of the incident, does not disclose details regarding Cornelius's prayer.

Cornelius sent three messengers to Joppa to seek for Peter. While the messengers were close to the house where Peter was staying, Peter had a vision. He saw a vessel coming down from heaven with all types of animals. Then Peter heard a voice, "Rise Peter; kill and eat. But Peter said, Not so Lord; for I have never eaten anything that is common or unclean" (Acts 10:13). Even though Peter was converted on the Day of Pentecost and preached a sermon, on that day, when three thousand souls were converted, he did not yet understand that his ministry was not confined to the Jewish people.

Peter would not dare eat meat or any flesh which the Jewish customary laws considered unclean. Neither would enter the house of a Gentile, which he probably considered unclean, if it were left up to him. Even though he had accompanied Jesus to Jairus—a Gentile house—when Jesus healed Jairus' daughter.

Peter had not learned that Jesus makes salvation available to people of all nations

God gave Peter a measured rebuke for his assertion that he did not eat anything common or unclean; God said to Peter, "What God hath cleansed, that call not thou common" (Acts 10:15). Peter got the message. In effect, God told Peter that he, Peter, did not decide who would receive salvation or to whom he would minister. He was God's servant, not His master.

Peter received Cornelius's message responded positively to his request and God's instruction. He journeyed to Cornelius's house at Caesarea to minister unto Cornelius. Peter avoided the consequences of disobeying God's instruction which the defiant Jonah experienced centuries before. When Peter arrived at Cornelius's house, he confessed that based on Jewish customs, it was unlawful for a Jew to keep company with people of other nations—a Gentile. Nevertheless, Peter shared his vision with Cornelius and all in the house. Cornelius then recounted his encounter with the angel, which I previously stated.

Cornelius ended the sharing of his experience with the angel in this manner, "Now therefore are we all here present before God, to hear all things that are commanded of God" (Acts 10:33). Apparently, Cornelius had invited others to his house to hear the message from God which Peter would deliver. The angel had told Cornelius that God had heard his prayers. Since his prayers were for good things, he wanted his neighbors to hear God's answer.

The devout Cornelius had now completed his testimony and was waiting for Peter's response. "Then Peter opened his mouth, and said, Of a truth I perceive that God is no respecter of persons: But in every nation he that feareth him, and worketh righteousness is accepted with him" (Acts 10:34). Peter now understood that the gospel should be preached to all nations— Jews as well as Gentile

Peter preached a sermon at Cornelius's house, starting with, "How God anointed Jesus of Nazareth with the Holy

Ghost and power: who went about doing good, and healing all that were oppressed of the devil" (Acts 10:38). Peter went on to proclaim that Jesus commanded them (the apostles) to preach unto the people and to testify.

Luke records, "While Peter yet spoke these words, the Holy Ghost fell on all them that heard the word" (Acts 10:44). The Jews who had accompanied Peter were astonished when they recognized that Gentiles received the gift of the Holy Spirit. "Then answered Peter, can any man forbid water, that these should not be baptized, which have received the Holy Ghost as well as we?" (Acts 10:46–47). Peter commanded that all the new Gentile converts be baptized in the name of the Lord. And Peter the Jewish apostle remained in Cornelius's (the Gentile's) house for a few days.

After Paul was converted, he taught, preached, and wrote that there are neither Jews nor Gentiles followers of Christ— they are all servants.

Peter was as blessed with the experience at the conversions and pouring out of the Holy Spirit at Cornelius's house as were Cornelius and his household. Peter and other believers learned that Jews did not enjoy monopoly on salvation. The experience was both humbling and exhilarating for Peter and the other Jews who had accompanied Peter to Cornelius's house.

Cornelius's continuous prayers, his devotion to God, and his generosity to the poor paid off in many ways. The obvious pay- off or reward is that Cornelius and all the Gentiles who heard Peter's sermon at Cornelius's house accepted Christ. They received the gift of the Holy Spirit and were baptized.

Even though Cornelius was already a devout man who prayed frequently a d was generous to the poor, he had not yet received the gift of the Holy Spirit. Now he was filed with the Holy Spirit. Cornelius was generous with material things, but more importantly he had now helped others to accept Jesus Christ and the gift of the Holy Spirit. He was an evangelist of sort. All the physical things he gave to the poor could not compare to the spiritual gift and salvation they received when they accepted Jesus Christ as Lord and Savior.

Cornelius's prayers were tremendous blessings to Peter as well. God revealed to Peter that his ministry included Gentile nations. God had told Abraham that the Jews would be a blessing to other nations. Peter now recognized that God is not a respecter of person or nationality and that the gospel must be preached to all nations.

We are thankful to God for the example of Cornelius, a Gentile man, who prayed continuously, even though for a long time he might not have seen results of his prayers. He applied the teaching of Jesus, "And he spake a parable unto them to this end, that men ought always to pray, and not to faint" (Luke 18:1). God's response to Cornelius's continuous prayers changed the trajectory of Peter's ministry—made it more inclusive, and even targeting Gentiles.

Non-Jewish people are beneficiaries of the prayers of Cornelius from the time of the early church to our time.

Do you pray always even though you don't see the manifestation of God's answer to your prayers? Or do you get discouraged and give up? You should strive to pray always and trust God to answer at the time and in the manner He chooses!

Prayer of Peter, a Jew

We recall that when Jesus was arrested and being tried by the Sanhedrin Council, Peter denied three times that he had known Jesus. Peter was with Jesus for more than three years and had made himself the spoke person for the rest of the apostles. He was in Jesus's inner circle. Before Jesus was arrested, Jesus told Peter that Satan wanted to sift—destroy him; however, Jesus assured him that He, Jesus, had prayed for him.

Before His crucifixion, Jesus commissioned Peter to minister to the other apostles after he was converted. Peter was converted on the Day of Pentecost and became a bold and dedicated advocate for Jesus. At his first sermon, on the Day of Pentecost, three thousand souls were converted. It is this transformed Peter who Luke describes in this incident of prayer.

Luke records that Peter and John were heading for the temple at the hour of prayer, the ninth hour (3:00 p.m.). Evidently, they were going to pray; public and private prayers were customary in the early church. This particular day and time of prayer were different from previous days and times of prayer.

As Peter and John reached the entrance to the temple, they encountered a man who was lame—physically disabled, paralyzed. He was born that way. His only occupation was that of a beggar. Someone took him to the temple each day that he could beg for something, anything. No doubt he had heard of the teaching of Jesus that the poor would be around and His followers should assist the poor.

When the physically disabled man saw Peter and John about to enter the temple, he probably thought that those apostles had compassionate faces and probably kind hearts as well. He mustered up all his strength and with his face looking away or looking down from Peter and John he made his usual plea for alms—just something, anything that you can spare.

Peter and John felt empathy for this unfortunate soul. However, quite likely they had no money on them. Jesus had sent them on an evangelical mission and told them not even to take their purse. Peter intended to give this poor beggar more than he asked for, expected, or could imagine. Peter was ready to deliver the amazing alms—gift to the man, "And Peter fastening his eyes upon him, with John, said, Look on us" (Acts 3:4). Peter gave this poor man a piercing, penetrating, unblinking, and steadfast stare. Would this man, who was probably a shame to look at Peter and John obey the command of Peter? Would he humble himself and receive the blessing Jesus had instore for him?

Well the physically disabled man mustered the courage and with a heart of great expectation looked at Peter and John. Those who had given him something in the past probably did not even want to make eye contact with him; yet these two apostles wanted him to look straight into their eyes. So he waited for the big gift.

To the astonishment of the paralyzed beggar, he was offered no coins, instead, "Then Peter said, Silver and gold have I none; but such as I have give I thee: In the name of Jesus Christ of Nazareth rise up and walk. And he took him by the right hand, and lifted him up, and immediately his feet and ankle bones received strength. And he leaping up stood, and walked, and entered with them into the temple, walking, and leaping, and praising God: (Acts 3:6–8). Peter prayed one short, intentional prayer and made an uncomplicated, single request, "In the name of Jesus Christ of Nazareth rise up and walk" (Acts 3:6). Jesus heard Peter's prayer, and answered it immediately, and the manifestation of His answer was evident to all present.

Peter believed in the efficacy of prayers. He had confident expectation that Jesus would answer his prayer. He demonstrated his faith by reaching out and holding the right hand of the paralyzed man and helped him to stand. Peter probably remembered what Jesus told the apostles while He was with them in the flesh, "If you shall ask anything in my name, I will do it" (John 14:14). What a powerful promise Jesus made to Peter, John and to His followers today.

This promise was made before Jesus was crucified. And now Jesus is sitting at the right hand of His Father in heaven, He delivered on that promise. And he delivers on all promises. He is never late and always gives the correct answer. Jesus answered Peter's prayer, and healed the paralyzed beggar.

However, the answer to Peter's prayer was not just about Peter, and John, and the paralyzed beggar. Rather, it was most importantly about glorifying God. Jesus had told the apostles, "And whatsoever ye shall ask in my name, that will I do, that the Father may be glorified in the Son" (John 14:13). Jesus took great pleasure in glorifying His Father while He was on earth as fully God and a fully righteous Man. He continues to glorify His Father as He sits at His right hand in heaven.

Therefore Jesus wants His followers to pray to and ask God, His Father, for our desire in Jesus's name—that Jesus will answer our prayers and glorify His Father!

Peter's short prayer of faith resulted in Jesus's immediate response. Jesus healed the paralyzed beggar and glorified His Father. The healed man entered the temple with Peter and John and was a living testimony of the power of Jesus to heal.

When Peter entered the temple along with the healed man, he used the incident of the healed (formally paralyzed) beggar to deliver a powerful sermon. He reminded the congregation that it was through the power of the risen Jesus, who they had killed and through faith in the risen Jesus, that the paralyzed beggar was healed.

Peter's prayer was brief, direct, and uttered with confident expectation for a specific desired outcome that the lame man would walk. Jesus answered the prayer and gave Peter exactly what he requested!

How about your prayer? Do you pray with confident expectation for a specific desired outcome? I urge you to consider the approach of Peter in his prayer for the paralyzed man; however, always leave the final outcome of your prayer to Jesus by asking that His will be done.

CHAPTER SIXTEEN

LORD, WHAT WILT THOU HAVE ME TO DO?

This chapter of the book is devoted to a man whose simple and sincere prayer "Lord, what you will have me to do?" resulted in the transformation of his life. He and became the greatest evangelist, preacher, teacher, and writer, and church planter in the New Testament. This is no other than Saul (Paul). Saul was a terror to the early at Jerusalem and surrounding areas and thought he was doing what God wanted him to do. After he prayed the short prayer cited above, he received the answer and made a 180-degrees turn around and kept going straight until he was executed in Rome.

You will be fascinated with the transformed Paul and his prayers, work, and commitment to Jesus and the spread of the gospel. All because he prayed!

Saul's Transformational Prayer

Paul is arguably the greatest human preacher, teacher, and most prolific writer and evangelist in the New Testament. And perhaps the greatest evangelist and church planter recorded in the entire Bible. His prayers are replete throughout the thirteen epistles which he wrote. Therefore, it was extremely difficult for me to select one or two of his prayers to include in this book which only includes a few selected prayers.

As I stated previously, I wanted to include prayers where the manifestation of God's answers to them was immediately evident. There are exceptions such as when persons prayed over an extended period, such as Hannah, Zacharias, Cornelius, and perhaps Isaac, and so forth. With these two criteria in mind, I selected Saul's (Paul's) prayers when he was on his journey to persecute Christians at Damascus and when he prayed for the Church at Ephesus, respectively.

Saul's Prayer on His Way to Damascus

Saul, a devout Jew, a Pharisee, a citizen of Rome, and educated by the master Gamaliel, had recently consented to the stoning to death of Deacon Stephen at Jerusalem. The death of Stephen pleased the religious leaders at Jerusalem. No doubt Saul was proud of the role he played in the notorious stoning of Stephen.

With a sense of pride and misguided loyalty and sincerity, Paul secured the outer garments of the murderers who were carrying out the horrendous act of murdering Stephen by stoning him to death. Saul was now energized to escalate the persecution of followers of the Jesus.

The Jewish religious leaders with Roman accomplices had crucified on a false charge that He blasphemed by claiming that He is the Son of God. Later on Saul would confess the fact that Jesus is the Son of God.

In his exuberance to destroy the followers of Jesus and their teaching that Jesus is the Son of God, Saul obtained a letter from the high priest authorizing him to persecute followers of Jesus. He had the authority to arrest and take to Jerusalem any men or women he found, between Jerusalem and Damascus, who were teaching that Jesus Christ is the Son of God.

The religious leaders had executed Jesus, on the cross, and though that was the end of Jesus and His teaching. However the apostles and other followers of Jesus continued to profess that Jesus rose from the dead and ascended into heaven. Saul wanted to stop, once and for all, what he thought was false teaching. So, with his letter of authority, from the high priest, in his hand and his co-conspirers with him, Saul set out for Damascus to persecute followers of the risen Jesus Christ.

Little did Saul know that Jesus was monitoring him every step of his journey. Saul was near Damascus to carry out, what he thought was, his sincere duty on behalf of God and to enforce the doctrines of the religious leaders in Jerusalem. Then the risen, living Jesus Christ confronted Saul. Suddenly a light from heaven—the Light of the world, Jesus Christ—shun around him. He fell to the earth and was immediately struck with blindness.

The blind Saul, laid prostrate on the ground in a humbling and trembling position. He heard a voice saying, "Saul, Saul, why persecutes thou me?" (Acts 9:4). Saul was a well-educated religious scholar and recognized the voice right away. However, in his state of fright and with a trembling voice Saul asked, "Who art thou Lord?" (Acts 9:5). Saul already knew the answer. Nevertheless, the voice said, "I am Jesus whom thou persecutes; it is hard for thee to kick against the pricks" (Acts 9:5). Saul was well familiar with God. He was a religious scholar and knew that he could not fight against God.

Jesus made it clear to Saul that when he persecutes the followers of Jesus, he is persecuting Jesus Himself. Furthermore, it is difficult for him to kick against sharp spikes. He could not fight against the risen Jesus Christ or the truth that the followers of Jesus were preaching and teaching.

Saul now realized that Jesus, who the religious leaders had crucified, is very much alive. He should have believed what Stephen said when he was being stoned, "And said, Behold, I see the heavens opened, and the Son of man standing on the right hand of God" (Acts 6:56). It is the same Son of God who Stephen saw when Saul was consenting to his stoning who had now confronted Saul.

Saul's Eight-Word Transformational and Impactful Prayer

In response to the admonition of the risen Jesus Christ that Paul cannot fight against Him, Saul humbled himself and prayed. The prayer is perhaps the most continually impactful and transformational, eight-word prayer of a human being in the New Testament and perhaps in the entire Bible Paul prayed, "Lord, what wilt thou have me to do?" (Acts 9:6). This prayer began the transformation of Saul and changed the trajectory of his life. From a life of sincerely wrong about Jesus to a life of sincerely correct about Jesus, and committed to and an effective advocate of Jesus Christ. The prayer was not a request to meet his immediate personal need—to restore his sight. Rather, it was a prayer recognizing Jesus and submitting himself to the will of Jesus. And Jesus used Paul in a most amazing manner which affected the early church, affected doctrines of developing church congregation, and is affecting humanity today.

Jesus Answers Paul's Prayer

Jesus answered Saul's succinct and submissive prayer by instructing him, "Arise, and go into the city, and it shall be told thee what thou must do: (Acts 9:6). Saul followed Jesus's instructions. Paul was now blind.

The men, who were accompanying Saul on his misguided mission to persecute the followers of Jesus, led the blind Saul to the city of Damascus. Saul could not see; therefore, he had to walk by faith—trusting his men to lead him to Damascus where he remained blind for three days.

While Paul was at Damascus without sight, Jesus instructed Ananias, a disciple at Damascus, to minister to Saul. Ananias laid his hands on Saul and he received his sight and the Holy Ghost fell up on him. Saul was now converted, "And straight way he preached Christ in the synagogue, that he is the Son of God" (Acts 9:20). One eight-word prayer and the answer of Jesus transforms Saul the persecutor of the followers of Jesus Christ to Paul the greatest advocate of Christ, the greatest preacher, teacher, evangelist, church planter in the Bible. And became the most prolific writer in the New Testament and perhaps in the entire Bible.

Years after the incident of Saul's conversion, the now Apostle Paul writing to the Corinthians proclaims, "For we walk by faith, not by sight" (2 Cor. 5:7). This statement, no doubt, had literal and spiritual implications for Paul. He probably thought of the time when he was both physically and spiritually blind and had to be led to Damascus. At Damascus, through the instrumentality of Ananias, Jesus restored his physical sight and gave him spiritual sight. It all started with his response to his encounter with Jesus and his eight words prayer, "Lord, what wilt thou have me to do?" Jesus answered his prayer and gave him an assignment. He accepted the assignment and never looked back.

Do you ever ask Jesus, what does He want you to do? Are you ready to accept and carry out the assignment to the best of your ability? Remember, there is no failure in carrying out God's assignment if you trust and obey Him!

Paul, the Obedient Servant of Jesus

Paul's preaching, teaching, writing, and praying contributed immensely to the physical and spiritual development and growth of the early Christian church, and fundamental doctrines of churches, congregations. Paul's writings, teachings and doctrines continue to influence the Christian church, body of Christ, and followers of Christ today. It all started with an eight-word prayer of a man who was transformed from a persecutor of followers of Jesus to an advocate of Jesus Christ the Messiah.

The significance of Saul's eight-word prayer is that he did not ask for something for himself a special gift or protection, for example. There have been many short prayers in the Bible, such as, "Lord, that I might receive my sight (Mark 10:51)," "Jesus, thou Son of David, have mercy on me (Mark 10:47, Luke 18:38)," "If thou wilt, thou canst make me clean (Matt. 8:2, Mark 1:40, Luke 5:12)," and many others. However, the short eight-word prayer of Saul if quite unique, "Lord, what wilt thou have me to do?"

Saul was ready to submit himself to the will of God. He was blind so it would have been understood if he had asked, "Lord, that I might receive my sight." Had he just received his physical sight and went his way he probably would have known that Jesus gives and can take physical sight. Instead he asked Jesus to reveal to him what He wanted him to do.

The disciple Ananias helped him to receive his physical sight and more importantly, his spiritual sight. Only Jesus gives spiritual sight; therefore, Ananias was the instrument through whom Saul received spiritual sight.

The world has not been the same since Saul submitted himself to the will of Jesus, and Jesus used him fully and completely in ministering to His people, especially the Gentile. Years after Paul was converted at Damascus, he continued to carry out the mission, which Jesus assigned to him, to minister to the Gentiles.

Paul was highly successful. However, he was reaping consequences of his earlier atrocities against the followers of Jesus Christ. He wrote to the Church at Ephesus, Ephesians, and expressed his situation in this manner, "For this cause I Paul, a prisoner of Jesus Christ for you Gentiles" (Eph. 3:1). This was a reversal of situation for Saul, who now goes by his Roman name Paul. He once persecuted people for teaching and preaching about Jesus, now he is imprisoned for the same reason.

When Paul was being persecuted for the same reasons he persecuted followers of Jesus he must have reflected on his past attitude and behavior. And how Jews and Romans in Rome were behaving toward him and wrote, "Be not deceived;

God is not mocked: for whatsoever a man soweth, that shall he also reap" (Gal. 6:7). One interesting thing about Paul is that he never complained about his circumstances, and except for the thorn in his side, he never asked God to deliver him from his tribulations. He accepted the consequences of his past misdeeds.

In fact, Paul asserted that he had learned to be contented with whatever situation he found himself (Phil. 4:11).

Saul, now Paul, who in the past did not believe Gentiles were worthy of salvation, was imprisoned, partially, because of his commitment to share the way of salvation with them. It all started with his eight-word prayer, "Lord, what wilt thou have me to do?" What an irony!

You might ask why Jesus chose a man who aided and abetted the murdering of His followers to be His great apostle? While I don't claim to know all the answers to that question, a few plausible answers come to mind: Saul was well educated in Jewish laws and customs and he was a Pharisee so he would be able to relate to the scribes and Pharisees and other Jewish religious leaders. Saul was a Roman citizen so he would have access to Roman leaders and other Gentile. Saul was a devout man and was sincere in what he did, even when he was misguided in sincerely doing wrong.

In addition, Jesus knew that once Paul knew the truth about Jesus Christ, he would be sincere in carrying out the message. Paul was well educated and was eager to learn, to teach, and to preach. He had tremendous and characteristics of o great leader. Jesus knew that Paul would be a great soldier for Him. Of course, only Jesus knows His reasons for selecting Paul for such monumental assignment!

I pray that when Jesus confronts or gently call you, you will humble yourself and ask the question as Saul did, "Lord, what will you have me to do?" And you will follow Jesus's instruction right away as Saul did. Furthermore, I pray that you will be ready to change your course, regardless of your sincerity, when you recognize that the course you are on is incorrect. I pray that you will take time on a regular basis to ask, "Lord, what will you have me to do?" And respond affirmatively when Jesus answers.

What will your prayer or answer be when Jesus calls you one way or another? What assets, characteristics, qualities do you possess which Jesus may use in His service? Are you willing to follow Jesus's instructions even when they are inconvenient?

Paul's Love for the Church at Ephesus

Paul did not establish the Church at Ephesus; however, he had special love for that church. In fact, on one occasion, he spent three years in Ephesus ministering to the church. One of the most heart rending and emotionally piercing incident recorded in the New Testament was when Paul was bidding goodbye to leaders of the Church at Ephesus.

When Paul was nearing the end of his third missionary journey, he truly desired to see the leaders of the Church at Ephesus. On his way to Jerusalem to attend the Passover Celebration, he wanted to pay another visit to Ephesus to meet with the church one more time. Perhaps, Paul thought or knew that it might have been his final visit with the church. He was pressed with time so he asked the elders of the church to meet him at Miletus.

When the elders got to Miletus, Paul recounted his experiences at Ephesus from the first day he got there. He recounted that he had served the Lord with humility. He had taught the church all he knew, everything that was beneficial to them. He had preached to both Jews and Greeks regarding salvation through Jesus Christ. Paul then poured out the burden of his heart, "And now behold, I go bound in the spirit unto Jerusalem, not knowing the things that shall befall me there. Save that the Holy Spirit witnesseth in every city, saying that bonds and afflictions abide me" (Acts 20:22–23). Paul had an intuition or discernment that he would not see the elders anymore, neither would he anymore visit the Church at Ephesus.

A Sad Farewell

Although Paul was not trying to cause sadness to the elders of the Church at Ephesus, he could not constrain himself. He said, "And now, behold, I know that ye all, among whom I have gone preaching the kingdom of God, shall see my face no more" (Acts 20:25). As I typed this quote, I could hardly hold by the tears from my eyes and my heart was in tears. What sad moment it must have been for Paul and the elders of the Church at Ephesus.

I can truly understand why Peter was beside himself when Jesus told the apostles that He would be leaving them soon to return to His Father in Heaven. Jesus at that time predicted that He would have been rejected and executed evil people. Yes, indeed, it was a sad time for Paul and the elders of the Church at Ephesus.

True love can be hurtful when there is physical separation of those who truly love. Paul and the elders love one another so much that Paul's truth was piercing and hurtful, at least, at that moment. Paul and the elders of the Church at Ephesus displayed true love mixed with sorrows by their embracing and weeping at the farewell ceremony for Paul. Yes, true love can be hurtful. It is so good to know that Jesus comforts the broken heart of those who turn to Him.

Paul Prays for the Church at Ephesus

After Paul had given his dear brothers and trustees of the Church at Ephesus further encouragement and instructions, he knelt down and prayed with all of them. "And they wept sore and fell on Paul's neck, and kissed him. Sorrowing most of all for the words which he spake, that they should see his face no more. And they accompanied him unto the ship" (Acts

20:37–38). Again, my eyes are teary as I experience the emotion of Paul and the elders of the Church at Ephesus. It was this type of love which Paul had for the Ephesians that moved him to write to them and to recount his prayers while he was a prisoner in Rome.

What was your reaction to the farewell incident of Paul and the elders of the church at Ephesus? How did you feel? What did you think? What comforts you or will comfort you when you must say goodbye to someone you may never see again? What comforts you when you must say final goodbye to a friend, colleague, or church congregation?

Paul's Epistle the Ephesians
(His Prayers from a Prison in Rome)

After Paul gave his farewell address to the elders of the Church at Ephesus when they met him at Miletus, he left Miletus and journeyed to Jerusalem to participate in the Passover Celebration. While in the temple at Jerusalem, Jews coming from Asia falsely accused Paul of "This is the man, that teacheth all men everywhere against the people, and the law, and this place: and further brought Greeks also into the temple, and hath polluted this holy place. And all the city was moved, and the people ran together: and they took Paul, ad drew him out of the temple: and forthwith the door was closed shut" (Acts 21:28). The religious leaders did not simply threw Paul from the temple and shut the door behind him; rather they rushed upon him and was beating him without mercy. They intended to kill him Paul.

Fortunately for Paul, he was saved by centurions and soldiers. Paul was arrested, but was allowed to address the Sanhedrin Council. He delivered a powerful sermon and a recounting of the incident of his conversion and his commitment to spreading the Gospel of Jesus Christ. He testified to his complicity in the stoning of Stephen. He revealed the incident of his conversion on his way to Damascus to persecute followers of Jesus. He proclaimed his Jewish and Roman heritage. He was spared additional flagging because of his Roman heritage.

The Jewish leaders in Jerusalem wanted to kill Paul, so Claudius Lysias, chief captain of Roman centurions provided two hundred soldiers to escort Paul to the Roman Governor Felix at Caesarea for trial by the Roman Governor. Jewish religious went from Jerusalem to Caesarea asked Felix to extradite Paul to Jerusalem for trial there. Felix agreed to comply with the request. However, Paul, on the basis of being a Roman citizen, appealed for trial by Emperor Caesar at Rome. Felix had no option but to comply with Paul's demand.

After a series events Paul arrived at Rome and was placed under house arrest. While under house arrest, he decided to write epistles—letters to some of his favorite church congregations. These became known as the Prison Epistles of Paul to the named church.

In the case of the Epistle to the Ephesians, Paul was not addressing any particular issue or doctrine. Rather, his primary purpose was to provide encouragement to the church. As recorded in Ephesians, Paul both prayed as well as recounted prayers which he had prayed. The Epistle to the Ephesians was written between AD 60 and AD 62.

As I indicated previously, I used two criteria, generally speaking, in selecting the prayers in the Bible which are included in this book. Firstly, the prayer should have a clear request. Secondly, there should be clear evidence or manifestation that the prayer was answered. Of course, I give allowance for implicit answers. The prayer which I have selected from Ephesians has a clear request and God's implicit answer.

In Ephesians Chapter 1, Paul greets the Church at Ephesus, "Grace be to you, and peace from God our Father, and from the Lord Jesus Christ" (Eph. 1:2). Certainly, this greeting is a prayer; however, it is a general prayer. Paul uttered (prayed) similar salutations (prayers) to other churches (congregations).

Paul's prayer recorded in Ephesians 1, seems to be a recounting of his prayer for the Church at Ephesus. He states, "Wherefore I also, after I heard of your faith in the Lord Jesus, and love unto all saints, Cease not to give thanks for you, making mention of you in my prayers" (Eph. 1:15–16). Apparently, Paul was praying for the church, Christians at Ephesus, even before his first visit to the church. He did not establish or plant that church. He helped to strengthen the church at Ephesus.

Then Paul went on to provide specificity regarding his prayer for Ephesian Christians-believers. Paul prayed, "That the God of our Lord Jesus Christ, the Father of glory, may give unto you the spirit of wisdom and revelation in the knowledge of him. The eyes of your understanding being enlightened; that ye may know what is the hope of his calling, and what riches of the glory of his inheritance in the saint" (Eph. 1:17–18). Paul is specific in his request to God for the Church at Ephesus. The salutation to his prayer was general in scope and would be applicable to any church; however, Paul addresses specific areas in which he was God's blessings on the Church at Ephesus.

What a powerful prayer on behalf of the Church at Ephesus! That God would give the Ephesian Christians a spirit of wisdom and revelation in the knowledge of God. No doubt Paul was very knowledgeable of the importance of wisdom as Solomon proclaims throughout the Book of Proverbs. Paul understood that only God can provide the spirit wisdom, and revelation in the knowledge of God. The leaders of the church and the Christians at Ephesus would need the spirit of wisdom and revelation, discernment, in order to pursue righteousness and justice.

Without biblical Knowledge, understanding, and wisdom, the church would have a difficult time, at best, and virtually impossible challenges at worse, fighting against the wiles of the devil. Paul demonstrates the importance of praying for the church even when the church appears to be doing well.

The Christians at Ephesus needed biblical wisdom and revelation in order for them to be effective evangelists as well as to edify the growing membership of that growing church. Paul was well acquainted with the teaching of James that, "If any of you lack wisdom, let him ask of God, that giveth to all men liberally, and unbraideth [God will not rebuke you for asking for wisdom] and it shall be given him" (James 1:5). Paul understood the principle that often, people cannot ask for what they do not know they need, or what they do not have.

Hence, sometimes, we must petition for others for what we believe they need, even when they are not aware and do not know what they need. Paul knew that God gives wisdom to those who genuinely seek it. He wanted to ensure that the church, Christians at Ephesus, would have wisdom and discernment.

The spirit of wisdom would provide revelation to the church. Paul was undoubtedly familiar with how God had given the spirit of wisdom to those He had selected to make Aaron's garment centuries earlier. God told Moses, "And thou shalt speak unto all that are wise hearted, whom I have filled with the spirit of wisdom . . ." (Exod. 28:3). Paul knew that it is God who gives biblical wisdom and that biblical wisdom supersedes all other types of wisdom.

No wonder Paul earnestly prayed that God would grant wisdom to the Ephesian Church, the Christians. Wisdom in this case is synonymous to righteousness.

Paul's prayer—the church, Christians at Ephesus—continues that, "The eyes of your understanding being enlightened; that ye may know what is the hope of his calling, and what the riches of the glory of his inheritance in the saints" (Eph. 1:18). Paul prayed that God increases the understanding of the Ephesian Christians that they may understand the hope which God gives His people. The hope of eternal life through Jesus Christ the Lord and Messiah. Understanding is necessary in order to apply to knowledge correctly.

As seen in the Book of Proverbs, when biblical knowledge and understanding are applied in a proper manner, God gives wisdom. No wonder Solomon says, "Wisdom is the principal thing; therefore get wisdom: and with all that getting get understanding" (Prov. 4:7). Although Paul does not explicitly say so, the Ephesian Christians were expected to study and learn in order to conduct themselves properly.

A few after writing to the Church at Ephesus, Paul wrote to the few later years Paul wrote to the young pastor Timothy: "Study to show thyself approved unto God, as a workman that needeth not to be ashamed, rightly dividing the word of truth" (2 Tim. 2:16). Paul wanted the Ephesian Christians to acquire information and knowledge so as to conduct themselves in a manner that meets God approval and brings glory to God.

Paul's desire and prayer for the Ephesian Christians were that as they continue to pray, meditate, and study Scripture, they would gain knowledge and understanding. And as they apply knowledge with understanding, God would grant them wisdom. And the circulatory process would continue.

No one understood more clearly than Paul, the importance of prayer in the process of gaining knowledge, understanding, and wisdom. God alone grants wisdom. James, the brother of Jesus, reminds the Church, followers of Jesus, that, "If any of you lacks wisdom, let him ask of God, that giveth to all men liberally, and upbraideth not; and it shall be given" (James 1:5). Prayer is essential for one to receive God' special gift of biblical wisdom.

Therefore, as Paul lovingly did, Christians and believers have a responsibility to pray that God will grant wisdom to those who earnestly seek it. Those who study learn and apply the knowledge and understanding they gain. In addition, Christians must pray that the hearts of God's people everywhere will thirst for, pray for, and seek biblical knowledge, understanding, and wisdom.

In the last four verses of Ephesians chapter 1 (19–23), Paul provides exhortation more so than praying. He proclaims the greatness of God's power, toward those who believe in Him, through the risen Christ. Paul proclaimed that it through the power of the risen Jesus, who sits at the right hand of God, that the Ephesians will receive wisdom.

Further, Paul declared the preeminence of the name of Jesus above all other names in the physical world and in the world to come. He affirmed that God has placed all things under the feet of Jesus and has made Jesus the head of the church. He reminded the Ephesian Christians that Christ is the head of the church.

Then Paul proclaims to the Ephesian, former Gentile, Christians the wonderful assurance, "And you hath he quickened (raised from spiritual death) who were dead in trespasses and sins" (Eph. 2:1). Paul had prayed that God would grant knowledge, understanding, and wisdom to the Ephesian Christians; now he assures them that they, through the risen Jesus Christ, possess the most important, continuing gift of all—resurrection from spiritual death, everlasting life!

It is noteworthy that Paul first prayed a passionate prayer on behalf of the Church at Ephesus. He then provided exhortation and assurance of eternal life to the believers. There is no doubt that God answered Paul's prayer and prospered the Church at Ephesus.

Paul prayed again for the Church at Ephesus, as recorded in Ephesians 3:14–21. He encouraged the Ephesian Christians not to worry themselves because of the tribulations he was experiencing—even in the prison in Rome. In fact, he informed the Ephesians that he bow his knees—prayed that they would not worry about him.

In his passionate prayer, Paul beseeched God, "That he would grant you [Ephesian Christians], according to the riches of his glory, to be strengthened with might by His Spirit in the inner man" (Eph. 3:16). Paul prayed that Christ would dwell in the hearts of the Ephesian Christians by faith. And that they will be grounded in love.

In the final chapter of Paul's Epistle to the Ephesians, he provides significant instructions to children, parents, and to Ephesians Christians, in general (applicable to all Christians). The Apostle went back to the theme of prayer. He said, "Praying always with all prayer and supplication in the Spirit, and watching thereunto with all perseverance and supplication for all saints" (Eph. 6:18). There is no other apostle in the Bible who has prayed nearly as much for the church and for individual congregations as Paul did.

Church leaders, in particular, and Christians, in general, will do well in modeling Paul as they/we pray for the church, Christians, and for people in general!

We give praise and thanks to God for the circumstances which converged to enable the Apostle Paul to write the Epistle to the Ephesians. We are particularly blessed to be the beneficiaries of the beautiful prayers contained therein. The Apostle Paul was a special person in many ways. Just to name a few. Firstly, Jesus Christ gave Paul a mission which he accepted and executed with enthusiasm, commitment, and persistency.

Secondly, Paul loved the Ephesian Christians and all followers of Jesus. Thirdly, Paul's physical body was in prison in Rome, but his mind and spirit were at liberty, and he had time on his hand to pray, meditate, reflect, and write. Fourthly, and perhaps most importantly, God inspired Paul to write.

The Epistle to the Ephesians is one of Paul's most significant declaration of the believers' assurance in and union with Christ. It does not matter if the believers were once devout Jews, Gentiles, or despised Samaritans. Paul urges the Ephesian Christians to live in unity as members of one body— the church, the body of Christ. He asserts that Christ is the head of the church, and all members are important for the proper functioning of the body.

Thank God! I trust that the forgoing discourse, on the teaching and prayers of Paul, is as inspirational and instructional to you as it is for me!

CHAPTER SEVENTEEN
JESUS TEACHES ABOUT PRAYING

Jesus Teaches His Disciples to Pray

When Jesus was on earth in the form of flesh as fully God and fully Man (God-Man), He (abided in) maintained close relationship (fellowship) with His Father in heaven. Jesus maintained fellowship with God His Father through regular and often prayers, fasting, and meditation. In this chapter, I will discuss a few of Jesus's prayers. I will focus on the teaching of Jesus about praying and the model prayer He taught his disciples.

As I searched the New Testament and studied teachings of Jesus regarding praying or a prayer of Jesus, the first times I read about the teaching of Jesus regarding prayer were in the Gospels of Matthew 6:9–15; Luke 10:29 and 11:1–4; and Mark 9:29.

I will begin with remarks Jesus makes about praying and then discuss, in some details, the Disciples' Model Prayer. According to the Gospel of Matthew, it was relatively early in Jesus's ministry when Jesus taught His disciples to pray.

Jesus was conducting His Sermon on the Mount. "And seeing the multitudes, he went up into the mountain: and when he was set, his disciples came unto him. And he opened his mouth and taught them saying" (Matt. 5:1–2). Jesus began this particular Sermon on the Mount with what is generally known as the Beatitudes—blesses and continues to teach fundamental principles for guiding the lives and behavior of those who are committed to follow Him.

Matthew records that Jesus had taught about the privacy of alms—giving to the needed privately, and that the heavenly Father would reward private givers-helpers openly. Jesus then turned to another significant private activity—praying. Matthew, unlike Luke, does not record that the disciples asked Jesus to teach them to pray. Luke states, "And it came to pass, that, as he was praying in a certain place, when he ceased, one of his disciples said unto him, teach us to pray, as John also taught his disciples" (Luke 11:1).

It is conceivable that Matthew just did not include the details that the disciples had asked Jesus to teach them to pray. Luke (the researcher, scientist, physician) included this little yet significant detail—the request by the disciples to teach them to pray. Later on, Jesus taught the disciples to "Ask, and it shall be given you" (Matt. 7:7). Regardless, Jesus taught His disciples to pray for what they desire.

For the purpose of this book, I am focusing on the prayer recorded by Matthew because it is a longer version than the version recorded in Luke. I have designated this prayer as the Disciples' Model Prayer.

Jesus Provides Guidelines for Praying: Avoid Praying to Impress

Before Jesus taught His disciples the Model Prayer, He provides some general guidelines for praying. He admonishes them not to pray in public places just to impress others. He gives examples of those who like to pray standing in the street corners and places of worship just that other will see and praise them. Jesus calls such people hypocrites—insincere. He mentions that those insincere persons will not receive any answer from heaven. Their rewards for their insincere prayer is the praise they receive from those they impress.

Jesus does not band public prayers which are sincere, such as praying at a place of worship, an assembly, or at a public gathering (see 2 Chronicles 7:13–14). Rather, He opposes to public praying designed to impress the hearers; rather than genuinely praying to God (Matt. 6:5). Prayers should be sincere and directed to God regardless of the purpose. Prayers should never be done to impress others or to infer piety of the person praying.

Praying in Secret and Sincerely for Results

Then Jesus provides instruction regarding the secret approach to sincere praying.

He told the disciples that they are praying to God, He is able see, hear, and answer secret prayers. Therefore, those who are sincere and are praying genuinely to God should go to a secret place at home and pray there. He uses the term "close the door of the closet and pray there." This implies praying at some secret place where they could pour out their heart—desires, griefs, and requests to God in confidentiality and without interference.

The sincere prayer is to God; therefore, it is not necessary for the public to always hear the sometimes grievous and intense prayer of one who is experiencing distress. God will keep the prayer a secret and might make the answer public.

There are somethings which are so personal that only God needs to hear them. Jesus does not suggest that the person for whom the praying is done at home or on whose behalf the disciples are making petition should not hear.

The key thing is that the prayer is sincere and it is to God; rather than to impress someone. Jesus affirms that God hears and answers secret prayers. He said, "And thy Father which seeth in secret shall reward thee openly" (Matt. 6:6).

Jesus then warns the disciples against using vain (meaningless repetitions) chanting in their secret praying (Matt. 6:7). In other words, praying is not magic requiring repetitions as the heathens did on Mount Carmel. They chanted for hours to Baal with no avail. They were chanting, asking Baal to accept their sacrifice (1 Kings 18:26).

The Lord Jesus does not suggest that praying on a particular issue should be a one-time thing. To the contrary, Jesus teaches "that men ought always to pray, and not to faint" (Luke 18:1). Jesus urges His disciples (followers) to be persistent and pray all the time and do not get weary in praying. Pray until the manifestation of God's answer is revealed.

Jesus Teaches His Disciples a Model Prayer

After providing guidelines, instructions about praying, Jesus taught His disciples a model prayer. If you were to ask a person, who is even minimally aware of Jesus or ask a devoted Christian, to tell you about the Lord's Prayer, you are likely to receive the same response from both. They are likely to mention the disciples' model prayer, recorded in Matthew 6: 9—13 and Luke 11:2. This is a wonderful model prayer which Jesus taught His disciples; however, this is not a prayer which Jesus often prayed to His Father in heaven.

As a prelude to the model prayer, Jesus told the disciples that they did not need to pray long repetitious prayers because the Father already knows their needs. Then Jesus said, "After this manner therefore pray ye" (Matt. 6:9). Jesus had the full and complete attention of the disciples. They had ears to hear and were ready to listen attentively, not only with their ears but with their hearts as well. This was a teachable moment for the Master Teacher from Nazareth.

He had been teaching His disciples for a while. He will now teach them a prayer. This prayer will become one of the best known passages in the Bible, perhaps surpass only by Jesus's proclamation, "For God so loved the world, that he gave us his only begotten Son, that whosoever believeth in him should not perish, but have everlasting life" (John 3:16). Jesus knows that His followers will memorize and teach the prayer to their children, and grandchildren and other children at their homes, at schools, at places of worship, and so forth. He knows that people, including children, will memorizing and pray the prayer even long after He returns to heaven; so He focuses on key components of a prayer and makes in succinct. He wanted it to be memorable, succinct, and yet comprehensive.

Then Jesus teaches this revolutionary prayer: "Our Father which art in heaven, Hallowed be thy name. Thy kingdom come. Thy will be done in earth, as it is in heaven. Give us this day our daily bread. And forgive us our debts, as we forgive our debtors. And lead us not into temptation, but deliver us from evil: For thin is the kingdom, the power, and glory, forever. Amen" (Matt. 6:9–13). I do not purport to provide an exhaustive analysis of this monumental prayer for who am I to analyze the prayer taught by the Master! Nevertheless, I make a few observations.

I mentioned that the prayer is revolutionary and that it is. Consider that Jesus asks His disciples to address God as "Our Father." The Pharisees and scribes accused Jesus of blasphemy when He declared that God is His Father. And now He is teaching the disciples to address God as Our Father—their Father.

This salutation certainly would have appeared presumptuous to the religious leaders in Judea (Judah). Interestingly enough, when Jesus taught the prayer, He had not yet sacrificed His life to make it possible for God to adopt His followers, so that they could call God Abba or Father. Jesus anticipated His death and reservation to restore relationship and fellowship between God and humankind. I elucidate elements of the prayer as follows:

Discussions on Elements of Disciples' Model Prayer

When Jesus taught His disciples to address God as "Our Father," He must have been anticipating, looking forward to His death, resurrection, ascension to heaven, and the pouring of His Holy Spirit of adoption on believers so that they could call God Abba or Father (Rom. 8:14–15). In any case, Jesus went on with another important component of the prayer. He taught His disciples to pray to their Father who is in heaven. No doubt the disciples knew Joseph or at least knew of Joseph, Jesus's step-father, who was like Jesus's earthly father. In addition, some people who were familiar with prophecies, such as blind Bartimaeus referred to Jesus as the Son of David. Jesus wanted to make it clear to the disciples that He was teaching them to pray to His Father in heaven.

Having taught the disciples to address God as "Our heavenly Father," Jesus then teaches the disciples to hallow the Father—to exalt Him to preeminence as the Holy One, deserving of all praise, glory and honor. Simply saying, there is none like the Father in heaven or earth with whom to compare Him. God has to have the central place in the believer's heart and life. To hallow God means to fear Him—reverence for Him, set Him apart as special, and to give Him the highest praise and glory! That's what Jesus calls on the disciples and on you and me to do!

God's Will Be Done

Moving along with this model prayer, Jesus teaches the disciples that their very first request of God is that God will carry out His will—plan throughout the earth as He has already done in heaven. What a day of rejoicing it will be when earth submits itself to the righteous will—plan of God and earth becomes like heaven, without sins and the consequence of sins!

When this happens, the answer to the remainder of this wonderful prayer will have been manifested—God's answer becomes evident. Jesus did not say that God's will on earth will happen overnight. No wonder He teaches, at another time, as I quoted previously, that men should pray always and not faint.

The will of God which is already done in heaven, in the presence of God, with love, righteousness, peace, contentment, and the absence of sin, will be done in earth. No wonder Jesus gives priority that God's will be done in earth. The fulfillment of part of God's will in earth was that Jesus Christ His only begotten Son gave up His life on the cross of Calvary so that those who believe in Jesus shall receive eternal life.

Physical and Spiritual Needs

Until God's will is completely accomplished throughout the earth humans will have physical needs even with the indwelling of the Spirit of God. So Jesus teaches His disciples to ask God to provide for two basic physical needs—the need for daily bread and the need for forgiveness. "Give us this day our daily bread" (Matt. 6:11). Give us daily bread may be interpreted as give us all we need to survive this day.

It is generally accepted that daily bread meant food, in general, including water. What might not be generally known is that in this prayer, more than likely, Jesus intends daily bread to include clothing and shelter as well.

At a later discourse, Jesus identifies physical needs of the disciples—food, drinks, clothing, and shelter. He tells them not to worry about those things because God knows their needs and will supply them (Matt. 6:31–34).

Forgiveness

In the Disciples' Model Prayer, Jesus turns to a physical, spiritual need—forgiveness. This is perhaps the greatest need of all humanity. A difficult need for humanity to meet for others; however, a need which God meets every minute of the day for humanity. A need which God h meets for those who seek to enter the kingdom of God. No one can enter the Kingdom of God without God's forgiveness.

Paul teaches, "For all have sinned, and come short of the glory of God" (Rom. 3:23). Consequently, God's forgiveness is necessary for anyone to enter the Kingdom of God. God's forgiveness is a spiritual gift because humanity does not earn, cannot earn, and does not deserve God's forgiveness.

God's forgiveness to humanity is made possible through the sacrificial death of Jesus Christ, who paid the wages of sin by the shedding of His blood on Calvary's cross. Again, in teaching the disciples that they should ask God to forgive their sins, Jesus anticipated that He would pay the wages of sin on Calvary' cross.

Jesus would not have taught the disciples to ask God for something that He did not know that God would give to them.

However, God's forgiveness is conditional. Consider that the request for daily bread did not stipulate any prerequisite. We know from the teaching of Jesus and from James—the brother of Jesus, and the writer of Hebrews, and others—that faith is required in order for God to answer prayers. Faith is understood to be a basic prerequisite!

In the case of asking for God's forgiveness, Jesus states another condition, "Forgive us our debts, as we forgive our debtors" (Matt. 6:12). It is clear in the teaching of Jesus that a person should first forgive those who have him or her before seeking forgiveness from God.

The Gospel according to Luke puts Jesus's teaching on the requirement of forgiving others before seeking God's forgiveness in a sharper way, "And also forgive us our sins; for we have also forgiven every one that is indebted to us" (Luke 11:4). In the prayer recorded by Luke, the person seeking God's forgiveness asserts that he or she has already forgiven those who are indebted to him or her and is then seeking God's forgiveness.

Humans forgiving humans can be both a physical and spiritual activity. Physical forgiveness due error or behavior caused by misunderstanding on the part of one person or the other or the person seeking forgiveness has met the requirements—and the consequences needed for forgiveness—and paid the price for the indebtedness.

Spiritual forgiveness is effectuated through the love of Jesus in the forgiver's heart. The love compels him or her to forgive, even though the perpetrator has not or cannot pay the price of forgiveness. This occurs without restoration of any indebtedness and is unconditional. This type of forgiveness is reflected in Stephen's prayer for those who were stoning to death. In any case, Jesus teaches the disciples that they must forgive others before seeking forgiveness from God.

Jesus emphasizes the need for the disciples (followers of Jesus) to forgive one another. He gave a profound admonition, "But if ye forgive not men their trespasses, neither will your heavenly Father forgive your trespasses" (Matt. 6:15). One of the great difficulties (challenges) that many Christians deal with on an ongoing basis is the difficulty of forgiving others; especially those who have done them egregious wrongs.

Christians will often profess that they have forgiven, but will not forget. Whenever the name of the offender is mentioned or whenever they come in contact with the person who caused their grief, anger and problem, their feeling of animosity and need for revenge are rekindled. The question is whether such Christians have truly forgiven the person(s) who have wronged them.

The Bible teaches, "For I will be merciful to their unrighteousness, and their sins, and their iniquities will I remember no more" (Heb. 8:12). The Psalmist reminds us, "As far as the east is from the west, so far hath he removed our transgressions from us" (Psa. 103:12). Jesus emphasizes that His disciples must forgive others before seeking God's forgiveness.

In addition, true spiritual forgiveness will allow the forgiver to forget the pain and suffering associated with the wrong doer(s). This type of true forgiveness is only possible through the Spirit of God (Jesus) who lives in the disciples' followers of Jesus Christ. That Spirit is available to all who believe in Jesus. This requires submitting oneself to God, abiding in the love of Jesus, and engaging in ongoing prayers and meditation.

Lead Us Not into Temptation and Deliver Us from Evil

Jesus knows and understands what it means to be tempted. This is to be enticed to do wrong; to disobey God or even to disobey legitimate civil laws. Imagine, right after Jesus was baptized and was embarking on His God-sent earthly mission, starting with fasting and meditation, Satan tried to tempt Him to disobey God.

After Jesus had fasted for forty days and forty nights, as a righteous Man, Jesus was hungry for physical food. Satan challenged Jesus to make bread out of stones to prove that He is the Son of God. This is something which Jesus could easily had done. However, if He had done it He would have been obeying Satan; rather than God.

Jesus rebuked Satan. Satan made two additional attempts to tempt Jesus. On the third attempt, Satan took the audacity to ask Jesus to fall down and worship him. He took his attempted temptations one step too far. Jesus now puts him in his place. Jesus said to him, "Get thee hence, Satan: for it is written, thou shalt worship the Lord thy God, and him only shalt thou serve" (Matt. 4:10). Jesus, filled with the Holy Spirit, rebuked Satan and there was nothing Satan could do about the rebuke but to leave Jesus alone.

Jesus resisted Satan and Satan fled from Him. Satan knows that Jesus Christ is the Son of God, the Messiah, yet he tried to get Jesus off course by trying to tempt Jesus. Satan tried to tempt the Son of God, not just an ordinary temptation. Rather, he asked Jesus, the Son of God, to fall down and worship him. Therefore, he will have no hesitation in trying to tempt even the saint of Gods! He will not hesitate to try to tempt you.

James admonishes followers of Jesus, "Submit yourselves therefore to God. Resist the devil, and he will flee from thee" (James 4:7). As a Christian, a believer, you must submit yourself to the will of God and abide in His love so that you are protected from Satan. In addition, you must have the desire to resist Satan so that he feels defeated and leave you alone that angels may minister to you.

The Apostle Peter reminds us, "Be sober, be vigilant: because you adversary the devil, as a roaring lion, walketh about, seeking whom he may devour" (1 Pet. 5:8). Peter could certainly remember how Satan wanted to sift him like wheat and how Jesus prayed for him (Luke 22:31–32).

The truth of the matter is that Satan pursues the saints of God, leaders of the church and Christians with determination and vengeance. The Apostle Paul admonishes that in order to stand against the devil, Christians—believers must, "Put on the whole armour of God, that ye may be able to stand against the wiles of the devil" (Eph. 6: 11). Paul describes elements of the spiritual armour as follows: (1) having the loins girt about with truth, (2) the breastplate of righteousness, (3) feet shod with preparation of the gospel of peace, (4) the shield of faith, (5) the helmet of salvation, (6) and the sword of the spirit—the Word of God.

Paul admonishes believers to be anchored in Jesus Christ who has already *conquered* the devil. As Jesus did so many times, Paul emphasizes to followers of Jesus the importance of praying without ceasing. He gave the instruction and urging of, "Praying always with all prayer and supplication in the Spirit, and watching thereunto with all perseverance and supplication for all saints" (Eph. 6:18).

Not only did the great Apostle, prayed for himself and prayed frequently for others and for churches; in addition, he frequently asked others to pray for Him. A robust prayer life of a believer is critical to God's protection from temptation and his delivery from the evil one, who is like a roaring lion seeking who he may devour, as previously discussed.

It is not surprising that Jesus teaches His disciples to ask God to deliver them from temptation and protect them from the evil one—Satan. Satan is the origin of temptation and all evil. The Bible teaches that temptation is always around the followers of Jesus. The Apostle Paul, one Jesus appointed as an apostle after His resurrection, puts it this way, "I find then a law, that, when I would do good, evil is present with me" (Rom. 7:21). Despite the ever presence of evil in earth until the will of God is fully accomplished, followers of Jesus must make intentional decisions and efforts to avoid opportunities for temptation and avoid the evil one as best as possible, while always praying and not fainting.

Kingdom, Power, and Glory Belong to God

Jesus ends the model prayer with the recognition that the Kingdom and all power and glory belong to the hallowed heavenly Father. He wants the disciples (His followers) to understand that God answers their prayers and that God receives the glory and honor when the disciple pray. Jesus suggests that prayers and the results of answered prayers should bring honor and glory to God. The greatest honor and glory will occur when God's kingdom is fully established in earth as it is in heaven.

Jesus's Closing Remarks to the Model Prayer

Jesus repeats, for emphasis, that His disciples (followers) must practice forgiveness. If they forgive those who do them wrong, the heavenly Father will forgive them of their sins and trespasses against Him. However, if they do not forgive others of their wrongs against them, neither will their heavenly Father forgive their sins and trespasses against Him (Matt. 6:14–15).

Later on in Jesus's ministry, Peter asked Jesus how many times he had to forgive someone seven times? To forgive an offender seven times was the Jewish customary law. Jesus told Peter that His requirement for forgiving someone for a wrong is not simply seven times. Rather, "Seventy times seven" (Matt. 18:22). To forgive a person 490 times for a given offence is symbolic of forgiving a person as many times as the person commits wrongs and seeks forgiveness.

This type of forgiving attitude requires spiritual (divine) love and faith, which Christians must strive to obtain and maintain. However, Jesus's illustration of the requirement for forgiving others is understood that a follower of Jesus Christ must forgive as often as the offender seeks forgiveness. Forgiveness is the essence of Christianity!

Forgiveness is fundamental to entering the Kingdom of God. Yet many Christians find it difficult to forgive others who have done the egregious wrongs against them. Often, some will say "I will forgive, but I will never ever forget what they did to me." Those who will not forget or cannot forget what others did to them have probably not yet really forgiven others! I frequently ask God to forgive my sins and remember them no more.

God promises, "I, even I, am he that blotteth out thy transgressions for mine own sake, and I will not remember thy sins" (Isa. 43:25). The writer of Hebrews puts God's forgiveness and forgetfulness of sins this way, "For I will be merciful to their unrighteousness, and their sins and their iniquities will I remember no more" (Heb. 8:12). Christians must strive to do for others what they want God to do for them. They must forgive and forget the wrongs of others as they want God to forgive and forget their wrongs toward Him.

To repeat, as a Christian, you must do to others what you are asking God to do for you. You must truly forgive others and do not allow the evil that others have done to you to perpetually linger in their hearts, and cause your heart to beat faster every time you see the forgiven offender or hear his or her name. This does not mean that you will put yourself in a situation for that person or persons to hurt you again.

A part of the Model Prayer is "Deliver us from the evil one." So forgive and ask God to help you to put the hurt behind you. It might be difficult or even impossible for you to forget, on your own, the willful hurt hurled at you; however, Jesus teaches that "The things which are impossible with men are possible with God" (Luke 18:27). God will help you forgive and forget if you have the desire and you are willing to try and take the first step.

So I pray that you will attach as much importance to Jesus's closing remarks after the Model Prayer as you do to the prayer itself. "For if ye forgive men their trespasses, your heavenly Father will also forgive you" (Matt. 6:14). And not only will you forgive others their evil toward you, but you will replace the pains of the evil with love and joy!

How and for what and for whom will you pray, knowing that you are honoring and glorifying God by your prayers? How will this discussion of the Disciples' Model Prayer influence your prayers? How will the Disciples' Model Prayer influence how you forgive, forget, and seek forgiveness? Write a prayer, based on the Disciples' Model Prayer.

Jesus's Disciples Are Unable to Cast Out a Demon

A concerned, caring, and hopeful father took his demon-possessed son to Jesus's disciples for healing. When the got to where the disciples were, Jesus, Peter, James and John were mot there. They had gone on another mission to the Mount of Transfiguration. The disciples who were present could not cast the demon out of the young man. When Jesus arrived on the scene, the disappointed father confronted Him with great sadness and disappointment.

The man, apparently, had heard of the great miracles Jesus had performed, including casting demons out of people. He had probably heard that the disciples had cast demons out of people as well. He must have believed that the disciples, who were present at the scene, would have been able to heal his beloved son. The disciples tried, but were not able the cast the demon out of the boy.

Alas, the father's excitement with the prospect for the healing of his son was shattered. His excitement had turned into disappointment, sorrow, and perhaps some degree of anger and disbelief. His desire for the healing of his son turned into frustration. No doubt, he was on the verge of losing his faith in the ability of the disciples to help his son. Or perhaps he thought that for one reason or another, they just did not want to assist him and his son.

Then the always on time Jesus arrived on the scene. He saw the scribes questioning His disciples. Jesus asked the scribes, "What question ye with them?" (Mark 9:16). Jesus already knew the situation; nevertheless He asked the scribes why they were interrogating His disciples. Perhaps Jesus wanted the father to state his case.

The disappointed and disillusioned father poured out his grief and despair to Jesus in a frank and accusatory manner. He sadly said, "Master, I have brought unto thee my son, which hath a dumb spirit; and I spake unto thy disciples that they should cast him out; and they could not" (Mark 9:17–18). The bottom line is that Jesus's disciples were not able to cast the evil spirit out of the father's son.

When Jesus heard the father's story, He was dismayed because of the lack of faith of the man and apparently of the disciples as well. Jesus chided them and said, "O faithless generation, how long shall I be with you? how long shall I suffer you? bring him unto me" (Mark 9:19). Jesus expresses His disgust with the rhetorical questions, for which He already knew the answers. Jesus was well into His earthly ministry for almost three years. Soon He would be returning to heaven.

He had already empowered His disciples to cast out evil spirit; yet His disciples were slow in exercising sufficient faith to cast out the demon from the boy. This was one of Jesus's strongest rebuke of His disciples as a whole. Essentially, he told them that He was losing patient with them and it was time for them to do the things He had taught them.

Some Miracles Require Praying and Fasting

As Jesus instructed, the father took his son to Him. Jesus asked the father how long his son has been possessed. Of course, Jesus already knew the answer. The father answered that since his son was a child. The father beseeched—prayed to Jesus, "If thou canst do anything, have compassion on us" (Mark 9:22). This was a direct appeal to Jesus. The man probably was not uncertain of the ability of Jesus to cast the demon out of his son. Rather, he was uncertain if Jesus would help him and his son.

Jesus responded to the father's plea, in His usual manner of "putting the ball in the person's court approach." He challenged the man with a conditional statement, essentially saying to him, it's up to you: "If thou canst believe, all things are possible to him that believeth" (Mark 9:23). Mark records the anxious and eager father's response, "And straight way the father of the child cried out, and said with tears, Lord, I believe; help thou mine unbelief " (Mark 9:24). The father expresses faith that he believed that Jesus could cast the demon out of his son. In addition, he asked Jesus to forgive him of any unbelief or doubt which might be lingering in him.

What a wonderful prayer uttered by a desperate father is search of assistance for his son. It is most noteworthy that the father asked forgiveness for any doubt-unbelief that might have been in his heart; considering that the disciples did not cast the demon out of his son

Jesus saw how eager the people were to witness the healing of the boy. "He rebuked the foul spirit, saying unto him, Thou dumb and deaf spirit, I charge the come out of him, and enter no more into him. And the spirit cried, and rent him sore, and came out of him: and he was as one dead; insomuch that many said, He is dead. But Jesus took him by the hand, and lifted him up; and he arose" (Mark 9:25). Jesus demonstrated that he had authority over even the toughest demons.

It is noteworthy that the demon demonstrated his anger with Jesus's command, but could not resist it. He had to obey Jesus. But he took a last stab at trying to inflict pains on the boy one more time before leaving him. Jesus commanded the foul spirit not to enter the boy in the future.

In addition to casting the demon out of the boy, Jesus helped the father in restoring and strengthening his faith in Him In addition, Jesus assisted the father in ridding himself of any unbelief or doubts which he might have been developing or harboring in his heart. Furthermore, Jesus demonstrated to the large number of onlookers that He has power over demons.

Christians and believers can learn much from the incident cited above, least of which is that they might have uncertainty and doubt when they pray. And like the desperate father, they should ask God to remove destructive uncertainties and doubts from their hearts, and strengthen their faith. They should apply the level of passion and persistency of the father who wanted his son healed.

When the disciples were privately, in the house, with Jesus, they asked Him why they were not able to cast the demon out of the boy. Jesus responded to their question with a fundamental principle of dealing with some difficult situations. He said, "This kind [of demon] can come forth [driven out] by nothing, but prayer and fasting" (Mark 9:29). More than four hundred years earlier, Esther, Mordechai, and other Jews, living in Persia, fasted and prayed for three days, for God's intervention, when Haman precipitated an existential threat against Jews in Persia. God answered their prayers and delivered them from the plot of the evil Haman.

It is conceivable that there might be difficult situations which you are facing which require both praying and fasting for their resolution. Jesus Christ Himself fasted and prayed for forty days and forty nights in order to be strengthened to meet the challenges ahead of Him—to defeat Satan, the tempter and to carry out His earthly ministry. So fasting was not a new concept to the disciples. Jesus fasted and prayed regularly during His ministry on earth.

Praying and Fasting

Jesus teaches that it is appropriate for His followers to fast. He provides guidelines for meaningful fasting. After teaching His disciples the Disciples' Model Prayer and providing complementary remarks about the importance of forgiveness, as discussed previously, He teaches about fasting.

Jesus teaches the disciples that when they fast, they should be sincere and should not make a public spectacle of their fasting. He puts His instruction on fasting succinctly in this manner, "Moreover when ye fast, be not, as the hypocrites, of a sad countenance: for they disfigure their faces that they may appear unto men to fast. Verily I say unto you, they have their reward" (Matt. 6:16). It is clear that Jesus approves sincere fasting. This type of fasting is done to communicate sincerely and intensely with God.

He had told His disciples that some miracles require fasting and praying. Why then fasting is seldom mentioned or regularly practiced by many Christian congregations or many individual Christians? It begs the question as to whether many prayers would be more effective if they were accompanied with fating!

In continuing His teaching on fasting, Jesus said, "But thou, when thou fastest, anoint thine head, and wash thy face; That thou appear not unto men to fast, but unto thy Father which is in secret: and thy Father, which seeth in secret, shall reward thee openly" (Matt. 6:17–18). The secrecy of fasting which Jesus teaches is similar to the secrecy of praying which He taught previously, in this same discourse.

It is quite interesting to note that Christians, in general, appropriate and apply the Disciples' Model Prayer; however, many seem to have little or no knowledge, understanding, and/ or appreciation of Jesus's teaching on the importance of fasting. As stated previously, it was the same teaching session—teachable when Jesus taught His disciples a model prayer and how to pray that He taught them the importance of fasting. Furthermore, as stated previously, Jesus teaches that some miracles require both prayer and fasting.

Christians, believers, who believe in the efficacy of prayers, and who are not yet applying the principle of fasting might want to consider and practice fasting, as appropriate.

If you are not familiar with the idea or practice of fasting, I suggest that you read Jesus's discourse on fasting, and identify a pastor or a church leader who can assist you with this complementary aspect of effective praying. There are different approaches to fasting; however, the general idea is to deny yourself of something your body needs, such as food, for some designated period and use that time in prayer and meditation. The idea is to communicate deeply with God regarding some important challenges, issues or decisions. Again, there are different approaches to fasting and I am not covering that subject to any extent in this book, suffice it to say that Jesus approves fasting, and I believe in fasting.

Persistent Prayers

Jesus teaches His disciples that regular and persistent praying is important. Just before Jesus taught His disciples the Disciples' Model Prayer, He told them that when they pray, they should not use vain repetition as the heathens do. Vain repetition may be similar to chanting over and over meaningless phrases and words as though they are invoking some type of magic. However, Jesus teaches that prayers should be persistent.

Luke records that Jesus teaches about the importance of persistent prayer by using a parable of a persistent widow who sought justice from a wicked judge. Luke records Jesus's emphasis on persistent prayers in this manner, "And He spoke a parable unto them to this end, that men ought always to pray, and not to faint" (Luke 18:1). Jesus then tells the parable of a wicked judge who at first refused to render justice to a widow.

The judge did not fear God neither did he respect anyone. There was a widow living in that city. Someone wronged the widow and she went to the judge seeking justice. At first the judge did not take any action on behalf of the widow. Then he realized that she would keep coming back to him until he gave her justice. She would not give up. The wicked judge concluded, "Though I fear not God, nor regard man. Yet because this widow troubleth me, I will avenge her, lest by her continual coming she weary me" (Luke 18:4–5). The judge was afraid that the widow would wear him out with her persistent visits, appealing to him for justice. So he decided to act on her complaint. She simply would not give up until she received justice.

Jesus uses the parable, illustration, to emphasize the importance of persistent prayers. Certainly, the disciples and followers of Jesus cannot wear out God by persistent prayers.

To the contrary, God is pleased when He hears from His people through prayers and praises.

You should continue to pray unto God regarding your issue or concern until you receive an answer from Him. It is important to bear in mind that you do not determine how and when God answers the prayer. God does not always answer a prayer in the affirmative or based on your timeframe. You must believe that when God answers your prayer, His answer is always correct and on time. He is omniscience and infallible and does not make mistakes!

Jesus Teaches to Pray to God in the Name of Jesus

From a Christian perspective, there two quintessential, fundamental requirements for effective prayers. Some Bible scholars and theologians, and other Christians will certainly list other requirements; however, I am focusing on two which Jesus teaches. They are (1) believing or having faith in Jesus, God, and (2) praying to God in the name of Jesus. These two requirements are discussed below.

Pray in the Name of Jesus and Believe

Jesus discusses with His disciples the principle of praying to God in His name and believing that God will answer their prayers. Jesus was coming to the end of His earthly mission. He had been sharing important principles with His disciples. He had taught them a model prayer and how to pray. He had taught them about fasting and about many other heaven-ward principles. For more than three years, He had been the source which satisfies their needs. Soon, He would be departing for His home in heaven and He would not be physically with the disciples to grant their requests.

Jesus wanted the disciples to know that sometime in the future, they would make their requests directly to God, His Father, rather than to Him. Jesus said to them, "And in that day ye shall ask me nothing. Verily, Verily, I say unto you, Whatsoever ye shall ask the Father in my name, he shall give it to you" (John 16:23). I had struggled to understand what Jesus means by "in that day." Then like an epiphany, it was revealed to me while I was half-asleep this morning, perhaps in a trance, visionary state of mind.

On that day when Jesus was crucified and died, He was not available to answer any questions His disciple might have had. On the Day of Pentecost when Peter and the other disciples were truly converted, they were able to pray directly to God, in the name of Jesus. Christians, believers today, continue to pray directly to God in the name of Jesus Christ. It is a fundamental belief of Christianity that prayers should be made, not to Jesus; rather to God. However, the prayers must be made in the name of Jesus—Jesus said it Himself.

John records Jesus's instruction to pray to God in His name in this manner, "And whatsoever ye shall ask in my name, that will I do, that the Father may be glorified in the Son. If ye shall ask anything in my name, I will do it" (John 14:13–14). Here Jesus provides additional information on why prayers should be made in His name. He wants to answer our prayer so that He will bring glory to His Father.

It is of interest to note that although prayers are made to the Father, it is Jesus who answers the prayer. Christians, followers of Jesus Christ, may assist Jesus to glorify His Father by praying God for our needs, in the name of Jesus.

When Jesus answers our prayers, He glorifies God. So our prayer requests are not just about our needs. Rather, they are also about Jesus answering our prayers and glorifying God, His Father. Consequently, it is a common occurrence to hear Christian prayers ending with, "In the name of Jesus, Amen."

Believe in Jesus

During Jesus's last week on earth, Jesus visited Jerusalem and returned to Bethany where He spent the night. The next morning Jesus was hungry. He saw a fig tree and looked for fruits on the tree, even though it might not have been the normal time of the season for mature figs. There was no fruit on the tree. Jesus cursed the tree by saying, "No man eat fruit of thee hereafter forever. And his disciples heard it" (Mark 11:14). The next day the fig tree had withered. Peter recalled that Jesus had cursed the tree and commented to Jesus that the fig tree which He cured is withered away.

Jesus used this teachable moment to emphasize the impact of having faith, belief, in God (Jesus). "Have faith in God" (Mark 11:22)—Jesus told the disciples. He continued, "For verily I say unto you, That whosoever shall say unto this mountain, Be thou removed, and be cast into the sea; and shall not doubt in his heart, but shall believe...he shall have whatsoever he saith" (Mark 11:23). There is no substitute for faith-believing in God-Jesus and believing that they can answer prayers.

Jesus concluded His discourse on the importance of believing in God in this manner: "Therefore I say unto you, What things soever ye desire, when ye pray, believe that ye receive them, and ye shall have them" (Mark 11:24). Jesus speaks to a condition for a successful prayer. There should be no doubt in the heart of the person praying. The person must believe with confident expectation that God will hear and answer the prayer.

I want to remind you of three important caveats, requirements already discussed, about effective prayers. Firstly, even though may answer the prayer immediately, the manifestation of His response might not be immediately evident to the person who has prayed or is praying. Secondly, God may answer the prayer in a variety of ways—yes, no, wait. Or He may answer the prayer differently from the request.

Thirdly, some miracles which you are asking God to perform may require fasting along with praying.

In the following subheading, I recapitulate on a very important requirement for successful prayers. If was discussed in a previous chapter of the book; however, I is so important that it is worth restating. It is asking in accordance with God's will.

Pray, Ask According to God's Will

The Apostle John makes a bold statement: "And this is the confidence that we have in him, that, if we ask anything according to his will, he heareth us" (1 John 5:14). The Apostle John was referred to as the disciple who Jesus loved. Jesus gave special revelations to John, who is the author of the Book of Revelation. He expresses great confidence that Jesus will answer our prayers if the prayers are in accordance with His will. Being in accordance with the will of God is another condition which a prayer must meet in order for Jesus to answer.

Recall that in the Disciples' Model Prayer, Jesus taught the disciples that they should pray that the Father allows His will to be done in earth as it has already been done in heaven. By extension, a Christian, a believer, should pray regularly that God will reveal His will for him or her, and that His plan for him or her is fulfilled.

It begs the question of how one who is praying knows God's will for him or her. While a person might not know for sure exactly God's will in a given situation, the individual can make the desired request to God, and then pray, Father, nevertheless, not just what I am asking for, but let Your will be done.

Recall the previous discussion about praying to the Father in the name of Jesus, the Son. Jesus promises that He will answer the prayer so that He will glorify the Father. It follows, therefore, that the prayer should be of such that when Jesus answers, He glorifies the Father.

In a previous chapter of the book, I discussed how your desire can be in alignment with God's will or plan for you. I quoted David, the man after God's own heart: "Delight thyself in the LORD and he will give you the desire of your heart" (Psa. 37:4). So the key to receiving what you pray for is to have great pleasure in the presence of God—to enjoy being with God.

The key to knowing God's will is to maintain close relationship and fellowship with God, to pray for discernment, and to listen attentively to His still, small voice which speaks to you. The closeness to God may be achieved through a lifestyle of prayer, meditation, reflection, and even fasting as may be appropriate.

When you delight in God, your heart's desire will be consistent with His will or plan for you. Your prayer will be consistent with God's will. And good will fulfill the desire of your heart

God has His plan for you. The words of God written by the Prophet Jeremiah is often quoted by believers when they discuss God's will or plan for them. The Prophet Jeremiah records, "For I know my thoughts that I think toward you, saith the LORD, thoughts of peace, and not evil, to give you an expected end" (Jer. 29:11). Jeremiah wrote God's message of encouragement to His people of Judah (Judea) when they were in captivity in Babylon. However, Christians, believers often appropriate and apply the encouraging message as a source of reassurance and inspiration.

When Christians, believers face challenges, they take comfort that God's will is being done in them or through them. God will reveal His will to those who seek it sincerely with perseverance.

You do not need to guess God's will for you. Firstly, you can pray and ask God to reveal His will; however, two conditions are required. You must believe that God will answer your prayer and you must be willing to accept God's will—answer to your prayer.

Secondly, as the Apostle Paul reminds you, "And be not conformed to this world: but be ye transformed by the renewing of your mind, that ye may prove [know] what is that good, and acceptable, and perfect, will of God" (Rom. 12:2). Paul admonishes the Christians in Rome and applicable to followers of Jesus of our time not to conform to worldly standards and criteria, not to allow the norms, requirement, and pleasures of society to influence them.

In rejecting society's standards—the values, ethics, expectations and behaviors—God will reveal His will to us. It is important to study God's requirements as revealed in the Bible. This means studying the teaching of Jesus Christ and of apostles such as Paul, James, Peter, John, and others. In other words, Paul teaches that those who want to know the will of God can diligently seek it, and God will reveal His will to them.

God answers prayers which are consistent with his will and plan. Anyone who desires to know God's acceptable, good, and perfect will can, you can too!

CHAPTER EIGHTEEN

PRAYERS OF JESUS, THE GOD-MAN

In this chapter, I review selected prayers of Jesus—prayers Jesus actually prayed. We know that when Jesus walked the earth, in the flesh, He was a fully righteous Man and fully God. So it is interesting to know that Jesus prayed regularly.

By praying regularly to His heavenly Father, Jesus demonstrates reverence for the all mighty—Almighty God. Undoubtedly, Jesus was modeling for Christians, believers so they will emulate Him in praying to the Almighty God. On the following pages, I discuss powerful prayers which Jesus prayed and the occasion of each prayer.

The prayers are not necessarily in the order in which they occurred, especially since they are not all taken from a single Gospel of Matthew, Mark, Luke, or John. In fact, one or more prayers are taken from each of the Gospels. It is noteworthy that most of Jesus's audible prayers are short and to the point. His longest audible prayer is when He prays for Himself and His disciples as He prepared to return to heaven.

I trust that these prayers and responses to them will enhance your faith in the efficacy of prayer, knowing that Jesus the Christ prayed on a regular basis. The details of Jesus's prayers are not always disclosed—the exact words He prayed are not always stated in the Gospels; however, the purpose and words of His audible prayers are always explicit or implicit. You may learn from, embrace, enjoy, and benefit from Jesus's life-changing prayers.

Jesus Prays When He Feeds Five Thousand Men

The Apostle Matthew records that early in Jesus's ministry, shortly after King Herod had John the Baptist executed, Jesus departed from Galilee by a ship and went to the desert. When the people heard that Jesus was in the desert, they followed Jesus, walking to many cities. This is presumably the same desert where John the Baptist preached before King Herod had him arrested and placed in prison.

Jesus saw a great multitude of people. He healed the sick among them. Jesus had been preaching, teaching, and healing all day, and it was now evening. The disciples went to Jesus and asked Him to dismiss the people so that they could go to the villages and buy food.

They were in the wilderness, and there was no place close by where the disciples could buy food to serve so many people. Moreover, it likely that the disciples had little or no money, and certainly Jesus had no money. Jesus's compassion for the people would not allow Him to send them to seek food on their own. "But Jesus said unto them [the disciples], They need not depart; give ye them to eat" (Matt. 14:16). The considerate and kind-hearted Jesus would in no way allow these hungry and tired people to fend for themselves. He already had a solution for what the disciples thought was a great dilemma.

The disciples canvassed the people and came up with a paltry five loaves and two small fishes which a young man had brought for his lunch. The disciples brought them to Jesus. What were they expecting? Did they believe that they were bringing proof to Jesus that there no food around and He should dismiss the multitude and allow them to go and buy food? Or did they believe that Jesus could do something great with such little bread and fish?

While the disciples were wondering what Jesus would do, "He said, Bring them hither to me" (Matt. 14:18). Matthew records that Jesus had done numerous miracles by this time in His ministry. He had turned water into wine at the marriage feast at Cana of Galilee, He had cleansed a leper, He had healed the centurion's servant of palsy, He had calmed the storm on the sea, and He had given His disciples power to cast out unclean spirits and to heal all manner of illnesses. Therefore, the disciples, more than likely, believed that He could multiply the five loaves and two small fishes.

Jesus took the loaves and fishes from the disciples, "And he commanded the multitude to sit down on the grass, and took the five loaves, and the two fishes, and looking up to heaven, he blessed [prayed)] and brake, and gave the loaves to his disciples, and the disciples to the multitude. And they did eat, and were filled: and they took up of the fragments that remained twelve baskets full" (Matt. 14:19—20). Jesus already had the power and authority to work miracles and did not need to pray openly. Nevertheless, Jesus prayed—probably as an example for the disciples and the multitude.

This is one of the rare times when Jesus prayed openly when He did a miracle. The exact words of Jesus's prayer of blessing are not recorded in this instance.

It is conceivable that Jesus was giving thanks for the abundant meals which He knew would be supplied. Rather than praying that the loaves and fishes would be multiplied— He already knew they would multiply.

Regardless, Jesus looked up to His Father in heaven and blessed the bread and fish. Although the content of Jesus's prayer is not revealed; however, He blessed the five loaves of bread and two fishes and they multiplied tremendously.

The multitude, consisting of five thousand men, not including women and children, had more than enough to eat. After the great feast the disciples picked up twelve baskets of fragment. Jesus did not want to waste anything from the miracle feast. He wanted the disciples to understand that He has the power to satisfy human needs above and beyond what they can imagine. In addition, by asking the disciples to gather the fragment, Jesus was teaching a lesson on stewardship—managing God's resources in an effective and efficient manner.

Was there inconsistency with the teaching of Jesus that the disciples/followers should pray to God secretly in their closed closet and Jesus's public prayer? Of course not. Notice that Jesus's prayer was not with eloquence of speech to impress the multitude. Rather, He prayed a private prayer even though He was in the public with the multitude. He wanted His disciples and the multitude to understand His connection with His Father and that praying in the public needs not be hypocritical-to impress others.

Jesus demonstrates that it is perfectly appropriate to let others know that you believe in the efficacy of prayer and that you pray. However, you don't need to try to impress anyone with your eloquent and repetitious words. Remember, God knows you well, and it is to God to whom you pray.

Jesus Prays When He feeds Four Thousand

Jesus's feeding of four thousand is quite similar to His feeding of five thousand. Jesus and His disciples were in the coasts of Tyre and Sidon—Gentile territory. He remotely cast out a devil from the daughter of a woman from Canaan. He then went to the region of the Sea of Galilee and sat on a mountain (hillside).

Great multitudes went to Jesus seeking healing from a variety of illnesses. Some of the ill people were carried, by others, and placed at the feet of Jesus. He healed them all. The people were astonished at the power of Jesus to heal all manner of illnesses. They glorified God.

The multitudes were with Jesus for three days and had nothing to eat. The compassionate Jesus assembled His disciples and said, "I have compassion on the multitude, because they continue with me now three days, and have nothing to eat: and I will not send then away fasting, lest they faint in the way" (Matt. 15:32). Even though Jesus had fasted forty days at the beginning of His ministry, He did not want to subject the people to hunger as they journeyed home.

Jesus was and is always concerned about the need—physical and spiritual—of others. That was a hallmark characteristic of Jesus which He demonstrates time and time again.

The disciples expressed an obvious observation that they were in a wilderness and did not have enough bread to feed so many people. To some extent, the disciples were slow learners. It was Jesus who had raised the need to feed the people. He had fed five thousand and others with five loaves and two fishes a few days earlier. So the disciples should have known that Jesus could feed the people, who were with them, on that occasion.

Perhaps, the disciples should have simply asked Jesus, what do you want us to do? Jesus was teaching His disciples not just that He is able to take care of physical needs; rather, He wanted to understand that they should be considerate of the needs of others. Later He would tell Peter to feed His lamb and His sheep.

Jesus already knew that there were some bread and fishes with the people. Nevertheless, Jesus asks, "How many loaves have ye? And they said, Seven, and a few little fishes" (Matt. 15:34). Jesus had something with which He could work—seven small loaves, two little fishes, and a whole lot of spiritual power. He instructed the people to sit on the ground.

Evidently, Jesus wanted people behave in an orderly manner as the loaves and fishes are served to them. There was no need rush to get to the front of the line; there would be more than enough food for all. Jesus was teaching the hungry people and His disciples the principle of patiently waiting, with confident expectation. In addition, Jesus wanted to reinforce in His disciples, the principle and ministry of serving others. Meeting the needs of the least among us.

All eyes were now on Jesus as He took the seven loaves and few fishes in His hands. Perhaps Jesus wants the people to see that what He has in his hands were not much; however, they could not see His enormous godly authority and power, which He was about to demonstrate. Matthew records, "And he took the seven loaves and the fishes and gave thanks (prays), and brake them, and gave to his disciples, and the disciples to the multitude. And they did eat, and were filled: and they took up of the broken meat that was left even baskets full" (Matt. 15:36–37). As in the feeding of the five thousand, Jesus again gave visible thanks and prayed to God, demonstrating the importance of acknowledging the source and sufficiency of all blessings and expecting plenty out of little.

Matthew records that four thousand men, not including women and children, participated in the miraculous great feast of loaves and fishes, and had much leftover. The disciples, perhaps with the assistance of some of the grateful multitude, gathered seven baskets of fragment—leftover from the feast. Here again, as in the incident of the feeding of five thousand, Jesus teaches the principle of stewardship—gather the fragment that nothing is wasted.

As in the incident of the miraculous feeding of the five thousand, the emphasis here is on the fact that Jesus prayed before the miracle and the manifestation of the answer to His prayer was instantaneous. Christians/believers must strongly embrace the efficacy of prayer, always pray before decisions and actions bearing in mind Jesus's assertion that that people ought to always pray and not faint.

Jesus Prays When He Was Rejected by Three Cities of Galilee

When Jesus began His earthy minister, at Nazareth of Galilee, where he grew up, His home town did not accept Him as the Son of God. Therefore, He did not do many miracles there. Consequently, He moved His headquarters to Capernaum about twenty miles from Nazareth.

Jesus did many miraculous work at Chorazin, Bethsaida, and Capernaum—cities of Galilee. However, the people refused to repent and turn to God. Jesus was particularly disappointed with Capernaum because He lived there for more than three years and did great works in that region. The people of Capernaum had every reason to believe in Jesus and to accept Him as the Son of God. However, they intentionally refused to accept Him in that manner.

Jesus Prays, Gives Thanks to God

Jesus did not allow Himself to become bitter, spiteful, or vindictive when He was rejected at Capernaum where he had ministered for more than three years. Rather, He prays, "I thank thee, O Father, Lord of Heaven and earth, because thou hast hid these things from the wise and prudent, and has revealed them unto babes. Even so, Father: for so it seemed good in thy sight" (Matt. 11:25–26). Luke records the prayer in Luke 10:21. This is seemingly the first prayer of Jesus recorded in the Gospel of Matthew.

Although the temporal, worldly wise adults in the aforementioned three cities of Galilee did not accept Jesus as the Son of God, perhaps because of the hardness of their hearts, God reveals Jesus to babes—children. Babes in this context could be physically or spiritually young persons. Solomon had already admonished people, "Be not wise in your own eyes: fear the LORD, and depart from evil" (Prov. 3:7). The people in the three cities were too wise in their own eyes to see that Jesus is the Son of God.

It is noteworthy that Jesus did not ask God to change the hearts of the people of Chorazin, Bethsaida, and Capernaum toward Him. Jesus had already done all that was needed for the people to recognize, acknowledge, accept Him, and turn from their sins. Jesus remarked that on Judgement Day, God will show more mercy toward Tyre and Sidon than He will show toward those three cities which intentionally rejected Jesus.

This thanksgiving prayer of Jesus clearly indicates that when followers of Jesus carry out His instructions there is no failure in the outcomes. Jesus gave thanks to God, even though He was disappointed with the hardness of the hearts of the people who saw, and (some) benefitted from His works. However, God revealed Jesus to the unlikely—babes—not to the wise and prudent, who did not want to know. Rather, God reveals Jesus to the humble and receptive at heart.

The people at Nazareth were skeptics, hence, they were the losers. They squandered the opportunity to obtain optimum blessings and benefits from Jesus—the home town God-Man. They epitomized the person described in Proverbs, "Seest thou a man wise in his own conceit? there is more hope for a fool than of him" (Prov. 26:12). In addition most people in Nazareth, at that time ignored the admonition of Solomon, "Trust in the LORD with all thine heart; and lean unto thine own understanding" (Prov. 3:5).

The incidents of the rejection of Jesus clearly teaches that the people who rejected and rejects Him had/have the free will to accept Jesus-Wisdom or to reject Jesus-Wisdom. Jesus is the personification of Wisdom. They chose and many today are choosing to reject Jesus.

Despite the fact the people of the aforementioned cities rejected Jesus, He prayed that God's will be done.

Those who reject Jesus intentionally or through indifference will receive the consequences of their wrong choice. You should be thankful to God for any result he allows you to achieve even when the result is different from what you asked. You should use your free will to intentionally accept Jesus, and not reject Him intentionally or by default or indifference.

Jesus Prays When He Raised Lazarus from the Dead

Lazarus was the brother of Mary and Martha; they lived in Bethany. They were all friends of Jesus. Mary loved Jesus so much that she anointed his feet with expensive ointment and wiped His feet with her hair. Lazarus got ill and Mary and Martha sent for Jesus to heal him. Jesus was in the Jordan region where John the Baptist had baptized Him. This was only a few miles from Bethany.

Jesus waited for a while before going to Bethany. When He finally arrived there, Lazarus had been dead and buried for four days. Based on the Jewish tradition there was no hope of resurrecting a person who had been dead for four days—no hope for Lazarus. The belief was that after a person had been dead for four days, the spirit leaves the body and will not return.

In other words, a person could be in a coma for three days and be brought back to life. But after four days there was absolutely no human intervention which could bring that person back to life—that was the common belief. This was the unfortunate situation with Lazarus, thought Mary, Martha, and other Jewish mourners at house of Mary, Martha and the dead Lazarus.

Before Jesus arrived at the house, Martha met Him on the way. Jesus taught her that He is the resurrection and the life, and that her brother would rise again.

When Jesus arrived at Lazarus's tomb, it was four days late, they thought. However, Jesus is never late, He is always on time. Martha overwhelmed with grief and sorrows said to Jesus, "Lord, if thou hadst been here, my brother had not died" (John 11:21). Martha's comment was an affirmation of her belief that Jesus could restore health to an ill person.

Martha went on to say that Jesus could ask God for whatever He wanted and God would grant it to Him. Here again Martha expressed faith in that God would grant Jesus anything He ask of God. It was all up to Jesus, in Martha's mind. In a subtle way Martha was expressing faith in the efficacy of prayer, especially the prayer of Jesus.

To the astonishment of Martha and the Jewish mourners, Jesus made the amazing declaration which defies Jewish logic, "Thy brother shall rise again" (John 11:23). Martha understood that her brother would rise at the general resurrection at the last day—Judgment Day.

Jesus took opportunity—teachable moment—and said to Martha, "I am the resurrection, and the life: he that believeth in me, though he were dead, yet shall live" (John 11:25). Martha, perhaps for the first time, really understood that their friend Jesus was more than just another ordinary man or prophet. Martha said to Jesus, "Yea Lord, I believe that thou art the Christ, the Son of God, which should come into the world" (John 11:27). After more than three years knowing Jesus, Martha is finally realizing and confessing that she believes that Jesus is the Son of God—who should come into the world.

Jesus's four-day delay might have done more for Martha—raising her to spiritual life—than it did for Lazarus, raising him to physical life. It is noteworthy that during Jesus's previous visits to the house of the three siblings, Martha was the one who gave more attention to physical things, while Mary gravitated toward spiritual things. Now, Martha is the one receiving spiritual enlightenment!

When Jesus saw Mary weeping over the death of her brother Lazarus, He demonstrated human empathy: "Jesus wept" (John 11:35). The Jews who were at the tomb remarked how Jesus loved Lazarus so much that He was weeping at his death. Jesus asked them to roll away the stone which blocked entrance to the tomb. Martha responded that by that time— four days after the burial there would be a terrible foul odor. Nevertheless, they rolled away the stone.

You can imagine what the Jews were thinking—there is no way this Lazarus can be raised from the dead, because they thought the spirit cannot be united with the body after four days after death.

There must have been a "you can hear a pin drop" moment of silence, just waiting to see. "And Jesus lifted up his eyes, and said Father, I thank thee that thou hast heard me. And I know that thou hearest me always: but because of the people which stand by I said it, that they may believe that thou has sent me" (John 11:41–42). It is important to note that Jesus did not ask His Father to raise Lazarus from the dead. Rather, He thank His Father for already hearing His prayer.

The prayer was for the benefit of the people that they would believe that God, the Father had sent Jesus Christ His Son into the world. Undoubtedly, Jesus had prayed before at the house of Mary, Martha, and Lazarus. Here, He was emphasizing the truth, for the benefit of the Jews, that He is the Son of God. This was arguably Jesus's most consequential and immediate impactful prayers at that time!

Note that unlike the inaudible prayers at the feeding of the four and five thousand, respectively, the words of Jesus's prayer at the raising of Lazarus are audible and recorded by the Apostle John. Jesus wanted those who thought that it was impossible to restore life to Lazarus to hear His prayer and acknowledge that He God's Son, on was on God's Mission.

When Jesus completed His prayer, He commanded Lazarus to get up and come out of the tomb. John records Jesus's command over the dead in this manner, "And when he thus had spoken he cried with a loud voice, Lazarus, come forth. And he that was dead came forth, bound hand and foot . . . Jesus said unto them, Loose him, and let him go" (John 11:44). Certainly, Martha, Mary, and the other Jews should now believe that Jesus is the resurrection and the life. He had done a miracle which Jewish traditions believe was impossible to do—restoring life to a corpse that has been without life for four or more days.

This is another incident when Jesus prayed and the Father answered His prayer, in the affirmative, even before He prayed. Jesus prayed audibly for the benefit of the people.

The Prophet Isaiah proclaims that God answers prayers even before they are prayed. Jesus affirms the proclamation, which Isaiah the great prophet made more than 700 years, before the incarnated Jesus came on earth, "And it shall come to pass, that before they call. I will answer; and while they are yet speaking, I will hear" (Isa. 65:24). Interestingly, Isaiah more than any other prophet, prophesied about the coming of Jesus Christ, the Messiah.

Do you have the fellowship with God and faith in Him to thank Him for answering your prayer even before you receive the manifestation of His answer? Isaiah proclaims and Jesus demonstrates that, yes, you can.

Will you devote as much of your prayer thanking God for what He has already done for you and what He will do for you as you devote to asking Him to do things for you?

Jesus's prayer at Lazarus's tomb is a model for thanking God, even before the manifestation of His answer to your prayer.

Jesus Prays That the Father Would Glorify His Name

Six days before the Passover Feast in Jerusalem, Mary, Martha, and Lazarus had a supper at their home, at Bethany, in honor of Jesus. The next day Jesus was riding a colt (young donkey) on His way to Jerusalem. This is commonly referred to as the Triumphal Entry.

This would be Jesus's last trip to Jerusalem. On his way to Jerusalem, certain Greeks who intended to participate in the Passover Feast celebration, wanted to see Jesus. When Andrew and Philip gave Jesus the message from the Greeks, Jesus answered them saying, "The hour is come that the Son of Man should be glorified" (John 12:23). Jesus made the remarks in reference to His pending sacrificial death.

Jesus went on to say that if anyone wants to serve Him that person should follow Him so that the follower would be with Jesus wherever He was going. He remarked if a person served Him, His Father would honor that person.

Jesus felt burdened. He said, "Now is my soul troubled" (John 12:27). Then He asked the rhetorical question, "What shall I say? Father, save me from this hour: but for this cause came I unto this hour" (John 12:27). At that time Jesus's heart was heavy. It was getting close to the time of, what He knew, His fate—His execution.

However, Jesus would not ask His Father to save Him. He knew that God sent him to earth for the purpose of His sacrificial death. So instead of asking His Father to save Him from the hour of His physical demise, Jesus prays this short prayer, "Father, glorify thy name" (John 12:28). Jesus always pleases His Father and wants His Father to receive glory. As soon as Jesus prayed, He receives an immediate response, "Then came a voice from heaven, saying, I have both glorified it, and will glorify it again" (John 12:28). John records that some of the people who heard the voice thought it was just thunder; others thought an angel had spoken.

Jesus responded, "This voice came not because of me, but for your sakes. Now is the judgement of this world: now shall the prince of this world be cast out. And I, if I be lifted up from the earth, will draw all men unto me" (John 12:30–32).

Even though Jesus was burdened, He did not ask God to relieve Him of His heavy heartedness; rather, He wanted to glorify His Father.

Jewish religious leaders and the Roman soldiers made the mistake of thinking that what they were doing to Jesus was of their own volition. However, they really could not avoid what they were doing, and were planning to do. They would be lifting up Jesus from the earth to Calvary's Cross. Jesus had already asserted that if they lift Him up, He would draw all men unto Him. They lifted up Jesus, and Jesus has been drawing people unto Him ever since.

In addition, people have been glorifying God's name ever since Jesus was lifted up and crucified on Calvary's Cross. As stated previously, Jesus asked God to glorify His (God's) name. God responded that He had already glorified is name and would do it again. God continues to glorify His name as He pleases. All because Jesus asked God, His Father, to do so.

What do you ask your heavenly Father to do to glorify His name? Do you give priority to glorifying God above all other interests? How will you strive to glorify God in your daily life?

CHAPTER NINETEEN

JESUS PRAYS FOR HIMSELF AND FOR HIS DISCIPLES

During His final supper with His disciples, Jesus broke bread and gave it to them to eat. He told them that the bread represented his body which is broken for them. He then shared wine with them and told them that the wine represented His blood which is shed for them.

Jesus exhorts His disciples to love one another and to continue to abide in Him. He consoles His disciples, telling them that He came from His Father in heaven and was going back to His Father. He forewarned His disciples of what would happen to Him and told them that even though they would scatter from Him (abandon Him, go into hiding) during His ordeal, His Father will be with Him. Jesus provides other insights, exhortations, and encouragement to the disciples.

Jesus knew that His disciples were merely humans, with good intentions; their hearts were willing but their flesh was weak. Therefore, He did not want them to feel so guilty for their lack of faith or their errors that they would not forgive themselves. He wanted His disciples to know that He would not be vindictive towards them, and He had forgiven them for their lack of faith, at that point.

Jesus Prays for Himself

After Jesus had completed His discourse with His disciples, He lifted up His voice to heaven and prayed a most passionate intercessory petition on His own behalf and on behalf of His disciples. Jesus does something which He had not done before. He prayed with a loud voice. His prayer was long, passionate, and heart rending.

Jesus prayed thusly, "Father, the hour is now come; glorify thy Son, that thy Son also may also glorify thee: As thou hast given him power over all flesh, that he should give eternal life to as many as thou hast given him. And this is life eternal, that they might know thee the only true God, and Jesus Christ, whom thou hast sent. I have glorified thee on earth: I have finished the work which thou gavest me to do" (John 17:1–4). Jesus was satisfied that He had completed the work which God had assigned to Him and He was ready to return to heaven.

Jesus asked His Father to bring him back into the glory He shared with Him before the world began. So Jesus prayed, "And now, O Father, glorify thou me with thine own self with the glory which I had with thee before the world was" (John 17:5). Jesus had given up His glory in heaven, for three years, was ready to return to haven to His position of glory at the right hand of God.

During His three-year ministry, on earth, Jesus had developed great relationships and friendship with His primary disciples and with many of His other followers. He had tremendous success with His ministry, despite obstructions from religious leaders and Satan.

Jesus had turned water into wine at Cana of Galilee, and was praised. He cleansed one leper and he became a follower of Jesus. He healed ten lepers and one went back and thanked Him. He cast out demons out of Mary Magdalene and she became a devoted follower. Jesus raised Lazarus from the dead, just to name a few of His accomplishments. He even did a few miracles at His hometown, Nazareth, before His hometown people, there, rejected Him.

Jesus established His headquarters to Capernaum and did great works at Chorazin, Bethsaida, and Capernaum; however, eventually all three places rejected Him. Jesus was disappointed.

It was keen desire to Jesus that His disciples and others would get to know the only true God, and to know that Jesus is the Son of God. In addition, Jesus wanted them to know that God sent Him-His Son to earth to provide the way through which humanity can be saved, from damnation, and receive eternal life.

Jesus shared God's Word with the disciples and they received it and believed that God sent Jesus into the world. Jesus asserts, "For I have given unto them the words which thou gavest me; and they have received them, and have known surely that I came out from thee, and they have believed that thou didst sent me" (John 17:8). Jesus validated, justified, the disciples before God. He knew that there was much that the disciples needed to learn; however, He was comfortable in recommending them to the care of His Farther.

Now, Jesus was satisfied that He had done most the works God had assigned to Him thus far. He still had to accomplish death on Calvary's cross and conquer death and the grave. This would be done soon.

Jesus was now ready to ask His Father to grant specific blessings on (His twelve) disciples who had been with Him since He began His earthly ministry.

By the time Jesus offered special prayers for His disciple, Judas had already left Jesus and the other disciples and had gone to the religious leaders to betray Jesus. Unfortunately, for Judas, he was not present to hear Jesus's passionate and heart-rending prayer on his and the other disciples' behalf.

Jesus Prays for His Disciples

As stated previously, Jesus had completed most of what His Father had assigned Him to do on earth. He would soon complete the most important assignment—Jesus would shortly demonstrate His unconditional love for humanity. He would sacrifice His life, dying on Calvary's cross, for the atonement of sins. He was ready to be lifted up: "That whosoever believeth in him should not perish, but have eternal life" John 3:15).

Jesus had prayed for Himself and now He prays specifically for His disciples and those who will subsequently believe on Him. He was going back to heaven, but could not take His beloved disciples with Him.

What would Jesus do for those men who had given up everything to follow Him for the past three years? He could not give them His earthly house because He had none. He could not give them expensive clothes because all He had was the outfit He was wearing. He could not give them silver and gold because He had none. In fact, He had instructed His disciples to take a coin from the mouth of a fish to pay tax to Caesar.

So what could He give or leave for His loyal disciples? He would leave for them what they needed most—He prays for them and leaves them in the hands of His Father!

So Jesus prays passionately for the disciples who, at that point, were only partially prepared to carry on His ministry. Jesus had already prayed for Himself as previously noted, He now directed His prayer specifically on behalf of His disciples, "I pray for them: I pray not for the world, but for them which thou hast given me; for they are thine, and thine are mine. And all mine are thine, and thine are mine; and I am glorified in them" (John 17:9–10). Oh, what depth of love Jesus has for His disciples. They were so special to Him.

Jesus had often prayed on behalf of multitudes, such as when He fed five and four thousand, respectively. He had prayed for families, such as when He raised Lazarus and Jairus' daughter from the dead, respectively. But this time, He prays for His beloved disciples who He could not take along with Him to heaven, at that time.

So Jesus pours out His soul to His Father in heaven. He needed help, not for Himself; rather for His disciples. On that occasion, He is not praying for the world or for the Jews in Jerusalem or Judea. He is not even praying for His close friends, Mary, Martha, and Lazarus, or for His mother Mary, or His half- brothers and half- sisters. No, He is praying for His close disciples and apostles. Even though Jesus knows that Peter will deny Him and Judas will betray Him, He still prays for them.

Jesus declared, in His prayer, that God gave Him the disciples and they belong to God. He also declared that the disciples belong to Him as well, because what God has belongs to Him—Jesus and what Jesus has belongs to God. There is a mutuality of ownership in whatever God and Jesus have. Jesus was simply giving the disciples back to God. Because God had given them to Him, He is giving them back, at least for a time.

It is of significance to note that Jesus was not giving the disciples back to the Father because He was tired of teaching them, or tired of being around them, or being frustrated by their slowness of learning. In fact, Jesus was proud of His disciples. He said of them, "And I am glorified in them" (John 17:10). The disciples brought glory to Jesus.

Jesus had asked the Father to glorify His own name, "Father, glorify thy name" (John 12:28) and to glorify the Son, "Glorify thy Son, that thy Son may also glorify thee" (John 17:1). Therefore, for Jesus to be glorified in the disciples speaks very highly of the disciples. Jesus is proud of His disciples. They gave him due reverence and respect, despite their familiarity with Him and His humility. Nevertheless, He had to leave them in the world, but not of the world, as He returns to heaven.

In continuing His prayer for His disciples, Jesus prayed, "And now I am no more in the world, but these are in the world, and I come to thee. Holy Father, keep through thine own name those whom thou hast given me, that they may be one, as we are one" (John 17:11). In the first part of the verse, it seems that Jesus is having a conversation, as the Son with His Father, noting that He is no longer in the world; He is heavenward bound, on His way to God, His Father in heaven.

Then Jesus appeals to His Father to keep as one, in unity (protect/defend) His disciples. God would do that through His own name. He did not need to act in the name of Jesus. He is God and acts in His own name.

The lifeless body, corpse of Jesus, the Master, Good Shepherd, would be resting in the tomb for three days, and the disciples would need God's protection especially during that period. God was able to fulfill Jesus's request to keep—protect and defend—His disciples. More importantly, Jesus prayed that the disciples will be in unity; that they will remain focus and in unity with one another and ultimately with Jesus.

Jesus knew that at the time of His imminent death, on the cross, the disciples would scatter as sheep without a shepherd. Because their Shepherd for the past three years will soon lay down His life for the sheep—them and others, they will be afraid and scatter.

Unless God protects the disciples, the sheep, they will not maintain unity among themselves nor with God. Jesus knew that God would answer His prayer. He would be returning to heaven soon and He needed His disciples to stay in unity and carry out His assignment. Jesus had told them earlier that if they are in unity, others will know that they are Jesus's disciples. In addition, when they are in agreement—unity on anything in His name—He will be in their midst to bless.

The need for unity within and between church congregations, among Christians/believers, among church leaders, and between Christians and Jesus is as great today as it was when Jesus prayed for unity among His disciples.

As recorded in John 17:12–14, Jesus continued His prayer, his conversation as a Son, with His Father. In verse twelve, Jesus proclaims that while He was in the world with the disciples, He kept them (safely), and He only lost one—the son of perdition, Judas—who betrayed Jesus. Judas's betrayal of Jesus was in fulfillment of the scripture.

There is an interesting question as to whether or not Judas was included in Jesus's special prayers for His disciples. This question becomes quite relevant in that Judas was not present when Jesus was praying. In fact, as noted previously Judas had already gone to betray Jesus by the time Jesus prayed the special prayer for His disciples. Nevertheless, more than likely, the unconditionally loving and ever forgiving Jesus included Judas in His prayer.

Considering that Jesus included Peter in the prayer, He more than likely included Judas as well. He knew that soon after His prayer, Peter would betray Him three times during a short period of time, yet He included Peter. In addition, Jesus taught His disciples/followers to pray for their enemies and to do good for those who do them evil. Later on, Jesus publicly forgives those who were executing Him on Calvary's Cross.

I will digress or pause for a short while and share my experience, or rather inspiration as I was writing this incident of Jesus's special prayer for His disciples. It had perplexed me as the reason(s) Judas apparently did not benefit from Jesus's prayer. Firstly, his love of money, was the root of his evil. Jesus stated toward the end of the Lord's Supper that Satan got into his heart. He was already consumed with the love of money so it was quite easy for Satan to tempt him. Later the Apostle Paul proclaimed, "For the love of money is the root of all evil . . ." (1 Tim. 6:10). Secondly, even though Jesus prayed for his disciple and God answered His prayer, Jesus or God did not deprive Judas of his free will. Therefore, he rejected God's protection in temptation and His deliverance from the evil one. I am no longer perplexed regarding Juda's rejection of God's grace and mercy at the time.

Jesus went on to converse with His Father. In verse fourteen of John 17, He remarks that He shared God's Word with the disciples and they accepted it. As a result the world hates them because they are not conforming to the expectations—behaviors, standards of the world. Jesus then picks up His intercessory prayer on behalf of His disciples, "I pray not that thou shouldest take them out of the world, but that thou shouldest keep them from the evil. Sanctify them through thy truth: thy word is truth. As thou hast sent me into the world, even so have I also sent them into world. And for their sakes I sanctify myself, that they also might be sanctified through the truth" (John 17:15, 17–19). Jesus did not ask His Father to allow His loyal, weary, and tired disciples to go with Him to heaven. They had work to do on earth—a great commission to carry out

The request of Jesus made of His Father was not for God to allow His disciples to sleep with their fathers quietly and peacefully as he had allowed Moses, His faithful servant to do centuries earlier. Or to take them to heaven as He took Elijah to heaven after his many years of ministry for God. Instead Jesus asked His Father to sanctify His disciples—set them apart, endow them with truth, and keep them from evil—Satan.

Jesus had commissioned His disciples to go out into the world and reach the unsaved. He will commission them again, after His resurrection, shortly before He ascends to heaven. The disciples have to remain in the world, in close proximity to those to whom they will minister; however, they will not be of the world. They will need protection, in order to carry out Jesus's great commission. In addition, Jesus asked His Father to reveal truth to the disciples and enable them to function effectively as His representatives on earth.

Often times, Christians/believers become tired and weary as they work for the Lord. Sometimes they cry out to God for relief. Sometimes they are scared to face the world in which they are commissioned to carry out their assignments. Well, Jesus anticipated the dilemma and took that into consideration in His prayer. See the continuation of Jesus's prayer in the next paragraph.

Jesus applies the concept of succession planning in His prayer. Firstly, He prays for His existing disciples, who would immediately continue His ministry while He is in heaven. Secondly, He prays for those who would believe in Him as a result of the teaching and preaching of His disciples-followers. He knew that the existing disciples would not live physically for centuries; they would need successors. Therefore, Jesus prays for their successors.

With a passionate appeal to His Father, Jesus prays for His successive disciples-followers in this manner, "Neither pray I for these [disciples] alone, but for them also which shall believe on me through their word; That they all may be one; as thou, Father art in me, and I in thee, that they also may be one in us: that the world may believe that thou hast sent me. And the glory which thou gavest me I have given them; that they may be one, even as we are one" (John 17:20–22). Jesus knew that the mission of the disciples to evangelize the world requires the successions of generation after generation of believers. The work would start with His existing disciples. He prays for the successive generations that will hear His Word, believe in Him, and apply His Word.

It is remarkable to note the emphasis which Jesus places on oneness-unity among His disciples, unity between the disciples and Jesus, and unity among those who will hear Jesus's Word, through the disciples, and accept the Word. And unity of believers with Jesus. The emphasis which Jesus places on unity cannot be overstated stated. Unity among followers of Jesus demonstrates love and fellowship with Jesus—that others will know that the disciples are followers of Jesus.

The disciples exemplified tremendous unity on and after the Day of Pentecost. Luke puts it this way, "And when the day of Pentecost was fully come, they were all with one accord in one place" (Acts 2:1). The manifestation of the fulfillment of Jesus's prayer for unity, among His disciples, and with Him occurred fifty days after Jesus rose from the grave and ten days after He ascended into heaven.

The fact that when Peter preached his first sermon, on the Day of Pentecost, and three thousand souls were converted, is one indication that the disciples were in unity with Jesus. Luke records that after endowment of the Holy Spirit on the Day of Pentecost, "And the multitude of them that believed were of one heart and of one soul . . ." (Acts 4:32). This oneness of the hearts and souls of the converts was clear evidence of the answer to Jesus's prayer for unity among His then disciples. The unity continues with His subsequent disciples-followers.

When followers of Jesus display unity, it is not simply for their benefit, although they benefit and are able to do great things by working cooperatively. Rather, more importantly, it is to convey the clear and unambiguous message that God sent His Son, Jesus Christ, into the world. And the followers of Jesus are endowed with the Holy Spirit.

Unity within a congregation among followers of Jesus indicates the answer to Jesus's prayer for His disciples, and conveys the ongoing message that God sent His Son, Jesus Christ, into the world to seek and to save those who are lost. And the followers of Jesus are His representatives, who are endowed by the Holy Spirit, and continuing Jesus's mission.

Jesus continues His prayer asking His Father to enable His disciples to be with Him so that they can see His glory and know how much God loves Him. Jesus prays, "Father, I will that they also, whom thou hast given me, be with me where I am; that they may behold my glory, which thou hast given me: for thou lovedst before the foundation of the world" (John 17:24). Jesus desires that His disciples be with Him so that they will see the glory which God gave Him before God laid the foundation of the world. This will likely occur when Jesus returns to take home His true disciples.

Jesus continues to emphasize His desire to glorify God and for God to glorify Him. Jesus wants the disciples to know how immensely God loves Him. The disciples would need to main fellowship with Jesus to experience how God glorifies His Son.

Then Jesus closed this prayer, "O righteous Father, the world hath not known thee: but I have known thee, and these [disciples] have known that thou hast sent me. And I have declared unto them thy name, and will declare it: that the love wherewith thou hast loved me may be in them, and I in them" (John 17:25–26). If there is a theme for Jesus's foregoing prayer, it might be: Love, protection and unity.

This is Jesus's longest, and perhaps most passionate, prayer on record in the Bible. Jesus prayed long and passionately for His existing disciples and subsequent disciples or followers. And God heard and answered His prayer.

Christians or believers can take comfort, when they face challenges, in knowing that Jesus Christ has already prayed for them. They need only to accept the answers to Jesus's prayer and walk by faith and in obedience to God.

The foregoing prayer goes well beyond the Disciples' Model Prayer. Jesus's prayer is passionate with specific requests both for Himself and for His then disciples and His subsequent followers. The prayer offers great assurance and comfort to those who believe in Jesus Christ and accept His prayer on their behalf.

Jesus Prays for Peter

Peter was a very special disciple of Jesus. Even though the Bible refers to the Apostle John as the disciple who Jesus loved; there is no question that Peter truly loved Jesus. However, apparently, Peter was quite emotional an`d reactive. He often spoke without fist thinking about what was about to say—he spoke his mind.

He was a person of action, a leader among the disciples, Satan wanted to destroy him. So Jesus prayed specifically for Peter.

Jesus had already prayed passionately for His twelve disciples. However, the disciples still had needs and concerns. He had shared with them that His execution was imminent. Instead of being genuinely sorrowful and prayerful about the imminent situation, the disciples were arguing about who would have the highest seat of privilege in the Kingdom of God. They still needed, within themselves, more selflessness, humility, compassion, and empathy.

Evidently, Jesus was not pleased, perhaps disappointed, with their behavior and their attitudes. Jesus politely rebuked the disciples and asserted that fighting, among themselves for high positions, is not appropriate. He told them that such rivaling for positions of privilege is something the Gentiles do. In other words, His disciples were acting as though they were Gentiles. He expected better attitudes and behavior from His chosen disciples.

Sometime previously, Jesus had severely rebuked Satan who was acting out in Peter. When Jesus told His disciples that He would be executed, Peter tried to prevent Jesus from accepting His cup of death on Calvary's Cross. Jesus told the disciples that He had reserved places for them in the Kingdom of God where thy might eat and drink at the table. In addition, they will sit at the throne judging the twelve tribes of Israel.

Then Jesus makes a profound and astonishing revelation, "And the Lord said, Simon, Simon, behold, Satan hath desired to have you, that he may sift you as wheat. But I have prayed for thee, that thy faith failed not: and when thou art converted, strengthen thy brethren" (Luke 22:31–32). What a bombshell that must have been to the disciples. They were probably thinking that if Satan is trying to destroy Peter, what would he try to do with or to them!

Peter was one of Jesus's earlier selected disciples and was in Jesus's inner circle. He had apparently assumed the role as spoke-man for the disciples. If Satan was trying to destroy Peter, then what would he try to do with the rest of them!

In His brief revelation, Jesus seemingly made at least three significant points, Firstly, Satan was going after the apparent human leader of the disciples. Satan had tried to go after Jesus many times and failed. If he could destroy the apparent human leader-spokesman among the disciples, the others would scatter and there would be no unity. He could destroy the rest of them one by one.

Secondly, Jesus revealed that He had made a special prayer request on behalf of Peter. Jesus had already prayed for all the disciples; However, He prayed specifically for Peter, based on Peter's particular need. Peter needed extra protection from the evil one. Here Jesus implied that sometimes general prayers might not be sufficient. Previously Jesus had prayed for the disciples—not for the world at that time.

Thirdly, Jesus knew that Peter will be converted on the Day of Pentecost; therefore, He told Peter to strengthen the other disciples when he is converted. At that time the disciples probably had little notion about the meaning and impact of true conversion. However, they would know and understand in a few days—on the Day of Pentecost. Although Peter was astonished that Satan had planned to destroy his, he could take comfort in knowing that Jesus had prayed. Furthermore, he could anticipate his conversion with great expectation.

Believers throughout the ages are thankful to Jesus Christ for praying for Peter. On the Day of Pentecost, Peter was converted, preached his first sermon and three thousand persons were converted. The church, the body of Christ, had its beginning on that glorious day. That might not have happened that way if Jesus had not prayed specifically for Peter.

Jesus had taught His disciples, in the disciples' model prayer, to pray for deliverance from the evil one, "But deliver us from evil" (Matt. 6:13). Prayer is central to Christians for protection and deliverance!

In His ministry, Jesus demonstrates, time and again, the efficacy of prayer. There is no doubt that Jesus's prayer protected Peter from the evil one-Satan. In addition, believers should be aware that Satan will try to destroy the human leaders of their congregations. After all, he tried to destroy Jesus Christ.

Later on, the Apostle Peter describes Satan "as the roaring lion, [who] walketh about, seeking whom he may devour" (1 Pet. 5:8). The Apostle James reminds us to, "Resist the devil, and he will flee from you" (James 4:7). We are thankful and grateful that Jesus prayed a special prayer for Peter. Followers of Jesus are beneficiaries of that prayer.

Jesus Admonishes His Disciples to Watch and Pray

Jesus was teaching in the temple when the disciples asked Him what signs will signify the end of the age-end of time. Jesus responded by warning the disciples against false Christs who will proclaim that they are the returning Jesus Christ. He told them not to allow false Christs to deceive them.

Then Jesus revealed to them some signs of the approaching end of time. He said, "Men's heart will be failing them for fear, and for looking after those things which are coming on the earth: for the powers of the heaven shall be shaken. And then shall they see the Son of man coming in a cloud with powers and great glory" (Luke 21:26–27). It is noteworthy that Jesus did not provide a specific date or time of His return; however, He provides significant signs which His followers, who are watching, will be able to discern.

After providing additional insights and instructions regarding the end of time, Jesus said, "Watch and pray always, that ye may be accounted worthy to escape all these things that shall come to pass, and to stand before the Son of man" (Luke 21:36). Jesus emphasizes the importance of His disciples being watchful and prayerful as the end of age (end of time) draws close.

As Jesus warned, false Christs (imposters) are already deceiving many. Jesus urges the disciples to pray continually and remain in fellowship with Him so they are not deceived by imposters pretending to be the returning Jesus Christ.

Followers, believers in Jesus Christ, must live godly, prayerful lives as they patiently await the return of the real Jesus Christ, the Son of God. Praying, watching, being alert, and waiting patiently with a godly disposition are essential qualities of those who await the return of Jesus Christ, and their hearts will not fail and they will not be anxious and afraid as the end of age draws nigh.

As a believer and follower of Jesus, you will do well to heed Jesus's instruction "that men ought always to pray, and not faint" (Luke 18:1). I urge you to become effective or increasingly more effective in utilizing the powerful offensive and defensive weapon that Jesus has given to those who choose to use it— prayer. When you combine prayer with love, faith, and fasting, if necessary, you will resist temptation and live in accordance with God's will!

CHAPTER TWENTY

THE LAST PRAYERS ON THE CROSS

Jesus Is Lifted from the Earth on the Cross

Was it a mere coincidence or was it divine providence that Jesus Christ, the Son of God, the Promised Messiah was hanging of a crucifixion cross between two common criminals who were hanging on their respect cross? The Prophet Isaiah more than seven hundred and forty years before Jesus came to earth in the form of Man, prophesied about the birth, suffering and death of Jesus. He said about his death, "Because he hath poured out his soul unto death: and he was numbered with transgressors; and he bare the sin of many, and made intercession for the transgressors" (Isa. 53:12).

The Prophet Zachariah, more than five hundred years before Jesus died on the cross, prophesied about the incident. "And I (GOD) shall pour upon the house of David, and upon the inhabitants of Jerusalem, the spirit of grace and of supplications: and they shall look upon me whom they have pierced, and they shall mourn for him, as one mourneth for his only son, and shall be in bitterness for him, as one is in bitterness for his first born" (Zech. 12:10). The fulfillment of Zachariah's prophecy was imminent.

No, Jesus's death and the type of death He endured were not by chance. Rather, they were ordained by God. In fact, Jesus, Himself, in signifying his death on the cross said, "And as Moses lifted up the serpent in the wilderness, even so must the Son of man be lifted up. That whosoever believeth in him should not perish, but have eternal life" (John 3:14–15). Jesus clearly indicates the significance of being lifted from the earth. He said, "And I, if I be lifted up from the earth, will draw all men unto me" (John 12:32). It was no coincidence that Jesus Christ was lifted from the earth on to the cross.

Jesus was lifted to the cross, crucified, and that Jesus will save those who look to the cross, to Him, and accept the gift of eternal life.

Eternal life is possible through the atoning death of Jesus on the cross. This is similar to how those who were bitten by the serpent in the wilderness, and looked up to Moses's bronze serpent on a pole, were healed. However, the difference is that the healing which occurred in the wilderness was physical and temporary; whereas, Jesus's death on the cross provides the opportunity for spiritual and eternal healing-wholeness. The lifting of Jesus from the earth was predetermined by God and serves God's plan and purpose-redemption and restoring of fellowship between God and humanity.

The Last Prayer of Man to the God-Man

I have discussed the predetermination of Jesus's death on the cross. The Jewish religious leaders (Sanhedrin Council) and the Roman officials gave Jesus the most severe punishment possible. They intended for Him to experience slow, painful, and torturous death on the cross. This was the type of punishment reserved for the worst of criminals in that society. Little did the Jewish religious leaders, Roman governor, and soldiers know that they were simply evil instruments in the hand and at service of the righteous God.

Situated on either side of Jesus's cross were two thieves on their respective cross. Their punishment was as harsh as that handed down to Jesus; however, they were paying the consequences for their evil deeds. Jesus was an innocent Man, a Son of God. Apparently, either the thieves knew about Jesus prior to the time they were placed on their crosses or they heard about Him from all the talk which going on around the crosses.

In any case, they knew that Jesus was not a common criminal and had done no wrong. Luke records that one of the criminals, who was being crucified beside Jesus, berated Jesus saying, "If thou be Christ, save thyself and us" (Luke 22:39). This was not a genuine request seeking salvation. This thief joined with the Jewish religious leaders in mocking Jesus.

In fact, the convicted criminal was behaving similarly to Satan when he tried to tempt Jesus at the beginning of Jesus's earthly ministry. Satan tried to tempt Jesus then with a similar proposition, "If thou be the Son of God, command that these stones be made bread" (Matt. 4:3). Satan had tried to tempt Jesus, at the very beginning of His earthly ministry, and failed miserably. No doubt Satan was using this criminal, dying on the cross, to try to tempt Jesus toward end of His earthly ministry. Satan failed again.

It was not necessary for Jesus to respond to the remarks of the convicted, disrespectful and impudent criminal. The other dying, repentant criminal responded immediately and appropriately. He rebuked his fellow criminal, saying to him, "Dost not thou fear God, seeing thou art in the same condemnation? And we indeed justly; for we receive the due reward for our deeds: but this man hath done nothing amiss" (Luke 23:40–41). Even a dying criminal knew and acknowledged that Jesus, who hung on the cross, is the Son of God and did nothing wrong. Yet, the Jewish religious leaders refused to recognize and accept Jesus as the Son of God.

One dying criminal confessed that he was guilty of the crime for which he was being crucified, and he rebuked the unrepentant criminal. But he did not stop there, he wanted Jesus to remember him when all was well with Jesus. Yes, Jesus had already touched him.

The Life-Receiving Transformational Prayer of a Repentant Dying Criminal

Having rebuked the irreverent, insolent, and guilty criminal, the repentant criminal confessed his guilt. He would soon die, and he was now ready to take full advantage of his physical and attitudinal proximity to the person who he knew could help him—Jesus, the Son of God. "And he said [prayed] unto Jesus, Lord, remember me when thou comest into thy kingdom" (Luke 23:42). His prayer was succinct, direct, specific, and consequential. He knew that Jesus was on His way to the heavenly kingdom and he just wanted Jesus to remember him once He got there.

It is worthy to note that the dying thief did not ask Jesus to save him from physical death. He did not want to get off the cross; he wanted to pay his dues to society by dying on the cross. Notice, he did not complain that the consequence for his criminality was too harsh. Rather, he confessed his guilt and, in a matter of speaking, he repented and prayed-asked Jesus to remember him. Undoubtedly, he knew that there is life after physical death. He must have known that Jesus would rise from the dead and he was seeking similar life from Jesus. Jesus did not need to wait until He got to His kingdom before He remember the dying repentant criminal. Jesus answered his prayer immediately.

Jesus Answers the Prayer of the Repentant Criminal Dying on the Cross

No sooner than the repentant criminal asked Jesus to remember him when He got to His Kingdom, Jesus gave him a transformational death to everlasting life response, "And Jesus said unto him, Verily I say unto thee, to day shalt thou be with me in paradise" (Luke 23:43). By the time Jesus was on the cross, He had raised a number of persons from physical death, including Lazarus and Jairus' daughter; however, more than likely they all experienced physical death again.

Jesus previously clearly stated that He is the Way, Truth, and Life—the means to the Kingdom of God He had forgiven the sins of some. However, this is the first record of Jesus promising someone that he will be in paradise with Him on a given day—today.

One of Jesus's greatest promises to His disciples is that He will return for them at some time in the future. However, He told the dying, repentant thief that he would be with Him in paradise that very day. Jesus saved gave eternal life to the repented dying thief in the nook of time. Because he confessed his guilt and asked Jesus to save him.

Even though the innocent Son of God would experience physical death—laying down His life in a few hours—He answered the sincere prayer of a repented dying, and gives him spiritual-eternal life. This incident reveals that Jesus is merciful and is able to give instantaneous salvation to those who sincerely seek it. He looked beyond His own physical pains and imminent physical death, and beyond the misdeeds of the dying thief and answered his prayer and saved him.

Jesus responded immediately to the prayer of the dying thief and gives him eternal life. This means that Jesus is instantaneous in His response to sincere prayers. However, no one should wait until his or her dying hour—on the dying bed or in an accident—before seeking the Lord. The Prophet Isaiah reminds us to, "Seek the LORD while he may be found, call upon him while he is near. Let the wicked forsake his way, and the unrighteous man his thoughts: and let him return unto the LORD, and he will have mercy upon him; and to our God, for he will abundantly pardon" (Isa. 55:6). It is incumbent on all to seek God's forgiveness right now! This is the right time to do so.

The dying thief was fortunate that through the Providential Will of God, Jesus-the Savior was being crucified, adjacent to him, at the same time. And that Jesus mercifully extended salvation to him. You may not have the opportunity to repent at your dying hour.

Today is the day to repent and seek salvation, if you have not already done so. Jesus will answer your prayer as He did for the repented criminal on the cross. However, you must repent and ask God's forgiveness, in the name of Jesus. Remember that tomorrow is not promised to anyone.

The God-Man's Greatest Forgiveness of Humanity: Jesus's Prayer

Herod the Roman-appointed King of Judah and Pilot, the Roman governor, representing Caesar the Emperor of Rome, examined Jesus and found no basis for the accusation of the Jewish religious against Him. And certainly, Pilot, who served as the judge at the fake trial of Jesus, found no crime which Jesus committed. And no accusation which remotely resulted in the penalty of death.

Nevertheless, the religious leaders at Jerusalem—Pharisees, scribes, high priests, and elders—accused Jesus of blasphemy. More importantly, as far as Caesar would be concerned was the false accusation of sedition against Caesar—Emperor of Rome. Herod the king Tetrarch of Galilee and Pilate the governor examined the case against Jesus and concluded that there was no evidence which warranted the crucifixion of Jesus. Herod Antipas's role was primarily in mocking Jesus by placing a gorgeous robe on Him and them removing it before returning Jesus to Pilate.

At the very worse, Pilate, who served as the trial judge, suggested that he would flag Jesus and release from custody.

Pilate's offer to flag the innocent Jesus and release Him, met opposition from the Jewish religious leaders. They would have no such lenient treatment of the innocent Son of God.

The Jewish religious leaders would not budge from their hardline decision. They wanted Jesus dead by crucifixion. They vehement in their demand that Jesus must be crucified. They wanted to kill Jesus and send a warning to His followers that they could suffer the same fate if they continued to preach and teach about Jesus.

After Palate made three unsuccessful attempts to get a compromise from the religious leaders to scourge Jesus and release, rather than crucifying Him, Pilate relented to their unfounded, malicious demand and reluctantly released Jesus to them. They could do as they wished—crucify the Man who he knew was innocent. Pilot washed his hands symbolizing that he was innocent of the shedding of the blood of the innocent Jesus!

Luke records that as soon as Pilate released Jesus to the chief priests, Pharisees, and other religious leaders, they took Jesus to Calvary, "There they crucified him, and the malefactors, one on the right hand, and the other on the left" (Luke 23:33). The chief priests, Pharisees, scribes, and other religious leaders, with the assistance of Roman soldiers, crucified the innocent Son of God.

Jesus came to earth to give His life for the redemption of humanity, so that those who believe in Him will have everlasting life. And the Jewish religious leaders with the weak enabler, Pilate conspired against Jesus and sentenced Him to die. This was the greatest atrocity in the history of the world—murdering the righteous Man, the Son of God.

The alleged crimes of Jesus were that He blasphemed, because He claims to be the Son of God, and that He committed sedition against Caesar—that He wanted to be king of Judea. Interestingly enough, Jesus is King of the whole world, Jesus simply testified to the truth that He is the Son of God. However, His murder—His laying down of His life—resulted in greatest redemption in human history. Those who choose to accept Jesus Christ as their Lord and savior receive eternal life.

Jesus has no vindictiveness toward His executioners. Rather, He had empathy and sympathy for their ignorance, misguided sincerity, envy, and cruelty. And most of all, Jesus has unwavering love for humanity, even for those who murdered Him. He came to earth to die for their sins and the sins of all humanity. .

So before Jesus commends His Sprit to God, He prays the greatest prayer of forgiveness ever uttered by the God-Man, Jesus Christ, on behalf of His executioners. "Then Jesus said (prayed), Father, forgive them; for they know not what they do" (Luke 23:34). Jesus knew that the religious leaders who wanted Him dead were ignorant and misguided in their atrocity.

Many of them misunderstood God and thought they were doing God's bidding by murdering a person they thought was a blasphemous imposter. Even so, some of the leaders wanted Jesus dead because they were envious and felt threatened by is growing popularity.

The religious leaders had failed to search the Scripture and they had a misconception of how the Messiah would enter the world. In a way, their hearts were hardened—they had eyes, but could not see and ears, but could not perceive. They refused to accept the words of Jesus that God is His Father. And they failed to accept the works of Jesus which clearly demonstrate that He was not just another ordinary Jewish man or even just another prophet.

While Jesus was giving up His life, on the cross for the sins of humanity, He prays loudly, asking God to forgive those who were responsible for killing Him. Regardless of their motivations— ignorance, jealousy, pride, misunderstanding, or whatever other reasons—He forgives them, and cries out loudly asking God to forgive them. Evidently, Jesus wanted His murders to know that He was praying for them.

No doubt, Jesus was setting an example for His existing and eventual disciples-followers. He wanted them to know that they must forgive others for their transgressions of others against them, regardless of how egregious the transgressions might be.

During His ministry, Jesus taught His disciples the quintessential requirement that His followers must have unconditional love for one another and for others—even their enemies. "But I say unto you, Love your enemies, bless them that curse you, do good to them that hate you, and pray for them which despitefully use you, and persecute you" (Matt. 5:44). On Calvary's cross, Jesus demonstrates what He had been teaching His disciples.

He was being executed, suffering pains as a righteous human being, yet His unconditional love supersedes His pains and anguish, and compels Him to forgive. He cries out to His Father as loudly as He could, so that His murderers would hear, "Father, forgive them for they no not what they do" (Luke 23:34).

Jesus's exemplary, supreme prayer of forgiveness did not go unnoticed by the dying Deacon Stephen. When Stephen was being stoned to death by misguided religious leaders at Jerusalem, he prayed similarly as Jesus did, "Lord, lay not this sin to their charge" (Acts 7:60). Stephen was murdered because he was testifying about the risen Jesus Christ.

What manner of forgiveness, precipitated by unconditional-divine love and compassion, Jesus shows on that cruel cross! Jesus did not say, as is commonly said, that "ignorance is no excuse for doing wrong—such as committing murder." Rather Jesus looks beyond the hate, envy, hypocrisy, and self-righteousness of His murderers and saw their need for forgiveness.

Jesus executes, not judgement, and justice; rather He chooses forgiveness and compassion through His unconditional-divine love. What a great example of forgiveness and love for followers of Jesus Christ to emulate! Jesus extends the same love, compassion, and forgiveness, which He extended on the cross, to you and me and to all humanity.

You might never have to sacrifice your life on a cross; however, you will have many opportunities to give love and compassion, and to forgive.

Jesus Prays for Himself on the Cross

Jesus was hanged-nailed to the cross at third hour (9:00 a.m.), on the day before the Sabbath. Some Bible scholars believe that the particular Sabbath referenced is the Day of Festival of the Passover, which would have been Thursday. Regardless of the day, at the sixth hour (12 noon), Jesus promised the repentant criminal, who was being crucified, that on that on that very day he would be with Jesus in paradise (see prior discussion). Luke records, "And it was about the sixth hour, and there was a darkness over all the earth until the ninth hour (3:00 p.m.). And the sun was darkened, and the veil of the temple was rent in the midst" (Luke 23:44–45). When Jesus was born in Bethlehem of Judea, a bright star symbolized His birth. And at His death, the sun refused to shine and plunged the earth in darkness from 12 noon until 3:00 p.m. because God deemed it so.

Jesus was on the cross for about six hours. During that time, as recorded by Luke, He asked God to forgive those involved in crucifying Him. And He promised a dying repentant criminal that on that day he would be with Jesus in paradise.

And significantly, the veil—curtain in the sanctuary of the temple split down the center from the top to the bottom; this signifies that through the death of Jesus Christ all humanity could pray to God directly without going through an earthly priest. The risen Jesus Christ is the Great High Priest in heaven, through whom all may pray to God.

Jesus was now ready to commit His Spirit to God. He was ready to take three days of physical death, to take some needed rest. He had a grueling previous night and a morning of foolish interrogation and physical abuses. Undoubtedly the God-Man, Son of God was tired. Luke records, "And when Jesus had cried with a loud voice, he said, Father, into thy hands I commend my spirit: and having said thus, he gave up the ghost" Luke 23:46). Jesus had completed His mission as the God-Man on earth. He would do a few more things as the risen savior before ascending to heaven—notably assign the great commission to His disciples, at the time, and subsequent ones, you me.

The last task He had to complete as God-Man was to sacrifice His life—die on Calvary's cross. He had control on when He would give up His life; so when the time was accomplished, He sent His Spirit to God and slept for three days-died. His very last prayer as a God-Man was to ask God to accept His Spirit. God accepts the Spirit of Jesus and Jesus went into a three-day sleep.

The religious leaders—chief priests, Pharisees, scribes, Sadducee, elders—thought they had finally executed Jesus and put His teaching to permanent rest. However, early Sunday morning—resurrection morning—Jesus rose triumphantly from the grave, never to die again. And because He rose from the grave, those who believe in Him, including His executioners—if they chose belief and repent—shall have life everlasting.

The greatest tragedy in human history, and the darkest hour of the day became and is the greatest blessing for humanity and the brightest light that shines on earth, respectively. Jesus gave His life on Calvary's Cross so that those who choose to believe in Him (will) have everlasting life. And Jesus gives forgiveness to those who murdered Him and to those who forgive others and seek His forgiveness.

Jesus prayed on the cross, not for his sins, because He had none. Rather, He prayed for the sins of those who were murdering Him. In so doing, He demonstrates God's unconditional love for humanity. Furthermore, He demonstrates the true meaning and reality of forgiving who despitefully use and abuse His followers, even in the most egregious manner.

THOUGHTS ON PRAYERS!

CHAPTER TWENTY-ONE

WHY PRAYERS FAIL AND WHY PRAYERS SUCCEED

I cannot remember asking my father for anything that he did not give to me or explain why he could not or would not give it to me. So can we expect our heavenly Father to give us what we ask of Him, or to respond to our request-prayer in one way are another? Yes, we can, you can, expect God to answer your prayer by saying yes, no, not now, or give you another appropriate response.

Jesus reminds us that God will respond to our request. He puts it this way, "If ye then, being evil, know how to give good gifts unto your children, how much more shall your Father which is in heaven give good gifts to them that ask him" (Matt. 7:11). Not only will God hear and answer your prayer, but He will also give the right answer or the appropriate gift to those who ask in sincerity with confident expectation.

You should not be concerned about how our heavenly Father answers your prayers or when you receive the manifestation of His answer. Rather, you should be quite concerned and even apprehensive-anxious if He simply ignores your prayer. Jesus teaches that if we ask our heavenly Father for anything in Jesus's name, God will answer our prayer, if we have faith—believe that He will answer. Believing is a condition required for God to answer prayers. Asking in the name of

Jesus is another condition for God to answer prayers. But what does it mean to ask in the name of Jesus?

In this chapter, I explore some conditions for answered and unanswered prayers. In addition, I discuss a few occasions when God appears to ignore prayers all together. Let me quickly say that when God says no to a prayer, it may appear that He has ignored the prayer; however, no is an answer. Therefore, only when there is no response from God, one may assume the prayer has been ignored. And we do not know for sure that God has not answered a prayer at a given time, because the manifestation of His answer might not yet de evident.

God is not on our timeframe, therefore, the manifestation of His answer may become evident at a future time. Again, it important to bear in mind that man's timeframe to for receiving God's answer a prayer might not be God's timeframe.

Following are incidents regarding prayers, God's responses or apparent lack of response, and plausible explanations for the apparent lack of response.

Misunderstanding God's Instructions and Promises

Sometimes God does not answer prayers because the prayers do not follow God's instructions. An excellent example is the promise which God made to Solomon. God promised Solomon that He would hear and answer the prayers of His people if they met certain conditions: "If my people who are called by my name will humble themselves and pray . . . I will hear from heaven and will heal their land" (2 Chron. 7: 14).

I was attending a church service recently when the distinguished pastor read 2 Chronicles 7:14, and then with great enthusiasm and eloquence proclaimed that if the current United States President (and he said his name) would humble himself and pray God would heal America.

The pastor received acclamations and a lot of amens for his proclamation. Undoubtedly the pastor and many in the congregation believe that it is the political leaders who have the responsibility to call the people together for repentance and healing of the land.

This happened in the Bible day. For example, the king of Nineveh assembled the people of that great city, and they all humbled themselves, repented, and turned from their evil way, and God spared that city from imminent destruction.

Certainly, God loves all people. He created all people, and there are some political leaders who accept Jehovah-Yahweh as their God. However, when God made that promise to Solomon, shortly after Solomon dedicated the temple, which he had constructed, God made the promise to Solomon and the children of Israel. The promise is now extended to God's people—members of the body of Christ, the church, the Christians.

So that pastor had very good intention and was quite correct in proclaiming the need for prayers for the healing of the land. However, it is the religious leaders, Christians, believers, who are called to carry out God's instruction to Solomon.

Christian leaders have the responsibility of calling God's people, believers in Jesus, to humility, repentance, and prayer on behalf of our nation, and for that matter, prayer on behalf of the whole world. This instruction from God cannot be relegated to political or governmental leaders and officials.

If you have accepted Jesus Christ as your Lord and your Savior, you are a Christian—one of God's people. If you are a pastor, bishop, priest, deacon or any other leader in church, the body of Christ, you are a leader of God's people. You share the responsibility of carrying out God's instruction, as recorded in 2 Chronicles 7:14. As stated previously, this responsibility cannot be relegated to political leaders or government officials. This is especially true in an environment where so much emphasis is placed on the separation of church and state.

The emphasis of the responsibility of Christian leaders to call on God's people to pray for the nation is not to suggest or imply that a president or other political or government leaders are not among God's people. The point I am making here is that our true religious leaders must assume the primary responsibility and leadership of calling God's people—members of the Christian Church, congregations—for the type of prayer which God demands in the Scripture preciously referenced.

In addition, the Apostle Paul reminds Timothy and us to pray, "For Kings, and for all that are in authority" (1 Tim. 2:2). This admonition indicates an expectation that Christians have an obligation of carrying out God's instruction of praying for the nation. This is an assignment that is far too important to leave up political leaders or government officials. We should pray that God will touch their hearts that they too will humble themselves, repent, and pray.

The implication of God's instruction to Solomon, recorded in 2 Chronicles 7:14, and Paul's instruction to Timothy, recorded in 1 Timothy 2:2, is that God might ignore prayers that are not consistent with His instruction. This might be particularly true with intercessory prayers. God instructs Christians to intercede on behalf of the nation. The Apostle Paul, inspired by the Holy Spirit, instructs Timothy to pray for kings and for all who are in authority. Christians must carry out their/our responsibility to provide leadership in praying for the nation and its leaders. Otherwise, God might ignore the intercessory prayers of nonbelievers, even if such prayers are organized by a president, governor, senator, or other government officials unless they are believers in Jesus as the Savior.

CHAPTER TWENTY-TWO

UNANSWERED AND SEEMINGLY UNANSWERED PRAYERS

Many people, including some devoted Christians, will confess that they do not know for sure if their prayers are being answered. Some will even say that despite their vigilant prayer lives they have no evidence at all that their prayers are being answered. The question is why individuals do not know if their prayers are answered or perhaps, and more importantly, why are their prayers not answered?

In the final analysis, only God knows why He has not answered particular prayer or why those who pray do not discern the manifestation of His answer. However, Jesus does provide conditions for answerable prayers and criteria for assessing the efficacy of prayers.

Perhaps, more importantly, the question ought to be, "Why does God not answer some prayers?" Again, only God knows the exact answer for such a question. However, God provides guidance for prayers which He answers. For example, Jesus taught His disciples a Model Prayer which is relevant and applicable today.

Insight to seemingly unanswered prayers as well as to actually unanswered prayers is provided, based on guidance in the Bible. Often one's refusal to accept the answer which

God gives is taken as an unanswered prayer. It is important to distinguish between a prayer for which God gives an answer, which is different from the request and one which He ignores— again, only God truly knows the difference.

Unanswered Prayers: God Does Answer Some Prayers

David and other writers of Psalms were concerned about God not hearing, and much less answering, their prayers. David expresses that apprehension as follows: "Hide not thy face far from me, put not thy servant away in anger; thou hast been my help; leave me not, neither forsake me, O God of my salvation" (Psa. 27:9). The Bible records that David was a man after God's own heart, yet David was concerned that God could decide not to hear his prayer.

One afflicted, unidentified psalmist prayed, "Hear my prayer, O Lord, and let my cry come unto thee. Hide not thy face from me in the day when I am in trouble; incline thine ear unto me: in the day when I call answer me speedily" (Psa. 102:1–2). Clearly, that psalmist knew that God could turn His face from the psalmist and refuse to hear his or her prayer. The psalmist was not as concerned about the answer that God would give; rather, the concern was that God would not give an answer.

In an urgent situation for David, it was not urgent for God, David appealed to God, "Hear my prayer, O Lord, give ear unto my supplications: in thy faithfulness answer me, and in thy righteousness" (Psa. 143:1). Once again, David recognized that it is God's decision to hear or not to hear his prayer. In this case, David was not asking God to answer his prayer according to what he requested, he just wanted God to give him an answer. David's prayer suggests that David recognized that God may choose not even to hear a prayer and much less to answer it.

Finally, in Psalm 88 for the sons of Korah, the Psalmist prays, "O Lord God of my salvation, I have cried day and night before thee: Let my prayer come before thee: incline thine ear unto my cry" (Psa. 88:1–2). Here again, apparently the psalmist had been praying night and day and had not received a response from God, or a response that he was able to identify.

In the foregoing examples, the psalmists desired that God would hear and answer their prayers; rather than ignoring them. Evidently, they were not as concerned with the answer which Gods gives them because they knew that God's answers are always the right answers. One who prays might desire that God answers the prayer in a favorable manner—giving him or her what is requested. However, one who prays must ask God to answer the prayer in accordance with God's will. Yet, apparently, there are situations in which God will not even hear, much less answer a prayer.

Reasons for Unanswered Prayers

The Bible is replete with requests from King David—a man after God's own heart—and others, including Solomon, pleading with God not to turn His face away from them. They pleaded with God to hear them when they pray. I have discussed a few of those prayers previously.

The implication is that God chooses not to hear and/or answer some prayers. There can be many reasons for God making His sovereign decision to hear or not to hear and answer prayers. First and foremost, no natural human is worthy to approach the throne of God in prayer. However, Jesus makes it possible for humans to approach God, in spite of our unworthiness.

You can petition God and expect His response when you meet certain requirements. God has established criteria for those who pray to Him and expect to receive His answer. Below are a few plausible explanations why God might choose not to hear or answer prayers. Again, only God knows the reasons for His decision in any given situation.

God Refuses to Hear the Prayers of
Those Who Do Not Obey Him

Solomon, the wisest man who ever lived, puts God refusal to answer some prayers in this manner: "Because I [God] have called, and ye refused: I have stretched out my hand, and no man regarded. When your fear cometh as desolation, and your destruction cometh as whirlwind; when distress and anguish cometh upon you. Then shall they call upon me, but I will not answer; they shall seek me early, but they shall not find me. For they hated knowledge, and did not choose the fear of the LORD" Prov. 1:27–29). The implication here is that God calls people to repentance and they refuse to respond. Yet when they need God's help, they call upon Him, pray, and expect God to respond to their prayers.

People have taken God for granted over the centuries—during the Bible times up to the present. They ignored and are ignoring God's instructions. Many feel self-reliant, independent of God or of anyone for that matter. Then in times of great needs-calamities, which are inevitable, they try to call upon God—to pray. Well, Solomon declares that God will not answer such prayers, as quoted previously (Prov. 1:27–29).

The great Prophet Isaiah, who was quoted previously reminds us that we must, "Seek ye the LORD while he may be found, call ye upon him while he is near. Let the wicked forsake his way, and the unrighteous man his thoughts: and let him return unto the LORD, and he will have mercy upon him; and to our God, for he will abundantly pardon" (Isa. 55:6–7). One must seek and obey God in order for Him to answer the prayer when His assistance is needed.

You cannot wait until you are in trouble or in great need before you try to develop relationship with God. It may be too late then. Isaiah's admonition to seek the LORD while he may be found is applicable today as it was when he made the proclamation centuries ago.

A good example of one who waited too late to pray and to ask for God's assistance was King Zedekiah, the last King of Judea. Before the Babylonian captivity, Zedekiah ignored the urging of the Prophet Jeremiah and others, pleading for him to return to God, and do that which was right in the sight of God.

Zedekiah waited until it was too late. Only when Nebuchadnezzar, King of Babylon and the Babylonians besieged Jerusalem did he asked Jeremiah to petition God to fight with Judea against the Babylonian. Zedekiah did not even repent and turn to God; he wanted God's assistance without repentance and turning to God. God's response was an emphatic no! In fact, God joined with the Babylonian against His own people of Judea. And Jerusalem was destroyed by the Babylonians in 586 BC. God refused to assist Zedekiah, who refused to obey Him.

God Refuses to Hear the Prayers of Those Who Pray Against His Will

Sometimes a person, even a devout servant of God, may pray for a given outcome without apparent success. The praying may go on for a long period of time. The person may be so sincere about the desired outcome that he or she might not be listening to God's voice or answer. I have already listed several possible reasons why God might not answer prayers. Again, I make a distinction between when God says no or give an alternative outcome, versus when there is no apparent manifestation of God's response. I have mentioned the incidents here and discussed them in a subsequent subheading "Seemingly Unanswered Prayers."

These prayers were against or inconsistent with God's Providential or Prescriptive Will. Two such prayers are one by King Saul and one by King David. God refused to answer the enquiry regarding the outcome of a battle between Israel and the Philistines. Similarly, God refused to give David an answer when he prayed to God to restore the health of the first son he had with Bathsheba.

God Does Not Answer Prayers of Those with Unforgiven Sins

Sometimes God refuses to hear and answer a prayer because the person who has prayed or is praying is aware of sins for which he or she has not sought forgiveness. A person might be praying to God for a blessing or to resolve a difficult situation while he or she has not asked God for forgiveness of that known sin or evil in the heart. David, the writer of Psalm 68 puts it this way, "If I regard iniquity in my heart, the LORD will not hear me" (Psa. 66:18). This is one reason that some people when they pray, they will ask God to forgive them of specific sins they know that they have committed. Then they will ask God to forgive them for all unknown sins—sins of which they are not aware which they might have committed. After seeking God's forgiveness for all sins, including the harboring—retaining evil thoughts in their hearts, they are now clear to make their other petitions known unto God.

The Apostle John reminds us that, "Now we know that God heareth not sinners: but if any man be a worshipper of God, and doth his will, him he heareth" (John 9:31). It is said that God hears the prayer of repentance coming from the sinner and is quick to forgive sins. The criminal who was on an adjacent cross to Jesus confessed that he was guilty of the crime for which he was charged. He then asked Jesus to remember him. Jesus heard his prayer and pardoned his sin.

Jesus Christ, through His death and resurrection, paid the wages of sins and makes it possible for sinners to pray to God for their sins, repent, and accept Jesus Christ as Savior. Then they can make other petitions to God. Confessing sins and seeking forgiveness must be the first of a sinner.

God Does Not Answer Vain and Insincere Prayers

Job, the man in the Bible, whose name symbolizes patience, acknowledges the sovereign God, and proclaims, "Surely God will not hear vanity, neither will the Almighty regard it" (Job 35:13). In other words, God will not listen to an empty cry, nor will He pay any attention to prayers which are insincere or prayed to impress others. It is understood from the proclamation of Job that false pride is synonymous with vanity. Job declares that when those with false pride cry out, God does not answer them because of their pride (Job 35:12).

James, the brother of Jesus Christ declares, "But he [God] giveth more grace. Wherefore he saith, God resisteth the Proud, but giveth grace unto the humble" (James 4:6). Not only does God refuses to hear the prayer of the proud, but He resists them. Jesus states the consequence of vanity-false pride more bluntly, He teaches His disciples—followers, "Except ye be converted, and become as little children, ye shall not enter into the kingdom of heaven. Whosoever therefore shall humble himself as this little child, the same is the greatest in the kingdom of heaven" (Matt. 18:3–4).

A prayer is communication between God and a person or persons. The person praying must approach God with humility, sincerity, and faith. God knows everything, therefore, there is no need for anyone try to impress God. Similarly, there is no need for pseudo-humility. It is perfectly okay for a person to accept with gratitude any accolades he or she receives, and give God appropriate acknowledgement, glory, and praise. Such acceptance and showing appreciation are not in and of themselves vanity or false pride. However, God will not hear and answer prayers of vanity or false pride.

God Does Not Answer the Prayers of Those
Who Refuse to Respond to His Call

God makes overtures to His people on a regular basis urging them to turn or return to Him. He also chastises them with grace and mercy as a loving father chastises his disobedient children. It is God's desire that His people take heed to His call and turn or return to Him. However, when God reaches out to His people and they refuse to respond to His call they will eventually reap the consequences of their rebellion against God. The writer of Proverbs records how God entreats His people, "Turn you at my reproof: behold, I will pour out my spirit unto you. I will make known my ways unto you" (Prov. 1:23). Despite the urging of God that His people turn or return to Him, they continue to ignore God's urging and His corrections. God wants to pour out special blessings on His people, however, they continue to resist God's simple condition—to turn or return to God.

Then God declares, "Because I have called, and ye refused; I have stretched out my hand, and no man regarded; I also will laugh at your calamity, I will mock when your fear cometh [when you are afraid]; Then shall they call upon me, but I will not answer; they shall seek me early, but they shall not find me" (Prov. 1:24, 26, 28). So God will not respond to prayers of those who deliberately and continually refuse His urging to turn or return to Him and accept His corrections. In fact, not only will God refuse to answer the prayers of those who refuse to heed His call, but He will laugh at them in their times of need and will mock them.

The writer of Hebrews, quoting from Psalm 95:7–10, declares that it is of critical importance that people, who desire that God answers their prayer, respond to His call before it is too late. Hebrews records, "Wherefore (as the Holy Ghost saith, to day if ye will hear his voice, harden not your hearts, as in the provocation, in the day of temptation in the wilderness: when your fathers tempted me, proved me, and saw my works forty years" (Heb. 3:7–9).

For emphasis on the importance of responding to the voice of God, the writer of Hebrews repeats, "While it is said, to day if ye will hear his voice, harden not your hearts, as in the provocation" (Heb. 3:15). The writer of Hebrews suggests that a person has the free will to respond to God's invitation and corrections. God usually does not force anyone to respond to His call—there are notable exceptions, such as Jonah and Saul of Tarsus—neither does God respond to the prayers of those who refuse to respond to His call. And Proverbs records that God will not respond to those rebellious persons at a time when they may need Him most. As previously quoted, God said, "I God also will laugh at your calamity' I will mock when your fear cometh" (Prov. 1:26). It is critical to respond to God when He calls, if you want God to respond to your prayers in the times of your need

God Does Not Answer the Prayer of the Doubtful Person

James, the brother of Jesus, who was converted after the resurrection of Jesus, perhaps on the Day of Pentecost, became the leader of the Church at Jerusalem. He was a practical apostle who teaches that faith and work must go hand in hand. He teaches that there cannot be one without the other. James teaches that a person may ask God for wisdom (or to supply another needs) and God will grant the request; however, such request must be in faith without wavering.

James emphasizes the importance of faith and unwavering mind when praying. He said, "But let him ask in faith, nothing wavering. For he that wavereth is like a wave of the sea driven with the wind and tossed. For let not that man think that he shall receive anything of the Lord. A double minded man is unstable in all his ways" (James 1:6–8). James lays out criteria for a person who desires God to answer his or her prayers. That person must have faith in the goodness of God to answer prayers and must believe, without doubt, that God is able to answer and to deliver.

A person cannot be doubtful about the ability or the willingness of God to answer his or her prayer. He or she must approach the throne of God with a positive mental attitude and confident expectation that God will answer the prayer. The writer of Hebrews stresses the importance of praying with faith in this manner, "But without faith it I impossible to please God: for he that cometh to God must believe that he is, and that he is a rewarder of them that diligently seek him" (Heb. 11:6). Some prayers are not answered because they are prayed with doubt and a wavering mind—lack of confident expectation. The Apostle James reminds us that God will not answer such a prayer.

You must practice believing and trusting God to answer your prayers according to His will, and your faith and trust in Him will grow. Remember, not only can you pray for wisdom, as the Apostle James teaches, you can pray for growing faith and trust in God as well! When you pray expect that God will answer your prayer and provide the best answer for you. Pray with confident expectation.

Praying for the Wrong Outcome

Have you ever prayed and asked God to bless someone who has turned his or her back on God and you don't seem to get a response to your prayer? Year after year you pray and you see no change in the person for whom you are praying and there is no apparent blessing on him or her. You believe that you are a devoted Christian, yet God has not answered that prayer. Well, you may be praying for the wrong outcome. Perhaps you should be praying, asking God to intervene in that person's life that he or she might come to know God for the first time or to return to God. God blesses those who humble themselves and submit themselves to Him.

Blessings are special gifts which God grants to whomever He chooses. God might choose not to grant His blessings to those whose hearts are contaminated with evil thoughts or desires. Therefore, rather than asking God to bless a person who has not yet accepted Christ or who has turned from God, perhaps the prayer should ask God to change the heart of the person. To help him or her turn or return to God and be ready to receive God's blessings. Not everyone who has physical possessions obtained them as a result of God's blessings.

It is right to pray for others even those who despitefully hurt you. Jesus teaches, "And pray for them which despitefully use you, and persecute you" (Matthew 5:44). However, such prayer should focus on asking for God's intervention in their hearts and lives to change them—turn their hearts toward God or that they will return to God.

In addition to praying for persons with whom you have relationship, there are religious and political leaders who need our continuous prayers for one thing or another. Those who are true believers may need to be strengthened in their spiritual life and abilities. Those who are not yet believers or non-believers need prayers that God will reveal Himself to them. Prayers must be intentional and the request to God should be guided by the situation and the Holy Spirit. But never, ever pray for an outcome that would not please God, such as revenge or curse!

Seemingly Unanswered Prayers

Do you recall how you have been taught to pray? You may have been taught to pray to God in the general domain, not to pray for anything in specific. Rather to pray for blessings, protection, supply of your needs, getting a job, and so forth? In this line to thinking and praying, people often believe that it is presumptuous to ask God for any particular thing.

They those who pray in general terms assert that God already knows their needs. They often cite this passage from the teaching of Jesus to justify their approach to praying, "For after all these things do the Gentiles seek: for your heavenly Father knoweth that ye have need of all these things. But seek ye first the kingdom of God, and his righteousness; and all these things shall be added unto you" (Matt. 6:32–33). Jesus had listed some specific things or needs which were distracting the attention of His followers, so He assured them that God knows their needs and they should turn over their physical needs to God and concentrate on their spiritual need-salvation.

The implication here is that it is quite acceptable and expected that believers will ask God to meet specific needs. If prayers are of a general nature the person who prayed may not know if the prayer has been answered. It is conceivable that God answers the general-type prayer in the best interest of the person who prayed, but he or she does not recognize that God has answered.

So the seemingly unanswered prayer has been answered. This type of prayer and God's answer I term a seemingly unanswered prayer. You cannot definitively declare that God has answered the prayer because you did not pray for a definite outcome. Yet God has answered the prayer, based on His will and plan for you in the given situation. God supplied what was appropriate at the time. The answer might even be no, not at this time.

Often when God gives a no answer, a prayer might think that God has not answered the prayer. A no from God is a real answer as a yes!

On the following pages are types of prayers which are sometimes considered or seemed or unanswered.

Failure or Refusal to Accept God's Answer

Sometimes people refuse to accept God's answer to their prayers because the answers are not what they wanted. God does not give them or do for them exactly what they requested. So as far as they are concerned, God did not answer their prayers. They did not give the omnipotent, all-knowing God the option of answering their prayers according to His will. In other words, they did not complete their prayers, acknowledging to God that although they prayed for what they desire; nevertheless, they are leaving the final decision to His will.

And even if they ended their prayers in that manner or a similar manner, they still expect God to grant what they requested. Such individuals are presumptuous, acting as though God does not know what is best in every situation. Individuals should pray only if they are prepared to accept God's answer.

There are times when I have prayed for an outcome, and the actual outcome of my prayer is exactly the opposite of that for which I prayed, but I always asked God that His will, not mine, be done. This has happened a number of times when I asked God to restore health to individuals who are ill and they died shortly thereafter. God is always correct in His answers.

You must be willing to accept God's answer to your prayers, even when the answers are different from what you desire. If you are not willing to accept God's answer just don't pray at all; unless you really don't expect God to answer. And if that's the case, why pray? You must believe that God is omnipotent, omniscience, and infallible; therefore, trust Him to give the correct and most appropriate answer to your prayers at the right time, and accept the answer.

Examples of Unanswered Prayers

As discussed previously, God answers prayers in a variety of ways, such as yes, no, not now, and gives different outcomes than requested, and so forth. He may also choose not to respond at all. I have discussed how King David and other psalmists were concerned and pleaded with God not turn His face from them and not to refuse to answer their prayers. They realized that God's answers are always correct, therefore, they wanted

God to answer. Below are incidents when seemingly God did not reveal His answers to prayers.

God Refused to Answer King Saul's Prayer

After the death of Samuel, the Philistines gathered at Shunem to fight against Israel. When King Saul saw the army of the Philistines, he was afraid and panicked and sought God's revelation pertaining the battle. "And when Saul enquired of the LORD, the LORD answered him not, neither by dreams, nor by Urim [sacred lots], nor by prophets" (1 Sam. 28:6). God did not answer Saul's prayer. He simply ignored Saul. That is the worse response one can receive from God (1 Sam. 28:3–25). Saul had turned from God and now needed God's assistance; God had taken away from Saul the ability to prophesy, and would not reveal anything to Saul. He refuses to answer Saul's prayer.

We do not want to God to ignore our prayers. Our desire should be that God gives us an answer to our prayer. If God ignores our prayers, we do not know what to do, we are lost as it were. God refuses to hear King Saul's prayer; therefore, Saul turned to divination.

God Refused to Answer King David's Prayer

This incident was mentioned previously. David took Uriah's wife Bathsheba and slept with her while Uriah was in the battlefield. Uriah was fighting on behalf of David. Bathsheba conceived and gave birth to a baby boy. God was displeased with David and sent the prophet Nathan to confront David. God severely rebuked David—a man after His own heart—and said, "The child also that is born unto thee shall surely die" (2 Sam. 12:14). David had repented for grave error before the birth of the child. God forgave David and spared his life; however, apparently he was not relieved of all consequences of his behavior.

The child was seriously sick. David fasted and prayed for seven days, appealing to God to restore health to the young boy, "David therefore besought God for the child; and David fasted, and went in, and lay all night upon the earth. And it came to pass on the seventh day, that the child died" (2 Sam. 12:16, 18). However David received no response from God. The Prophet Nathan did not return to David and give him an answer from God.

It may be construed that God said no to David's prayer, affirming the prophecy of Nathan, because the child died. However, the Bible does not record that God revealed to David His answer to his prayer. Nathan did not return to David to reveal to him God's answer to his prayer on behalf of the child.

Of significance to note and to emphasize is the point that although God had forgiven David for his egregious wrong and spared him from death, God had not completely exonerate David. God mitigate the full consequence of David's behavior; however, he suffered a great deal of consequence—the child he loved dearly died.

Even though David was a man after God's own heart, yet God refused to answer his prayer on that occasion and held him accountable. Therefore, God might refuse to hear or answer prayers which are not consistent with His will and plan.

CHAPTER TWENTY-THREE

GOD ANSWERS SOME PRAYERS BY SAYING NO!

God Said No to Abraham

Sometimes a seemingly unanswered prayer is one which God did not answer according to the request or desire of the person who prayed. God sometimes gives a better and more appropriate answer than the outcome requested. An excellent example is when God said no to Abraham—God's righteous servant.

God had promised Abraham that he would be the father of many nations. However, Abraham apparently thought he and his wife Sarah were advancing in age—he was ninety years old and his wife, Sarah was eighty years old. He needed to speed up the process of having a descendant who would carry out his legacy—he thought. He would wait another ten years before Isaac was born.

So Abraham asked God to allow Ishmael—his son with Sarah's Egyptian maid, Hager—to be his heir. This request-prayer was not consistent with God's plan. God's answer was no: "And God said, Sarah thy wife shalt bear thee a son in deed; and thou shall call his name Isaac: I shall establish my covenant with him . . ." (Gen. 17:19). God had a better plan for Abraham. He and his wife Sarah would bear a son—Isaac, who would be his heir and carry out his legacy. God gave Abraham an affirmation of His promise, with additional detail—the name of his son.

Even though Abraham was a righteous man he did not have full knowledge and understanding of God's Providential Will and Plan. God's answer to Abraham's prayer was in accordance with God's Providential Plan and the prayer of Abraham could not change God's Plan of making Isaac his heir.

Isaac, Abraham's primary heir, was humble, obedient, and godly. He was so obedient and humble that as a young man he was willing to allow his father to lay him on an altar, tie his hands and feet, and was about to offer him as a burnt offering. Of course, God intervened, provided a substitutionary sacrificial ram and spared his life.

It should be noted that although God did not permit Ishmael to become Abraham's primary heir to carry on his legacy, God blessed Ishmael. Ishmael's descendants began years before Isaac's (Gen. 17:20; 25:21).

God Said No to Abraham's Prayer-Appeal to Spare Sodom and Gomorrah

God appeared to Abraham, through three messengers (angels), and affirms His promise to Abraham that He and Sarah, his wife, would indeed have a son within one year. Sarah and Abraham entertained the messengers and fed them well.

The messengers were on their way on another assignment to destroy the wicked cities Sodom and Gomorrah. God disclosed His plan to Abraham: "And the LORD said, Shall I hide from Abraham that thing which I do [imminent annihilation of Sodom and Gomorrah]" (Gen. 18:17). The messengers were now heading toward Sodom, but Abraham stood in their way.

Then Abraham conducted a persistent prayer of intercession, for Sodom and Gomorrah, even greater than he did on behalf of Ishmael. For one thing, His nephew and his family were living in Sodom. And he did not want them to be destroyed with the rest of the people there.

Abraham's appeal-prayer to God began with Abraham asking God, "Wilt though also destroy the righteous with the wicked" (Gen. 18:23). Abraham then ask God if He would spare Sodom if there were fifty righteous people there; then he went to forty-five, then to forty, then to thirty, then to twenty, then to ten (Genesis 18:24–32). Not as many as ten righteous people could be found in Sodom. Abraham ceased his appeal-prayer at the low threshold of not being able to find ten righteous persons in Sodom. Bearing in mind that his nephew, Lot and his wife, two daughters, and two sons-in law—eight members of his family—were living in Sodom at the time. Yet ten righteous persons could not be found there

God said no to Abraham. He completely annihilate Sodom and Gomorrah; however, He saved Lott and his two daughters. God spared Lott and his daughters despite Lott's relevancy to leave Sodom. God spared him, no doubt, as a favor to Abraham—His righteous servant.

God Said No to Moses's Prayer for His Death; God Had a Better Plan for Him

Moses prayed for death when he was frustrated by the rebellious children of Israel who he was leading out of slavery in Egypt. He was leading those rebellious people in the wilderness toward the Promised Land (Canaan).

God had provided manna and water for them along the way. Sometimes water was not readily available to them. However, in the end, God would always provide water for them. They only needed to exercise a little patience.

On one occasion, the children of Israel complained that they were tired of eating manna, which God Himself provided for them. Their complaint displeased God as well as Moses. The people cried unto Moses and Moses, in turn, cried out unto God for assistance.

Moses told God that the multitudes of people were not his children and he had no way of giving them the flesh for which they were craving. Moses went on: "I am not able to bear all this people alone, because it is too heavy for me" (Num. 11:14). The burden was truly great for a man who was eighty years of age when God gave him the awesome assignment.

He was leading some 2.4 million children of Israel—600,000 men in addition to women and children—out of slavery in Egypt. They had been wondering in the wilderness for some time, and Moses was now more than eighty years old.

Seemingly, out of frustration, despair, and perhaps a reaction to the ingratitude of the children of Israel, Moses continues his prayer, "And if thou deal thus with me, kill me, I pray thee, out of hand, if I have found favour in thy sight; and let me not see my wretchedness" (Num. 11:15). Moses was tired of hearing negative remarks of the ungrateful and rebellious people who he was trying to lead.

He wanted to give up, or perhaps, he just needed reassurance from God, that God was there for him. And God not blaming him for his shortcomings. Little did Moses know, at the time, that he would be leading the children of Israel for more than thirty-five additional years, for a total of forty years!

God fully understood the plight, disappointment, and frustration of Moses. He was the greatest human leader the world has ever known, yet he felt like wanted to die before he had completed his assignment.

Perhaps God was teaching Moses a lesson that he was not autonomous or independent of God. So the faithful, merciful, gracious, and forgiving God, answered Moses's prayer with a "No, Moses, I will not take your life. Rather, I will provide assistance for you." God gave Moses a mission instead. "And the LORD said unto Moses, Gather unto me seventy men of the elders of Israel, with whom thou knowest to be leaders of the people, and officers over them; and bring them unto the tabernacle of the congregation, that they may stand there with thee" (Num. 11:16). The LORD provided a perfect solution for what Moses thought was an unsurmountable problem. He probably did not consider the fact that there is no failure in doing God's mission. And God would provide any provision he needed to accomplish the mission.

Once Moses selected the seventy elders, God ordained them and shared Moses's leadership responsibilities with them. Undoubtedly, Moses was pleased with the new arrangement. Moses prayed. God did not give him that for which he prayed. Rather, God gave him what he needed.

Moses's prayer for his death was not consistent with God's plan for him. So God said no to Moses and gave him a better alternative answer. God provided Moses the assistance he needed to complete God's mission during the next thirty-five years.

If your prayer will not bring glory to God, think about it and meditate on it before you pray it. When you pray, even though your request may be specific, always ask God to let His will be done. God might have a better plan for you than the plan for which you are praying.

God Said No to Jonah's Prayer for His Death

In a previous chapter of the book where I discussed God's answers to prayers in the Old Testament, I mentioned how God answered the prayer of Jonah when Jonah prayed from inside a fish. Well, Jonah, after his exciting fish experience, obeyed God and went to Nineveh and carried out God's assignment.

You will recall how the king and the people of Nineveh responded to Jonah's preaching and warning and humbled themselves before God and repented. God accepted the repentance of Nineveh and through His love, grace, and mercy spared Nineveh from utter destruction. Jonah was utterly displeased with God's decision to spare Nineveh.

Jonah thought that the great City of Nineveh, that capital of Assyria, deserved to be destroyed because of its wickedness. Furthermore, his ego was hurt. Because he had preached destruction to the city of Nineveh and God spared the city, he thought that his credibility was in question.

So Jonah wanted to die. The same Jonah who God had rescued, days earlier, from drowning in the sea, or being eaten by a sea monster, now behaved as though he knew more than God—with a holier than thou attitude. He thought that his only way out was for God to take his life. And get him out of his self-righteous indignation, affliction and psychological pains. "And Jonah prayed unto the LORD, and said, I pray thee, O LORD, was not this my saying, when I was yet in my country? Therefore, I fled before thee unto Tarshish: for I knew that thou art a gracious God, and merciful, slow to anger, and of great kindness, and repentant thee of the evil. Therefore now, O LORD take, I beseech thee, my life from me; for it is better for me to die than to live" (Jon. 4:2–3). If there was any doubt about the love, mercy, and grace of God toward rebellious people—and these were not Jewish people; such doubt must dissipate, in light of God's response to the Jonah

After all, Jonah had disobeyed God's first direct instruction to preach to the City of Nineveh, and now he was displeased and angry that God, in His infinite wisdom and mercy, decided to spare the City of Nineveh. At that time Nineveh had 120,000 people and animals, from annihilation.

God extended Mercy to Jonah by not taking his life for his unmerciful and unforgiving attitude and disposition and for his anger over the Sovereign God's decision to spare Nineveh. In fact, God told Jonah that he had a right to be angry.

Nevertheless, God answered Jonah's prayer for his immediate death with, no Jonah, I will not take your life.

God did not take Jonah's life at that time. The prayer was not consistent with God's plan for Jonah.

God wanted to teach Jonah another lesson about caring for others. Jonah should have been so pleased to know that God used him to preach one sermon for three days. As a result, a great King, a great city, and one hundred and twenty people repented and were saved from destruction, in addition to animals. Instead of being delighted, Jonah was sulking and angry with God.

Throughout this book, it has been emphasized that it is important to pray for outcomes that will please God and glorify His name. That's why one should not pray for evil to befall others or for evil on oneself.

When you feel that someone does not deserve mercy or kindness, pray that God will change his or heart and, perhaps change your heart as well. As the Apostle Peter reminds us that "The Lord is not slack concerning his promise . . . but in long suffering to usward, not willing that any should perish, but that all should come to repentance" (2 Pet. 3:9). The incidents of Jonah not only inform us that God answers prayers by saying no. Perhaps more importantly. They affirm God's willingness to forgive and to save those who are willing to seek His forgiveness. In addition. The incidents instruct followers of Jesus to assess their/our attitude regarding our belief on those we might consider as unworthy of God's grace, mercy and blessings. Further, the incidents inform followers of Jesus to rejoice over every decision of God when it is revealed!

When you feel that you are at the end of the rope and there is no way out, pray that God will bring you out or provide you with what you need to endure. Finally, when you feel angry about a situation, pray that God will turn your anger into compassion and action to deal with the situation. Give God thanks that He does not always give you the outcomes for which you pray! And remember that there might be a little part of

Jonah in you, so strive to be obedient to God. And to accept God's decisions and actions.

God Said No to Zedekiah

Nebuchadnezzar and the Babylonians besieged Jerusalem about 587 BC. They had invaded Jerusalem in 607 BC and took people from Judah into captivity, including Daniel, Shadrach Meshach, and Abednego.

Things seemed different this time. Zedekiah, King of Judah was scared to death. He had refused to take heed to the warnings of God, which was delivered him through the Prophet Jeremiah. However, this time he felt more threatened than he had ever been. He felt that the Babylonians meant business.

Zedekiah sent two men—Pashur and Zephaniah—to Jeremiah for assistance. He wanted Jeremiah to pray and enquire (urge) God to protect and fight with the people of Judah against Nebuchadnezzar and his Babylonian army. Zedekiah's desperate plea Jeremiah was, "Enquire, I pray thee, of the Lord for us; for Nebuchadnezzar king of Babylon maketh war against us: if so be that the Lord will deal with us according to all his wondrous works, that he may go up from us" (Jer. 21:2). This was Zedekiah's indirect prayer, of sort, to God through the Prophet Jeremiah. The people of Judah were God's special people; therefore, King Zedekiah thought that despite his and their rebellion against God, He would certainly deliver them from Nebuchadnezzar and the Babylonians.

God had delivered Judah from the Philistines and the Assyrians in the past, so Zedekiah thought that surely, He would deliver them this time from the fierce Babylonians, Zedekiah might have thought. Evidently, Zedekiah did not remember the proclamation of his predecessor, King Solomon, the wisest king who ever lived, "He that being often reproved hardeneth his neck, shall suddenly be destroyed" (Prov. 29:1). Zedekiah had been reprimanded, corrected and warned time and time again to turn to God. There was no more time to tolerate his evil ways. .

God's response to Zedekiah plea-indirect prayer was swift and fatal. Unfortunately, Zedekiah was not humbling himself before God, repenting of his evil and seeking God's forgiveness. No, he wanted to keep disobeying God and expected God to join with him in battle against Nebuchadnezzar and the Babylonians.

Unlike the incident, previously discussed, when God did not send Nathan with a response to David's prayer, God gave Jeremiah an immediate answer for Zedekiah's request.

God's answer to Zedekiah's prayer was more than a diametrically opposite to what Zedekiah requested God's response to Zedekiah was devastating, "Thus saith the LORD God of Israel; Behold, I will turn back the weapons of war that are in your hands, wherewith ye fight against the king of Babylon, and against the Chaldeans, which besiege you without the walls, and I will assemble them into the midst of this city. And I myself will fight against you with an outreached hand and with a strong arm, even in anger, and in fury, and in great wrath" (Jer. 21:4–5).

Zedekiah might have been better off if he had not asked for God's intervention against the Babylonian. Perhaps God would not have joined with the Babylonians to invade and destroy Jerusalem—Judah.

In addition to the capture and destruction of Jerusalem, including Solomon's beautiful temple, Nebuchadnezzar inflicted severe humiliation and pain on Zedekiah. "Then the king of Babylon slew the sons of Zedekiah in Riblah before his eyes: also, the king of Babylon slew all the nobles of Judah. Moreover, he put out Zedekiah's eyes, and bound him with chains, and carry him to Babylon" (Jer. 39:6–7). God saying no to Abraham, Moses, and Jonah were to their benefit; however, the no to Zedekiah was devastating Zedekiah and his sons, to Jerusalem, and to all Judah.

Years earlier God had told the Prophet Habakkuk that he will not believe the punishment that He (God) will inflict on Judah through the Babylonians (Hab. 1:5–7).

The execution of God's judgement—invasion of Judah by the Babylonians and the destruction of Jerusalem, including Solomon's Temple in AD 586 must be one of the most atrocious events in the Bible, against God's Jerusalem and the Kingdom of Judea. Perhaps only by the crucifixion of Jesus, the Son of God supersedes this atrocity. And even so, the crucifixion of Jesus was in fulfilment of God's Providential Will to redeem humanity and reestablish fellowship with mankind.

As I type this page of this book and observe what is going on in our nation and across the world, I pause to wonder what will happen to our nation! On the one hand, Zedekiah was much too late in seeking God's assistance—intervention. On the other hand, he had not repented and submitted himself in obedience to God; yet he expected God to join with him in battle against Nebuchadnezzar and the Babylonians. I hope that we are not making similar mistakes to those of Zedekiah, his predecessors and the people of Judah. Zedekiah was the last king of Judah. May God help us to seek His forgiveness while there is time and to obey His instructions!

CHAPTER TWENTY-FOUR
GOD ANSWERED MY PRAYERS

God Said No to My Prayers for Healing No to the Healing of My Cousin (niece)

I previously mentioned this incident. One of my favorite first cousins—she is more like my—niece was struck with COVID-19 (Coronavirus) in June 2020. She was my father's last sister's third and last daughter—Romaine/Claudette Edwards. She was the nicest, kindest person you could ever meet. I really love her dearly.

She was more like one of my nieces. She came to the university where I was an administrator and earned her master's degree in economics there. In addition, her only child—son matriculated at the same university where I was employed. I generally stayed at her home when I traveled in that part of the United States of America.

When my sister, a medical doctor, informed me that my cousin-niece had contracted COVID 19-coronavirus and was hospital, I was saddened. In fact, I was devastated. She and I had exchanged text messages just a few days earlier, and I had spent several days at her home nine months earlier.

What could I do? One of my favorite cousins-nieces was ill in the hospital, hundreds of miles away and I could not even visit her, because of hospital regulations. God had heard and answered my urgent—urgent to me—prayers in the past. I would ask God for one more favor. I was confident that God would hear and answer my prayer on behalf of my cousin-niece.

So I went into my room and closed my door and fell to my knees. Then I poured out my request to God. I knew that niece was a Christian who believed In God. She grew up in the same Baptist Church as I did I did not need to ask God to convict her heart so she would be able to receive God's blessing, because she was a believer. Instead, I pleaded with God to intervene in the coronavirus illness spare her life and grant her recovery.

As I prayed, I thought about King Hezekiah—previously discussed in this book—prayed for an extension of his life, and how God extended in life by fifteen years (2 Kings 20:1—6).

Yes, I prayed as passionately and sincerely as I knew how. I am a teacher-believer in the teaching of James, "Is any sick among you? let him call for the elders of the church; and let them pray over him, anointing him with oil in the name of the Lord" (James 5:14). Well, I was unable to physical visit and anoint my niece with oil; however, I visited her in spirit and I did that quite frequently.

In addition, I complied with another of James' admonitions, James teaches, "Confess your faults one to another, and pray one for another, that ye may be healed. The effectual fervent prayer of a righteous man availeth much" (James 5:16). I have applied James' teaching regarding prayer and praying many times.

I have taught the principle in my sermons, Bible study class, and Sunday school classes. Now I was applying the principle on behalf of my niece. Not only was I praying, but I asked my Bible study class members and my Sunday school class members to join me in praying as well.

In addition, we pray corporately as a class. We prayed passionately and sincerely. And at the end of my prayer, our pray, we say: Nevertheless, Father, not just my will, our will, respectively, but Thy will be done.

My niece's son, went the hundreds of miles just to speak with the doctors regarding his mother's situation. When I spoke with him, he told me that his mother was improving. However, within one week of our conversation, his mother, my niece transitioned. God answered my prayer, but not according to my preference or permissive will, Rather in accordance with His Prescriptive Will.

I deeply believe in the efficacy of prayer and the infallibility of the omnipotent, omniscience, and Sovereign God. God spoke and though my heart-our hearts are heady with sorrows, we accept God's decision; knowing that He will see us through our sorrows. I previously stated that a person who is not willing to accept God's answer to his or her prayer, probably should not pray!

God has the sovereign right to answer or not answer prayers when and how He chooses. God said no to His only begotten Son when He prayed, "O my Father, if it be possible let this cup pass from me: nevertheless not as I will, but as thou wilt" (Matt. 26:39). God did not allow His Son's substitutionary sacrificial death to pass away. Rather, Jesus died on Calvary's Cross, and humanity is the beneficiary.

Jesus accepted God's providential sovereign decision. So who am I to question or not to accept God's decision regarding the passing of Romaine? I take comfort in the teaching of Paul that, "And we know that all things work together for the good of them that love God, to them and are the called according to his purpose" (Rom. 8:28). While the good of my niece's death, at a relatively young age, might not be quite evident to me and her family right now, I am confident that there is good in her death.

What about you? If you are a Christian, a believer, how have you reacted to God's response to your prayer, or how will you react? What do you do if you are not sure of God's response to your prayer? Are you ready to accept God's decision, regardless of your personal desire?

Three Emergency Prayers and the Manifestation of God's Immediate Response

A well-revered vice president for financial affairs—Jones at a renowned university—took pleasure in reminding poor planners and no planners that their lack of planning does not constitute an emergency or state of urgency for the Department of Financial Affairs.

Similarly, an urgency or emergency for humans does not constitute an emergency or urgency for God. God knew all along that whatever it is it would have been and had already dealt with it.

The Prophet Isaiah reminds us that God will answer our prayers while we are yet praying. The Prophet puts God's rapid response. In fact, His proactive answer to prayers in this manner: "And it shall come to pass, that before they call, I will answer; and while they are yet speaking, I will hear" Isa. 65:24). Yes, we know that God answers a prayer even before the prayer is uttered or completed.

However, sometimes the manifestation of the answer is not immediately revealed or evident. For example, when the children of Israel were in slavery in Egypt, after the death of Joseph, they prayed consistently for God's deliverance. God heard and answered their prayers. But the manifestation of His answer might not have been revealed to them for years.

It is likely that only after God called Moses and instructed him to lead the children of Israel out of bondage in Egypt was God's answer to their prayers manifested to the children of Israel. And perhaps it was only after Moses spoke with the children of Israel that they realized that God was answering their prayers and had sent deliverance for them.

The fact of the matter is that sometimes there is a delay between the time God answers a prayer and His answer is revealed or manifested to the person or persons who prayed or praying. Sometimes the immediate manifestation of God's decision or intended action is critical to the person or persons who have prayed or are praying; however, there is no emergency on the part of God.

I want to share three incidents when the manifestations of God's answers to my prayers were immediate or almost immediate. Such immediate manifestations of God's responses were critical for me. I will discuss the incidents in the chronological order in which they occurred.

Hopefully they will help to reaffirm your confidence in the efficacy of prayers and the faithfulness of God to hear and answer sincere prayers, in our times, of those who believe in Jesus Christ. In addition, these personal incidents might assist you in your striving to feel the very presence God with you and enhance your belief in His willingness to act on your behalf.

1. Prayer for the examination I could not fail—Third Jamaica Local Examination (JLE)

I had taken the Third Year National (Local) Examination (JLE). It was a national examination, but because it was graded in Jamaica, rather than in England, it was considered a local examination. This national examination was one key which opens the door for a primary school student to be eligible for admission to a tertiary institution in Jamaica. Such tertiary institutions included teacher colleges, technical institutions, and the Jamaica School of Agriculture, among others.

It was difficult, almost impossible, for a thirteen to fifteen-year-old primary school student, or a past primary school student to obtain additional formal education in Jamaica if he or she did not succeed in passing the Third Jamaica Local Examination. This was a gatekeeper exam, so to speak.

When the official results of all Jamaica Local Examinations were published in the Jamaica Gazette, the official government publication of legal notices, my name was not included among the names of successful candidates. First, I panicked. My hope of further formal education, was diminishing or at least was dwindling in my mind's eyes.

I was scared that my key to admission to the Jamaica School of Agriculture was deactivated-destroyed and my dream for attending that fine institution had now become a nightmare, so I thought.

My shattered dream of attending the Jamaica School of Agriculture was secondary only to my embarrassment of failing the examination. I had to face my teachers, parents, siblings and friends with the sadness of failure all over my face. I almost gave up on any opportunity of furthering my education.

That was my doom day. But it was not quite over. I still had Auntie Melworth's unfinished house as my study and prayer closet. After taking off to a property adjacent to our house and stayed there for a few hours. My classmate and friend, Kenneth came to my place of mourning and consoled me. That was one of the saddest days of my life. Only my experience in Canada, which I discussed later came close.

I decided to retreat to my study and prayer closet—Auntie Melworth's unfinished house on the hill above my house. And I did the only thing that I believed that I did well; I prayed and I prayed, and I prayed! I needed only one outcome, that God would intervene I the examination and the results. The angel told Abraham that he and Sarah would a child at their old ages with a rhetorical question, "Is anything too hard for the LORD?"(Gen. 18:14). I believed that God could and would do something on my behalf for his name's sake.

God answered my prayer immediately, however, the manifestation of God's answer was one week later. I had prayed, at the prayer closet for God's assistance many times before, but this time my prayer was urgent for me, not for God and most consequential.

I really needed God's immediate intervention. My name was not among the names of students who had passed the national examination. So I cried out, literally cried out, to God for help. I did not know how God would help, but I knew He would.

My cries were with tears running down my cheeks. Luckily for me there was no other house or person close by. No one to disturb me, and no one for me to disturb. No one to take my attention off God. I needed God's immediate help.

After the intense praying and crying and sobbing, there was a calm that came over me. God must have answered my prayer at that time. Or perhaps, He had answered even before I prayed or completed my prayer, God gave me no sign regarding His answer other than a feeling of calmness that came over me. I heard no voice, but I believed that God had answered my prayer. My feeling of distress and embarrassment dissipated and I had the feeling that everything would work out well.

I cannot say that I was contemplating sitting for the examination the following year. That examination was only administered once each year and a person could retake it every year, if desired, until he or she was successful or just give up. All subjects had to be retaken each time. There was no partial passing.

Well, with God's help, I survived the weekend. I felt that God had heard and answered my prayer. The one daily national newspaper, came out on the Monday, after my serene and somber weekend. The paper carried an official supplemental notification (an addendum) to the monthly gazette, which had published the previous week, with the names of success candidates of the examinations.

The national newspaper included names of additional students who had passed the examination, but were inadvertently omitted from the previous week's publication. My name was included on the supplemental list of successful students. My name was inadvertently omitted from the original listing in the gazette—that's what the government said.

But I believe that God answered my prayer according to His way. Let me quickly say that mine was not the only name omitted from the origin publication.

There was great joy among my family, teachers, and friends. For us, God had answered my prayer and the prayers of my family, especially that of my mother, who was perpetually praying for and encouraging me.

Had God not said yes to my prayer then, I probably would not have been writing this book. Yes, God answered prayers in the Bible times, and He continues to answer prayers in our times!

Do you believe in the efficacy of prayer? Do you believe that God will answer your sincere and fervent prayer? I do, yes, I really do!

2. Prayers that held my car together so I could attend Jessy's funeral.

I met Jessy White a few years after I became a member of and deacon at Hollywood Baptist Church at Powhatan Virginia. I had known this gentleman—wanted to be a cowboy who hailed from Texas—for about seven or so years. He had married a lady originally from Powhatan. When they retired, he from the military and she from a telephone company, they decided to relocate to Powhatan.

Jessy, as everyone called him, was the nicest person you could hope to meet. He was known for his numerous antique cars, cowboy hats, cowboy boots, pleasing personality and big smiles. I was drawn to Jessy and we had many jovial moments together.

Jessy had been in the hospital on many occasions, sometimes very ill. He was a fighter for life, just as many military persons are. Well, I left Virginia and returned to Mississippi where I had lived for many years. However, I maintain contact with Hollywood Baptist Church and the members there.

The news came to me that Jessy was very ill and I was planning to go to Virginia to visit him. Then I got the sad news a few days later that he had passed. Transitioned before I could say good bye, farewell to this larger than life, cheerful Texan. Not only that, but jokingly, he promised me one of his antique cars and a Texas cowboy hat to go along with it.

Well, the only thing I could do was to go to his funeral services in Powhatan and say a few words—tributes on behalf of the man we all loved.

The funeral services were set for a Saturday in June. I decided to drive my seventeen-year-old Honda CR-V 2000. This is the vehicle my sister gave to me. It worked well once I replaced the transmission. I had been driving it for almost ten years, almost all the years I was in Virginia. I had driven it from Virginia to Mississippi one year earlier and had been driving it in Mississippi without any problem.

I packed up and left Mississippi Thursday about 5:00 a.m. On my way on the 1,100 miles (seventeen hours for me) drive to Powhatan. Nothing would prevent me from attending Jessy's funeral services. Within one 160 miles of the trip the engine of the Honda CR-V was hot. I stopped in Meridian, Mississippi and bought a new radiator cap and refilled the radiator with coolant and tapped up the three one-gallon containers with water which I carried in the trunk of the CR-V.

By the time I got to Tuscaloosa things had gotten worst. The new radiator cap had placed additional pressure on the radiator and it was leaking worse as I drove on the highway. I took the vehicle to several mechanic shops in Tuscaloosa but none was able to accommodate me. The last one ran a pressure test on the engine. He told me that the head gasket blown.

He advised me against replacing the head gasket and offered to locate an engine which was used, which he could install in about five days. He was charging almost twice the book value of the Honda CR-V 2000 to procure and install the used engine. I might have accepted his offer if he could have installed the used engine by midday, Friday. I told him no thanks, paid him for running the pressure test on the engine and took my vehicle from him.

I was determined to attend Jessy's funeral in Powhatan, Virginia, more than one thousand miles from where I had reached in Tuscaloosa, Alabama By this time I paid the mechanic forty dollars for the pressure testing the engine and receiving his dismal report it was after 5:00 p.m. CT. I did the most logical and only thing I knew to do, I prayed.

Then I called Deacon Tammy Woodson, with whom I served as deacons at Hollywood Baptist Church and told her my dilemma. She was conducting Vacation Bible school in Powhatan.

I asked her to inform others of my situation and asked that they all pray for me, and my safe journey to Powhatan. They knew how I felt about Jesse White and that I would not want to miss the funeral—celebration of life and homegoing.

After making three stops between Tuscaloosa and Birmingham to allow the engine to cool down and refill the radiator with water, I finally got to the Birmingham High 20 East Bypass. I had to hurriedly pull off the highway because the temperature indicator was registering dangerously hot.

It is a blessing that I had three one-gallon containers, filled with water, at all times. I must have learned to carry, in my vehicle, from my father. The extra water was precious to the vehicle and to me.

When I got off the highway in Birmingham and pulled to the shoulder of Highway 20 East, two highway help patrol officers stopped with their flashing lights. I explained the situation. They empathized with my situation and stayed with me long enough for the engine to cool off and for me to refill the radiator. It started to get dark. One of the highway patrol officers asserted that it would take a miracle for me to Virginia with that vehicle. Little did he know how prophetic he was!

The highway safety officers offered to call the tow truck. I responded no, thanks. I asked the highway patrol officers if they believe in miracles. One said, "Yes, and you will need one to get to Virginia in that CR-V."

I called Deacon Woodson again and gave her an update on my journey. Not only was she a deacon, she was also and still is the chair of the deacon ministry. She assured me that they were praying for me. The highway patrol officers left, perhaps thinking that I was hardhearted.

Something interesting happened from that point. I got in the CR-V and this time was able to drive about one hundred miles before I had to stop to allow the engine to cool and to refill the radiator. This was more than twice the distance I had previously been able to drive, before refilling the radiator, since I left Tuscaloosa. From that moment, I did not need to stop by the side of the highway. Rather, I stopped at rest stops to cool the engine, pour water in the radiator, and refilled the water containers. This was a significant improvement in my rate of travel as well as my safety—not having to stop by the side of the highway. All this time prayers are going up for me—my own and those of my friends—friends in need.

After a stop at a rest stop in northern Alabama, and refill the radiator, the temperature gage did not register very hot anymore. I did not need to pull over on the side of the highway to cool the engine and refill the radiator. But I stopped at rest stops just to allow the engine to cool and refill the radiator as needed.

There is no doubt that God had answered our prayers. I will say more about this in the next paragraph. No repairs had been done to the vehicle, however, it was now running almost as good as normal as far as the temperature gage was concerned

My expectation, when I left Mississippi on Thursday morning, was to arrive in Virginia about 10:00 p.m. on Thursday. Instead, I got there at about 5:00 p.m. on Friday. But that was great. I would not, could not, miss Jessy's funeral.

On Saturday morning I took the CR-V to the best one-man work at home mechanic I knew—Chris. Perhaps the best and fairest (value for price) person in that business.

Chris replaced the radiator hoses and the thermostat, which I had bought in Tuscaloosa, and had tried, unsuccessfully, to pay someone to install—replaced the old ones. I thought that the engine was losing water (coolant) because faulty radiator hoses and/or the thermostat might have been defected, or even because of a faulty radiator cap.

After Chris completed his work on the CR-V 2000, he told me the vehicle was good to go.

So I went to the church building, which is adjacent to Chris's place, and spoke at Jessy's funeral—celebration of life homegoing services. I briefly shared, with the congregation, my experiences, on how I got to Powhatan. The response was unanimous, "It was nothing but God who brought you here." Little did we know the extent of the miracle!

After attending Hollywood Baptist Church—Jessy's church, my church—on the following Sunday, I was on my way to the hotel where I was staying. I was less than half of a mile from the church building and from the mechanic's shop when the temperature gage hit the dangerously hot temperature mark. Of course, I pulled to the side of the street, and my Pastor O, who had just preached at Jessy's Church, stopped behind to offer his help. He had already helped; he had already prayed for my safe return to Mississippi. I refilled the radiator with water and drove my CR-V back to Chris's shop.

When Chris poured water into the radiator it just ran out from the front of the radiator. On removing the radiator, we all saw with amazement that the radiator had rotted at the concealed front toward the bottom. He/we could not understand how it was possible for that radiator to take the vehicle from Mississippi to Virginia. The words of the highway patrol safety officer, in Tuscaloosa, Alabama, rang clearly in my ears, "It will take a miracle for that CR-V to take you to Virginia." He said that he believed in miracles. And it was a truly a miracle. Some people may say it was good luck; I say, a great miracle!

Evidently, the radiator had been slow-leaking all along and the new hoses and radiator cap placed additional pressure on the radiator causing water to push through the rotted part at the bottom of the radiator.

It must have been God's intervention which prevented the several mechanic shops I went to in Tuscaloosa, Alabama from assisting me. Undoubtedly, if the new radiator hoses and the thermostat, which I had already purchased had been installed in Tuscaloosa and the new radiator cap was put on, the additional pressure in the radiator would have, more than likely, caused the radiator to fall apart on the highway between Alabama and Virginia. And I more than likely would have missed speaking at Jessy's homegoing celebration. God intervened for me and, perhaps more importantly, for Jerry's wife, family and loved ones

During my brief talk at the homegoing celebration, I mentioned, jokingly, that Jessy had promised me one of his Texas cowboy hats; he had many. Within three weeks of the going homegoing celebration services, Jessy's wife, Elouise, sent me one of Jessy's brand new Texas cowboy hats.

Well, we bought a new radiator for my Honda CR-V, which Chris installed. This allowed me to drive the vehicle, with confidence, back to Mississippi. The return journey to Mississippi was calm and peaceful without a single problem.

Because God answered our prayers and we applied faith and workmanship and fix the problem with the vehicle.

Yes, God answered my prayer and the prayers of Deacon Tammie Woodson and her Vacation Bible School's teachers and students who prayed for me. Other members of Hollywood Baptist Church, including Pastor O (Rev. Otis B. Lockhart) prayed for me as well.

This incident reminds us that obstacles may get into our way, but they should not prevent us from doing what we really want to do. If we trust God to help us, God will make a way somehow, or He will provide for an alternate outcome! That's the reason that in our prayer we say "Father, not just our desire, but let your will be done" because God knows best!

I pray that by sharing my experience on how God came through for me will inspire you to trust in God, especially when you see no way out. And will encourage you to never give up on what you desire to do. But always pray and accept God's guidance and decision!

3. Prayers to turn my darkness to light.

In my book, *When God Says No: Listen for the Yes!* I discussed the circumstances of how I was employed at Alcorn A & M College (Alcorn State University) and my wonderful experiences at that lovely institution. I will not include that discussion to any extent here. Suffice it to say that when I was employed there as an assistant professor, in the mid-1970s, there were not many administrators, faculty, and staff who held and earned academic doctoral degrees. I had just completed all the requirements for my doctorate at the University of Illinois in December but had to wait until the next May for the conferring of the degree.

I was employed at Alcorn in an approved United States Department of Immigration and Naturalization Services' Practical Training Program. The training was for eighteen months and could be extended for another eighteen months, if the institution wanted to continue my employment.

The college wanted to offer me permanent employment because it was difficult to identify and recruit candidates with terminal degrees in my field of education. Acorn filed a permanent residence application, with the US Immigration and Naturalization Services (INS), on my behalf. The application was filed on the basis that I had expertise and qualifications which the college needed, but it was difficult to identify and recruit appropriate candidates. The college filed that I could receive permanent visa—known as a green card. This involved retaining an immigration attorney to assist with the process.

Some seventeen months or so after the application was submitted, we received a response INS that the application was conditionally approved, pending my final interview by US Immigration and Naturalization Service's officials. That sounded really great.

I contacted the immigration attorney who was assisting us. He told us there was no problem; I just needed to go out the United States, to a US Immigration and Naturalization Services Office. This would be a routine interview and INS would issue the permanent visa—green card to me. This would have been the first week in January.

There was a stipulation that a person could not go to his or her country of origin for the interview and to pick up the permanent visa; therefore, I decided to go to Canada.

I arrived in Canada that cold Thursday night. There was more snow on the ground than I had ever seen. Fortunately, I was staying with a person who was living relatively close to the American Embassy. Early the next morning, Friday, I caught a cab and went, through the heavy snow, to the American Embassy. The cab fare was about five dollars. It did not take long for me to get to an immigration official. It was a cold and snowy day, a day to stay home if you could.

My excitement about receiving a permanent visa quickly turned into anguish and disillusionment. The immigration officer went through a folder he had on me and said, "I am sorry, sir. You are out of status. We cannot issue a permanent visa to you. And not only that, we cannot allow you to go back to the United States."

O my God, I was dumbfounded. I was petrified. Yes, I was absolutely beside myself. I want to make it perfectly clear that the Canadian Government had nothing to do with my plight.

As I write this page of this book, I can hardly fight back the tears from my eyes as I think about children who were separated from their parents at the American-Mexican border, some of whom are still separated. I compare the plight of those children and their parents with how I felt in Canada that snowy Friday!

I pleaded with the immigration officer to just allow me to return to Mississippi to, at least, pick up, some of my belongings. He appeared sympathetic with my plight, but he insisted that he could not allow me to return to Mississippi. He said that my only option was to seek a flight home to Jamaica.

Was this a nightmare I was experiencing? Was the world crushing in on me? My pleading did not change the decision of this immigration and naturalization officer. He was undoubtedly doing his job. Or perhaps, God wanted me to know that He answers prayers in Canada as He does in Mississippi, Alabama, Virginia and wherever sincere prayers are uttered with confident expectation!

So I took a cab back to where I was staying. And I did the only thing I knew to do. I dropped on my knees and I cried out to God for His assistance. I literally cried with tears running down my cheeks. I needed to get back to Mississippi. Then I called my dear friend in Mississippi, Joyce, who only one year earlier had graduated from the University of Illinois and joined the faculty at Alcorn. I had graduated from the University of Illinois one year before she did and had somewhat recruited her to Alcorn.

She was my colleague and closest friend in Mississippi at the time. I asked her to contact the senior US Senator from Mississippi and Mayor Charles Evers, a graduate of Alcorn, to inform them of my plight and seek their assistance.

I then went back on my knees in prayer, calling on God for His intervention. I needed to get back to Mississippi.

While I was on my knees praying, I must have been praying most of that afternoon, the telephone rang. It was about 4:40 p.m. I nervously answered the phone and heard the most beautiful words in the English language, to me at that time, "This is the United States Embassy, please come over here, we need to talk with you."

With lightning speed, I rushed outside, waved a cab, and said, please take me to the American Embassy; here is twenty dollars. The cab got in motion. The snow could not get in its way. When we reached the Embassy, a man was closing the external door. He said, "Who are you?" I told him my name. He responded that they were waiting for me.

The same man who had refused to permit me to return to the United States to pick up my belongings there, approved my immigration and naturalization documents. He informed me that the permanent visa would be mailed to my address in the United States.

On that memorable Friday afternoon, the manifestation of God's answer to my pleas and to the prayers of others on my behalf was instantaneous. My nightmare and my dark-cloudy day were transformed into a dream come true and a bright light at the end of that dark tunnel.

This is the most consequential and traumatic experience I have had in my life. But glory to God, that darkest day of my life was transformed into many delightful days, indeed years, in the United States of America.

If I had not been able to return to the United States when I was trapped in Canada, the trajectory of my life would have changed and undoubtedly not for the better. God answered my prayer, perhaps long before that cold winter Friday afternoon in Canada, as He has always done and continues to do!

Years after this incident, I was granted American citizenship by choice and have worked hard to live up to the patriotic duties and responsibilities concomitant with the privilege of being an American citizen by choice and desire.

God answered my desperate plea for assistance when I was stranded in Canada. God's answer to my earnest prayer enabled me to be and do what I have since that day. God answered my prayers as I exercised my faith and deeds by praying and calling on those who were in a position to assist me.

Prayer, faith, and deeds really work well together! I do not know which of the two public servants, Mayor Charles Evers or Senator John Stennis, who had greater impact on the American Embassy in Canada; however, I do know that Joyce would not have stopped calling their offices until they had assured her that they had done what they could. But in the final analysis, I know that it was God who intervened on my behalf. And as usual, in my situation, God intervened through humans.

I hope that by sharing, with you, my experience in Canada, your faith in the efficacy of prayer will be strengthened. God did not give me an verbal answer to my prayer. Rather, He answered through orchestrating appropriate assistance of humans. Perhaps, you are having an experience that only God can see you through. Remember that God works through humans to answer prayers. Cooperate with God, in faith, as He intervenes on your behalf—perhaps through humans!

CHAPTER TWENTY-FIVE

ACCEPT JESUS'S PRAYERS AND LIVE WITH CONFIDENT EXPECTATION!

The primary purpose of this short chapter of the book is to encourage disciples, the followers of Jesus Christ to accept the particular prayer which Jesus prayed for them/and foryou. The prayer is discussed in detail in chapter eighteen, "Prayers of Jesus, the God-man."

If you speak with anyone who is nominally familiar with the Holy Bible and ask about great promises in the Bible, you are likely to hear about God's promise in the Garden of Eden. This is when God promised to send an offspring of the woman—Eve (Jesus) who would crush the head of the offspring of the serpent. Through this promise God would restore fellowship between God and His creature—humanity (Gen. 3).

In addition, you are certain to hear about the prophecy of Isaiah, "Behold a virgin shall conceive, bear a son, and shall call his name Immanuel" (Isa. 7:14). You are also likely to hear quotes from Isaiah chapters 53 and 61) regarding the coming Messiah.

Then you are almost sure to hear about the Great Promise of Jesus Christ, recorded in the Gospel of John, "Let not your heart be troubled: if ye believe in God, believe also in me . . . I go to prepare a place for you . . . I will come again and receive you unto myself; that where I am, there ye may be also" (John 14:1–3). This is the Promise for which Christians/believers live and would die. The Promise of Jesus to return to earth for His people for them to live with Him forever.

If you press a bit further and ask about great prayers of Jesus, you are most likely to hear about the Disciples' Model Prayer, Jesus's prayers in the Garden of Gethsemane, and His prayer on Calvary's cross.

What you are not likely to hear about is Jesus's passionate prayer for His disciples then, and subsequent disciples/followers. He prayed this prayer shortly before He was crucified. It is about that prayer which I discuss in this short chapter of this book.

I have discussed this prayer in the chapter of this book on Prayers of Jesus. In this current chapter, I focus on the implications of believers accepting the prayer as though God has already answered it. Because He has already answered. The Prophet Isaiah, reminds us that God answers our prayers while we are yet praying or even before we pray (Isa. 65: 24)

God answers the prayers of mere mortals while they are praying or before they pray; how much more is God likely to answer the prayer of His Son! Therefore, certainly God answered when Jesus, His Son, prayed on behalf of His then existing disciples/followers and subsequent ones.

Christians/believers are looking forward with great expectation to the return of the Messiah to take His people with Him that where He is, they will be with Him also. So the question is why many believers are seemingly not aware of or act as though they do not accept the prayer which Jesus has prayed on their behalf?

Jesus knew that His disciples, and those who subsequently believe Him as a result of the ministry of the disciples, would encounter trials and tribulations in their ministry. He was leaving them on earth, while He went back to his heavenly

Kingdom, so He prayed for them, and those who would subsequently believe in Jesus.

Therefore, Jesus prayed specifically for His disciples, "I pray for them, I pray not for the world, but for them which thou hast given me; for they are thine" (John 17:9). As stated previously, discussed the prayer in the chapter of the book on Prayers of Jesus. So I am not discussing the prayer in detail here. Rather, I ask that you review the entire chapter, and note how passionately Jesus prayed for His disciples and subsequent believers.

Nevertheless, I am repeating portions of the prayer as I discuss the importance of followers of Jesus accepting the prayer, because Jesus has already prayed for them. And they need only to accept the prayer and conduct their daily lives as though the prayer has been answered.

A most powerful element of the prayer is when Jesus asks God to, "Sanctify them through thy truth; thy word is truth. Neither pray I for these alone, but for them also which shall believe on me through their word" (John 17:17, 20). As a believer in Jesus Christ, who accepts the answer to Jesus's prayer on your behalf, you are set aside through the Word of God. You are a special messenger of Jesus Christ. You are in the world to deliver the message, but you are not under the domination of worldly lifestyles.

Jesus prays passionately for His disciples and those who would subsequently believe in Him. God answered the prayer; however, many believers are not appropriating the God's answer to Jesus's prayer and acting in accordance with the prayer.

It is important that as follower of Jesus, a believer, you understand that Jesus's prayer empowers you to be effective in the ministry to which Jesus assigns you. Consequently, as a believer, you are equipped to carry out your Christ-like ministry with love and unity.

No Need to Recreate the Wheel

When you, the believer, accept Jesus's prayer for you, as discussed previously, you will function in the love, unity, power and light of God, Jesus. This is the primary focus of this chapter in this book. God is already protecting the believer, you, from evil, and His Spirit and love of Jesus are in you; therefore, there is no need for you to continually beseech God for protection and for unity among believers. Jesus has already prayed. Jesus tells us that we should always pray and not faint and there are many outcomes for which you can pray. There is . no need to recreate the wheel.

I am encouraging and urging, believers, to accept the "done deal"—God's answer to Jesus's prayer for them, for you endowment of God's love, sanctification, protection from evil, spirit of unity, and remembrance of the teaching of Jesus. Then you are able to step out in faith and carry out the wonderful ministry which Jesus has assigned to you.

The ministry includes your role in the great commission: "And ye shall be witnesses unto me both in Jerusalem, and in all Judaea, and in Samaria, and unto the uttermost part of the earth" (Acts 1:8). The Apostle Matthew records the great commission in this manner: "Go ye therefore and teach all nations, baptizing them in the name of the Father, and the Son, and of the Holy Ghost. Teaching them to observe all things whatsoever I have commanded you: and, lo, I am with you always, even unto the end of the world" (Matt. 28:19–20). Jesus did not leave His disciples and subsequent believers to fend for themselves. Rather, He prayed for them and promises to be with them throughout the ages. Jesus's Word is His bond which cannot return void. He pledges his Word and is following through every day.

Jesus has already prayed for you and for me and has endowed us with His Holy Spirit. It is now up to us to trust and obey Him. May He help us on our journey as we pray, with faith and confident expectation, and step out and do!

I trust that you are inspired to review, study, and accept Jesus's prayer for you. And you will strive with, faith and endurance, to live the life which Jesus has prayed for you, and you will encourage and assist others to do likewise!

CHAPTER TWENTY-SIX
CONCLUSION

Your Effectual, Fervent Prayer Works, Expect an Answer

As I write the concluding chapter of this book, I want to encourage you, and in fact, urge you to believe in the efficacy of prayers, if you are not yet convinced. Perhaps you have never had to pray as though your life depended on the answer to your prayer or you have not faced an obstacle where you could see no way out—over or around it. If your prayers have been answered in the past, there is no need for me to convince you that God responds to sincere prayers.

The Bible is replete with prayers that God answered instantaneously and where the manifestation of His answers were immediately known. Then there are those prayers which God answered immediately; however, His answers were not evident for years and even for centuries. In addition, there are prayers which God answered before they ended. However, the manifestations of the answers might or might not have been immediately evident.

Some prayers were prayed just once, while others were prayed over a long period of time—years. An example of a one-time prayer, previously discussed, was when Abraham prayed and appealed to God that Ismael, his son, would be his heir and carry on his legacy. God answered immediately with a no. In some instances, prayers were prayed over and over again, as in the incident of Hannah praying to conceive and have a child.

God might have answered the prayer immediately, However, His answer might not have been immediately revealed. Examples of prayers prayed over a long period of time are when the children of Israel prayed over and over for deliverance from Egyptian slavery. And when the people of Judah, in Babylonian captivity, prayed for their deliverance.

No doubt God heard and answered their prayers right away. Even though the manifestation of God's answers was not known immediately to the children of Israel in Egyptian slavery and the people of Judea in Babylonian captivity, respectively, God had answered their prayers.

After much pleading with God, God finally appeared to Moses on Mount Sanai and instructed him to lead the children of Israel out of slavery in Egypt. God permitted the Persians, and perhaps assisted them in defeating the Babylonians in 538 BC and in releasing the Jewish people in Babylonian Captivity so that they were free to return r to Judah.

Sometimes God answers prayers by giving a different and better answer than the answer-outcome requested. An example is when God refused to heal David's first son with Bathsheba. Rather David and Bathsheba a son—Solomon—the wisest and richest man in Bible times.

I have discussed examples in my book, *When God Says No: Listen for the Yes!* when God said no to me many times and then enabled me to receive, have, and/or gain better or more appropriate alternative yeses.

The book includes many examples of effective prayers—prayers for assistance, prayers seeking forgiveness, prayers for deliverance, prayers for direction and guidance, prayers for protection, prayers of thanksgiving, and so forth.

I want to encourage you to look at the prayers again and determine those which speak to your current situation, and accept them as prayers for you. I particularly encourage you to carefully review, with new insight, the prayer which Jesus prayed for His disciples and subsequent believers. You are covered by that prayer.

Use Jesus's prayer as a baseline for your prayer, knowing that Jesus has already prayed for you and God has answered. Then believe that God will really answer your prayer, when you pray in accordance with His will, and when you make your requests in the name of Jesus. You can expect with confidence that God will answer your prayer, in accordance with His plan and His timeframe.

In the book, I urge you to trust God more than you trust your most loyal friend because God is in fact your most loyal friend and Jesus is your advocate. Jesus wants to answer your prayer in order to glorify His Father.

I encourage to continue to pray until you receive an identifiable response. And be prepared to accept God's answer. Remember that a no to your prayer is a valid answer; "wait" and "not now" are answers as well.

In addition, remember that God may give you an answer entirely different or diametrically opposite to what you desired or requested. Remember that God's answer is always the best answer for you, even though you may not know it at the time.

Please remember not to try to hurry God for His answer or the manifestation of His answer. And do not to get discouraged while you are waiting for an answer from God. God does not want you to guess His answer; therefore, it is quite appropriate for you to ask Him to reveal His answer so that it is clear to you. God promised that in the last days, "I [He] will pour out my Spirit upon all flesh; and your sons and daughter shall prophesy, your old men shall dream dreams, your young men shall see visions" (Joel 2:28; Acts 2:17). So you must be open to the method(s) that God might use to reveal His answer to your prayer.

God sent Moses to tell the children of Israel, trapped in slavery in Egypt, that He had heard their prayers and had sent him (Moses) to deliver them. The people accepted God's answer and followed Moses out of Egypt.

Cornelius received God's answer to his prayers through a vision. In the vision, Cornelius saw an angel who told him that God had heard his prayers and saw his good deeds. The angel reveled to Cornelius what God wanted him to do. And Cornelius accepted god's answer to his prayers, and was converted (Acts 10:1–8).

Peter meditated on his vision and God revealed to him that the Gospel should be shared with the Gentiles. Peter obeyed God. And Cornelius became the first Gentile convert recorded in the New Testament (Acts 10:9–36).

God sent the Prophet Isaiah to inform King Hezekiah that God heard his prayer and extended his life by fifteen years (2 Kings 20:1–6).

There are different ways and means through which God reveals the answer to prayers. These ways include dreams, visions, Scripture, spoken words of His religious leaders and other believers. God makes revelation during prayer, meditation, fasting, and quiet moments with God, and through personal experiences, and in other ways as God chooses.

The key thing is to remain alert to God's response to your prayers and wait patiently with confident expectation. While you are waiting do the things which you know are right, based on your understanding of the Word of God. And be ready to make a 180-degree change, if God says so.

Remember that sometimes doubt or uncertainty may flash across your mind. At such times, whisper a quiet prayer that God will strengthen your faith and act as though He has answered your prayer. Never, never doubt the power of God or

Jesus to fulfill their promises. It is important to remember that some challenges that you face will require two or more people praying together. Jesus promises that He will be in the midst to assist and to answer prayers when two or three are gathered praying (Matt. 18:19–20).

In addition, remember what Jesus said about casting out demons, "This kind can come forth by nothing, but by prayer and fasting" (Mark 9:29). By inference, you may conclude that some difficulties and distresses-tribulations, obstacles which are hindering you, standing in your way and holding you back, and some miracle for which you are praying may need the combination of prayer and fasting.

Jesus endorses fasting. He told His disciples, "But thou, when thou fastest, anoint thine head, and wash thy face; that thou appear not unto men to fast, but unto thy Father which is in secret: and thy Father, which seeth is secret, shall reward thee openly" (Matt. 6:17–18). If you are not familiar with the concept and practice of fasting, find a Christian person who can assist you in the combination of praying, fasting, and meditation.

I pray that this book has been, and will continue to be a blessing to you. I hope that it has inspired you and will continue to inspire and assist you in your prayer life and in your desire and ability to share ideas about prayer with others. And above all, I earnestly pray that the book will help to strengthen your faith in God and in the efficacy of prayer.

Blessings and love to you and to all with whom you share and or discuss this book!

If you enjoy this book, please check out my two other books: *When God Says No: Listen for the Yes!* and *Becoming a Joy-Fulfilled Christian in the Twenty-First Century and Beyond*. Thank you.

THE AUTHOR

The author is an inspired individual who began to write religious books at a relatively later age after serving in numerous academic and administrative positions. He holds a bachelor's, master's, and a doctoral degree from outstanding universities in the United States of America. He holds a Certificate in Evangelism, Mission, and Global Christianity from one of the premiere schools of theology in the United States of America. He has served in academic and administrative positions at several universities before embarking on his current writing and evangelism endeavors.

The desire of the author is to write in a reader-friendly manner that makes it easy for even individuals who are not theologians or Bible scholars to comprehend his writing and be inspired. He believes that the most important thing that one human can do for another is to assist him or her to come to know Jesus Christ as Lord and Savior.

He is passionate about the Word of God and receives great joy in sharing the Word. He believes that prayer is the greatest and perhaps one of the least understood and most underutilized tools available to a Christian as he or she lives in our challenging world. His desire is to assist Christians understand and apply prayer as a fundamental means of accomplishing God's will for their lives, including winning souls for the Lord, and strengthening other Christians in their faith. It is his great desire that those who have not yet given their lives to Christ will read this book and be moved through the power of the Holy Spirit to pray and ask God, in the name of Jesus Christ, to grant him or her everlasting life!

CPSIA information can be obtained
at www.ICGtesting.com
Printed in the USA
LVHW041004080621
689682LV00004B/61

9 781647 493233